THE
DAVE MATTHEWS BAND:
STEP INTO THE LIGHT

THE DAVE MATTHEWS BAND:

STEP INTO THE LIGHT

MORGAN DELANCEY

ECW PRESS

CANADIAN CATALOGUING IN PUBLICATION DATA

Delancey, Morgan
The Dave Matthews Band: step into the light

ISBN 1-55022-342-9

1. Dave Matthews Band – History. 1. Title.

ML421.D24D33 1998   784.4'8'0973   C97-931572-7

Front cover photo: Ilpo Musto/London Features
Back cover photo: Sydney Burtner/*The Observer*
Epigraph: Reprinted with the permission of Simon & Schuster from
Zen Guitar by Philip Toshio Sudo. Copyright © 1997 Philip Toshio Sudo.

Cover design by Guylaine Régimbald.

Imaging by ECW Type & Art, Oakville, Ontario.
Printed by Printcrafters Inc., Winnipeg, Manitoba.

Distributed in Canada by General Distribution Services,
30 Lesmill Road, Don Mills, Ontario M3B 2T6.

Distributed to the trade in the United States
exclusively by LPC Group-InBook,
1436 West Randolph Street, Chicago, Illinois, USA 60607.
Customer service: (800) 626-4330, fax (800) 334-3892.

Published by ECW PRESS,
2120 Queen Street East, Suite 200,
Toronto, Ontario M4E 1E2.

www.ecw.ca/press

PRINTED AND BOUND IN CANADA

A band is not merely a collection of individuals. Its essential character must be for the whole to exceed the sum of the parts. When the right people get together, be it in music or sports or business or marriage or sex or whatever, a kind of spiritual fusion takes place. This fusion cannot be bought or forced or manufactured. . . . No one knows how this magic happens. But when it does, we feel the presence of something divine and everyone who's there knows it. Cherish the chemistry of great bands wherever you find it. You're onto something big.

— Philip Toshio Sudo, *Zen Guitar* (1997)

CONTENTS

1
PLAYFUL BEGINNINGS

"Learn your history. Have some fun. Stay awhile." A tourist brochure for Charlottesville, Virginia, population 50,000, entices visitors to savor breathtaking Blue Ridge mountain vistas and to step back in time by visiting Thomas Jefferson's favorite haunts, Monticello and the University of Virginia. The third American president's ties to the area were emotional and deep; he once proclaimed, "I am happy nowhere else, and in no other society, and all my wishes end, where I hope my days will end, at Monticello."

Jefferson's strong ties to Albemarle County, Virginia, derived from his father's initial interest in it. Peter Jefferson, upon surveying the region in 1735, loved it so much that he acquired 1,000 acres of land and settled there. Thomas eventually inherited his father's legacy: a vast property and an unwavering passion for this special place. Monticello, the mountain-top estate the family erected on that property, became the home of Thomas's dreams, and the University of Virginia was his treasured "academical village."

It was due to the legacy of *his* father that a David John Matthews, 19, found himself in Charlottesville, Virginia, in 1986, not long after graduating from high school in his native Johannesburg, South Africa. Facing the prospect of a stint in the military, mandatory for subjects of South Africa's apartheid-torn government, he conferred with his family about relocation options. His father, John Matthews, a physicist of international acclaim, had worked at the University of Virginia before David was born. Although

John Matthews had died in 1977, nearly a decade earlier, his ties to Charlottesville — and his wife's love of the place — were strong enough to motivate the entire Matthews family to emigrate from South Africa to this small college town in the United States.

And the rest, as they say, is history. Rock and roll history. By the end of 1997, the Dave Matthews Band had sold over seven million CDs, performed at President Bill Clinton's second inauguration gala, won a Grammy Award, and become one of the top-grossing touring acts in North America. And Dave had acquired an eighteenth-century estate on 65 acres in the Blue Ridge Mountains, near Monticello.

The other members of the Dave Matthews Band — drummer Carter Beauford, bassist Stefan Lessard, saxophonist-flutist Leroi Moore, and violinist Boyd Tinsley — had been residents of Virginia long before Matthews arrived. By 1986, Beauford, Moore, and Tinsley had all established strong ties to the burgeoning local arts scene; at that point, Lessard was probably still contemplating the perils of junior high in Richmond. But "C'ville" is the kind of place where, as one insider put it, "Everyone knows everyone knows everyone about everything." A musical meeting between these five guys seemed destined.

From 1986 through the early 1990s, the youth sector of the C'ville social scene displayed a dual nature: a trendy college culture as well as an active, Bohemian café society. Either way, or perhaps because of its double character, it was a site that was hard to leave. People tended to "have some fun" and to "stay awhile." The town's attractiveness still enchants many UVA graduates: it's not uncommon to have people with Ph.Ds waiting on you in restaurants on the Downtown Mall — not far from where Jefferson used to practice law. C'ville is not just a small place. It's a small place populated by a lot of bright people.

The history of Charlottesville goes back several centuries. Located in central Virginia — about 100 miles southwest of Washington, DC, and 70 miles northwest of Richmond, Virginia — the town nestles on the upper Piedmont Plateau, in the foothills of the Blue Ridge Mountains, at the headwaters of the Rivanna River. Established in 1762 by the Virginia General Assembly, with its governing laws linked to Albemarle County, the town was named after Queen Charlotte-Sophia of Mecklenburg-Strelitz, the young bride of King George III of England. It was officially granted a separate city charter in 1888. Today it encompasses over 10 square miles ("Monticello Avenue").

According to longtime residents, there is something palpable in the atmosphere of Charlottesville, something that extends beyond its history and demographic makeup. Musician Dawn Thompson, currently a member of the band Code Magenta, along with Greg Howard and the Dave Matthews Band's Leroi Moore, first moved to Charlottesville in 1981 with the idea of staying just for the summer. She's been there ever since. Thompson explains: "The same magnetism that engenders the musical atmosphere here is something that's been going on as long as I can remember. Thomas Jefferson may have even felt it. There's a kind of energy here that just feels right to me."

Musician-journalist-deejay David Wellbeloved, formerly of the popular Charlottesville band the Hogwaller Ramblers, describes other conditions that make Charlottesville unique: "You easily cross-pollinate here. In most places it's too difficult to cross genres. But here, everyone knows each other, so you can have a punk player doing country stuff, for example. Or a rock musician doing jazz. And there aren't that many venues."

A complex synergy between college town and Bohemian vibrancy, as well as the alchemical mix of atmosphere and artistic cross-pollination, served as a distinct backdrop for key events that occurred in late 1990 through early 1991. These would ultimately lead to the formation of the Dave Matthews Band. The site of much of this shaping was a Charlottesville bar: Miller's. A charming establishment located on the historic Downtown Mall, Miller's has long been considered a musical nexus in Charlottesville.

Everyone plays there sometime. Some musicians have regular weekly gigs at Miller's. Dawn Thompson singles it out as a focal point "for a lot of the musical interaction around here. It's always been that way." Housed in a three-story, turn-of-the-century brick building, the bar still displays vestiges of its original use — it was a drugstore. Quaint apothecary notices adorn both the storefront and the bar area inside. Immediately to the right of the front door, there's a small stage; old-fashioned wood paneling and mirrors line the walls. The bar is straight ahead, and tables are ranged throughout. The place has a relaxed atmosphere and a unique character.

Paths crisscross at Miller's: to sort them out you'd need a time-line chart. What *is* apparent is that Miller's was a clearinghouse for the talented musicians who would later coalesce to form the Dave Matthews Band. Five intersection points define the Miller's/DMB connection:

1. In November of 1990, fledgling songwriter-guitarist-vocalist-actor David Matthews, who had worked as "sandwich boy" and bartender at Miller's (often with a keyboard-harmonica player named Peter Griesar at his side), recorded his first demo of four songs. Musical entrepreneur Ross Hoffman, who frequented Miller's, helped set up the recording session. It included "The Song That Jane Likes," "Recently," "I'll Back You Up," and "The Best of What's Around." Greg Howard (on Chapman Stick, alto sax, drum samples, and backup vocals), John D'earth (on trumpet), and Kevin Davis (additional percussion) were also featured on the demo. Howard, who occasionally played his own gigs at Miller's, engineered the recording. The purpose of all this? Not to form a band, but to see if Matthews could sell the songs he'd written.

2. Soon afterward, with Hoffman's encouragement, Matthews approached Carter Beauford. Dave had seen Carter perform and had waited on him at Miller's. As before, the plan was not to form a band — it was to record even more original Matthews compositions. Matthews explained the situation to a local newspaper: "We really got together for more of a recording team, we really didn't get together to play live" (Jones).

It took guts for him to approach the more experienced Beauford; Carter had played in many bands and was doing a jazz show on Black Entertainment Television. Matthews had never even been in a band. He recollects: "I had been a fan of Carter's for a very long time. He didn't know me from a bar of soap. I had served him a couple of whiskeys. I went to him and said 'Would you like to play with me? Maybe we can do some recording'" (Kelley). After hearing a tape, Beauford agreed.

3. Matthews also asked a regular Miller's performer named Leroi Moore — who often took the stage with the John D'earth Quintet — to practice with him. This was also encouraged by Hoffman. Moore, Dave recalls, "was at Miller's making these heartfelt sounds and I was pouring drinks" (Blackwell, "Dave Matthews"). Moore and Matthews had already bonded during drinking and late-night conversation sessions at Miller's — the favored topic was the evils of apartheid. Moore was one of the most respected sax players in C'ville.

    It was a courageous move for Matthews to seek Moore's participation, too: "He was just amazing," says Dave. "I never told him I played music. . . . I was still playing in my bedroom" (Granados). Upon listening to the same tape Beauford had heard, Moore accepted the recording invitation.[*]

4. John D'earth, who played regularly at Miller's on Thursday nights with various jazz configurations, invited the Tandem School student jazz combo, the Yabanci Jazzites, to showcase there. Then a junior, bassist Stefan Lessard's 1989–90 debut performances grabbed everyone's attention. Matthews had met

---

* In interviews, Matthews has sometimes reversed the order of numbers 2 and 3. See Jones versus Chenoweth; Kelley versus Passy. By most accounts, these events occurred at the same time, as listed in Caputo, for example.

Lessard while visiting John D'earth's music classes at Tandem. Lessard was soon asked to play with Matthews, simply, in Matthews' words, to make "a recording . . . we didn't really have plans" (Cadigan). By the early spring of 1991, Beauford, Moore, and Lessard had begun to play with Matthews (Deck). Lessard had only recently taken up the electric bass, but he had been playing the upright for a while. Had Matthews once poured some juice or soft drink for Lessard at Miller's?

5.   Boyd Tinsley can pinpoint placing an order. "I remember playing with Down Boy Down at Miller's. Dave was the bartender there, and he would serve me Cokes" (Blackwell, "Dave Matthews"). Of course, by early 1991, most people in town had seen the electric violinist perform; he was, after all, also the star of the Boyd Tinsley Band. Tinsley would initially be asked to play on one song on the next Matthews demo, entitled "Tripping Billies" (Bledsoe). Busy, at that point, with his own heavily booked group, Tinsley couldn't seriously consider joining another band, but he was interested in helping out on the demo. In fact, all the musicians Matthews approached were in other bands: Beauford and Moore were playing in a jazz trio with Jeff Decker; Lessard was playing with a jazz group. Tinsley's band had major gigs scheduled up and down the coast, as well as at a bigger venue in the C'ville area named Trax.

There would be other C'ville musicians who would sit in with the various incarnations of DMB in its early period (1991–92), and they had all, at some point, commanded the small stage at Miller's: guitarist Tim Reynolds, drummer Johnny Gilmore, drummer Ian Moore, and saxman-flutist Richard Hardy, to name a few. Peter Griesar, for a time DMB's keyboardist, had worked there, too.

This Miller's inventory illustrates how the C'ville music community was functioning around the time the Dave Matthews Band coalesced. Matthews once summed it up like this: "There's kind of a school of musicians in

15

Charlottesville, an incestuous group of people" (Brown, "Coming In"). But before any of this, Dave Matthews of Johannesburg, South Africa, had to end up in Charlottesville, Virginia. His personal hegira was the essential overture to the formation of DMB.

"I think my mom was in a Vivaldi phase when I was in her womb, because I'm so inexplicably insane about Vivaldi," Matthews has mused (Considine). David John Matthews left the womb and took his place in a music-loving household on January 9, 1967. Home was a suburb north of Johannesburg. John and Val Matthews, Dave's parents, both had family ties in South Africa. John was a respected physicist; Val is a painter and was once an architect. The Matthews family would eventually expand to include four children — Anne, Peter, David, and Jane — all raised in the Quaker tradition. In addition to Vivaldi, Dave also remembers hearing Tchaikovsky, Bach, Beethoven, and Stravinsky during his very early years. A grandfather introduced him to Glenn Gould's recording of Bach's *Goldberg Variations*; he told *Rolling Stone* in 1995 that Bach was like pop music to him when he was a kid. Clearly, classical was Matthews' first major musical influence (Matthews, "Raves").

Because of the nature of his father's work, Dave's childhood years were peripatetic ones. Dave Matthews, it seems, was born to tour. "I was actually born in South Africa, but my family left almost immediately a couple of years after that. I grew up in New York" (Brown, "Coming In"). That move, which came about because John Matthews began working for IBM, landed the clan in the New York City suburb of Yorktown Heights (Colapinto). America rapidly introduced young Dave to a whole new set of musical references: "I liked the Jackson Five for a little while, because I was five" (Considine). Soon, he started listening to Bob Dylan.

When Dave was seven, the family was again uprooted. They resided in Cambridge, England, from 1974 to 1975, and Dave's new musical heroes became the Beatles — the Fab Four. "I was very young . . . and I couldn't understand how anybody could make such perfect things. It made me think extraordinary things were possible if people could so consistently make great music" (Considine). His taste in British pop and rock was as diverse as his taste in American influences: Matthews also started listening to the Sex Pistols around this time.

At this stage in his successful career as a research physicist, John Matthews was building an international reputation as — in Dave's words — "one of the granddaddies of the superconductor." In 1975, the family moved back to Yorktown Heights. These transcontinental shifts did not adversely affect their home life, however; the Matthews were a close-knit and loving unit (Colapinto).

The Matthews family was keenly aware of cultural events wherever they happened to be living, and this gave each member a unique perspective on the arts in three different countries, continuing through the 1970s and the 1980s. This provided a fascinating background for a future artist — even as a child, Dave managed to sample an international cultural smorgasbord on three different continents.

Soon, his interest in playing the guitar manifested itself. At the age of nine, he took guitar lessons, but it wasn't a pleasurable experience. "I was a terrible student," says Matthews. But he admits his teacher did offer a piece of advice that he never forgot: " 'Keep your foot tapping whatever you do.' That always stuck in my mind. If you miss a note or you miss a chord, as long as you keep the rhythm going, it really doesn't matter" (Morse, "How Dave"). He also remembers learning a couple of simpler Beatles tunes when he first started. Sometime during this period, Matthews developed an affinity for Sly and the Family Stone, but, sadly, his record collection was stolen, and his Sly albums were lost.

Matthews has given us a few insights into the halcyon days of his childhood: "Although there were no musicians in my family, there was always music playing in the house. And there was the appreciation of long hikes through the woods and family quiet time, where we could listen to the sounds of things around us, heartbeats and footsteps" (Gulla). Quaker philosophy is an important element of his roots. He recalls gathering with his family and fellow worshipers in a quiet building in eastern New York State — in times of both sorrow and happiness — and watching respectfully as members of the Quaker congregation rose, one by one, moved by the "inward light" to share their thoughts (Marzullo and Leta).

Matthews' love of serenity may, in fact, be linked directly to Quaker teachings. The Quaker (or, more formally, the Religious Society of Friends) meeting for worship is based on silent meditation; those moved by the spirit can offer prayer or exhortation unrestrained by ritual or the intervention of ordained clergy. This is one of the basic tenets of the teachings of George Fox, who, in 1652, founded the movement in Britain as a protest movement against the Church of England. Fox and his followers believed, among other things, that the utterance of oaths recognizes a double standard of truth. To be frugal and plain in speech was considered honest, and such a resolve brought one closer to Christ ("Quakers").

Serenity aside, there was also plenty of sound-making activity in the Matthews home. "I've been singing since before I can remember," Dave insists (Cadigan). He was pounding the piano keys, to boot: "When I was a kid, I loved to play the piano like it was a drum kit. I would open it up — we had an upright in our house — and I'd pull the front off and take off the top so I could look at the strings, stick my head in and just pound away" (Mettler). Around the time he turned 10, his brother, Peter, introduced him to Led Zeppelin and Jethro Tull. Dave was — by this time — steeped in folk music, as well: James Taylor, John Denver, Cat Stevens, Joan Baez, and Buffy Sainte-Marie were already favorites. Matthews also took in the offerings of Joni Mitchell and Carly Simon; he then got into Pink Floyd and Deep Purple and entered a heavy-metal stage.

In 1977, tragedy struck. John Matthews died of lung cancer, possibly as a result of handling radioactive material in the course of his research (Colapinto). The loss was devastating. The family entered a time of mourning and profound grief. Val Matthews made the decision to leave New York and go back to South Africa. Dave explains: "It was for family that we went back there . . . a single mom with four kids, she wanted to get some support. But then we all left, pining for the States. . . ." (Jones).

Dave Matthews became a US citizen in 1980, but continued to reside in South Africa with his family. He loved it there. He developed a flair for art, and continued listening to music. According to his sister Jane, Matthews listened much more carefully than the rest of them. While a student at a British-style private school, he was reprimanded for behavioral "antics" (Colapinto).

It was in South Africa that Dave underwent passage from adolescence to adulthood. Recalling those crucial years, he comments: "I lived in three environments in South Africa. . . . There was my family. There was [private school]. And there was the one that was to sort of go out and sit out in the field, go out in the bush and hang out with some guys who worked at my uncle's dairy who were mostly black and maybe smoke a little pot and drink a little beer, stay up late and tell stories" (Kelley). He relished the physical beauty of South Africa's landscape and its cities. He developed a special fondness for Cape Town, the country's legislative capital: "There's a sense of comfort there. When I lived in South Africa — even through apartheid — that city was so beautiful that it made things seem . . . hopeful" (Matthews, "Raves").

Matthews was mature enough to absorb the cultural and political aspects of South Africa. He listened to South African music — artists like King Sunny Ade, Salif Keita, and Hugh Masekela. He participated in protest marches to end apartheid. He witnessed people singing "the most incredible music in the face of police with tear gas and bats" (Morse, "How Dave"). And he also experienced overwhelming feelings of helplessness, because he knew that the rest of the world was unaware of the level of atrocity occurring daily in the streets of Johannesburg: "The violence was there whether it was international news or not" (Jones).

Val Matthews was an activist in the anti-apartheid movement, thereby upholding a long Quaker tradition of fighting social injustice. The Matthews children were raised to believe that bigotry and racism are absolute evils (Colapinto). Dave was able to observe, firsthand, the power of culture as a political force. He is circumspect in describing this power: "It seems as if the struggle to survive, along with the struggle to create, are driving forces. . . . I've gotten great inspiration from a people — and this is before they even thought of freeing Mandela — who have been suppressed but made their culture grow and, in a way, surround the oppressors. Their culture was their last voice, and no one could take it away" (Snider).

Matthews also observed the role that organized religion plays in South African politics, and this later affected his personal convictions: "My politics are I'm an anarchist. . . . Growing up in South Africa was part of the reason, because there's a government telling you what's wrong and right, and you can see that it's not. And then they can pull the Bible out, because it's a great place to find quotes. And that was a good thing, because in turn, the revolution came from the church" (Mervis, "Crashing Through").

Dave's plaintive song "Cry Freedom," first performed in 1991, addresses the political plight of South Africa: "Cry freedom, cry from deep inside / Where we all are confined / While we wave hands in fire." With the additional lyric line "How can I turn away," he speaks to the continuing responsibility he feels to encourage peace in that ravaged country to get involved — an extension of the political activism he embraced as a teenager.

From about 1982 to 1986, Matthews played the guitar "all the time. That's all I did" (Colapinto). His vocal stylings began to develop. He began to emulate Bob Marley and Marvin Gaye. Elaborating on Marley's influence on him, he remarked: "I think the person that inspired me the most when I was a teenager was Bob Marley. . . . He was on the edge, at least socially. . . . And I loved the rhythm. That was the thing I thought was missing from a lot of music that was on the edge then. . . ." (Considine, "Songs"). Matthews played electric guitar for a brief time at the age of fifteen.

As the South Africa years unfolded, Matthews accumulated a wealth of experience. Some of his adventures he would relate to DMB fans, at length, during concerts. Some highlights: seeing the genitals of monkeys in the wild (told at the Jones Beach concert, 6/9/96); being astounded by the size of elephant genitals (recounted at an acoustic concert with Tim Reynolds, 2/17/96); traveling the road to Zimbabwe — an epic, scatological tale involving a bus trip, Fanta, cheese puffs, beer, and hiding things from border guards (told at the University of New Hampshire, 2/19/96). He has also said that the song "Tripping Billies" is about a real-life high-school escapade during which he found himself tripping on hallucinogens while visiting a beach on the southeast coast of South Africa. Leaving their crackling campfire, Dave and friends climbed a cliff, which crumbled beneath their feet. Everyone jumped clear in time except Dave, who landed facedown in the sand (Marzullo and Leta).

Matthews clearly enjoyed himself in South Africa. "It really is a great place. I love the music and I love the people. I go back at least once a year, and I really hope to live there again some time" (Riemenschneider).

In 1986, Matthews decided to leave South Africa in order to avoid the draft. According to him, "it's what about 65 percent of the people do" (Jones). His avoidance of military service is consistent with Quaker philosophy, which is fundamentally pacifist. Quakers do not sanction taking part in war because they feel that war causes spiritual damage through hatred. How much this directly affected

Matthews' decision is hard to determine, but, in any event, Quakers also advocate that individuals should be true to their own convictions.

Returning to New York City, alone, at the age of 19, Matthews landed a temporary job at the same IBM research center where his father had once worked (Colapinto). Later that year, 1986, he joined the rest of his family, which had taken up residence in Charlottesville. Matthews would never choose to be far away from them for long: "I'm a family boy, I'm a good boy, the kind of boy your mom would like you to bring home" (Mervis, "Crashing Through"). The family chose C'ville because John and Val had lived there before, when John worked at UVA. Val had fond memories of the town. "She liked it here and always thought she would come back," Dave explained (Jones). "My family moved to Charlottesville before I was born, so that's how I ended up in Charlottesville" (Silverman).

The next few years were filled with travel and study. He shuttled back and forth between Virginia and South Africa several times. He entered a local community college on a limited-enrollment basis; there, Dave did well in philosophy (Colapinto). His dreams expanded to include drama and art as possible career paths. He was searching for his métier, and the search was fascinating.

It was around this time that Matthews began to play and sing in public, performing solo at open-mike nights around Charlottesville. He also played with Tim Reynolds, whom he met in 1987 while Reynolds was performing at Miller's. Matthews approached Reynolds, asking if he knew a certain Bob Marley tune. Later, Matthews occasionally sat in with Reynolds' band, TR3. Reynolds remarks: "We started hanging out, having fun in Dave's basement and messing around with little four-track recordings. I remember this one song that was dark-sounding. I had to go to a gig, and I said, 'Have at it, man.' When I got home that night, he'd left me a tape and it floored me — very creative and angular" (G. Brown, "Chance").

Dawn Thompson recalls enjoying Matthews performing a Bob Marley tune with TR3 at the now-defunct club portion of the C & O, a once-thriving music venue in C'ville that currently operates as a restaurant and bistro. Matthews remembers that Leroi Moore was unimpressed by one Matthews guest stint with TR3. Dave confides: "That was before Leroi knew me. Leroi loved TR3, and he walked in and heard me playing this song with them. It really is funny, he said that was the worst thing he heard in his life" (Blackwell, "Dave Matthews"). But, obviously, Moore didn't let that performance define his opinion of Matthews.

Another witness to a Matthews/TR3 performance was John D'earth. "He sang incredibly well," D'earth says of Dave, "and had great stage presence. You could tell he really felt the music. He was superb."

In September of 1989, Thompson and Matthews sang a duet in a multimedia dance performance with a theatrical format. D'earth composed the song they did, and was pleased with their effort: "They sounded really good together." Each had a solo. The pair continued to sing together, off and on, for a few years. Throughout this period, Thompson says, Matthews "was always singing and playing guitar. He has a natural instinct for performing. He's a unique, natural talent."

It was in 1990 that Matthews seriously began writing songs. Taije Silverman, interviewing Matthews for the Charlottesville *Observer*, asked him about the genesis of his songwriting talent. He replied that he hadn't been writing very long before the band got together: "I'd thought about, or dreamt about, being a musician but I hadn't really done anything. I hadn't written any songs." Silverman repeated: "You hadn't written songs when the band came together?" Matthews responded: "No, not like for a year before. That's when I started writing."

By 1990, Matthews had met Ross Hoffman; they became close friends. Hoffman had owned a local recording studio and was a songwriter. "I started writing songs in 1990," explains Dave. "Before then, I had only doodled around on the guitar and never finished a song, until Ross Hoffman encouraged me, steered me towards writing" (Chenoweth). As the summer wore on, Matthews could often be found hanging out at Hoffman's apartment in the now-famous pink warehouse — also known in Charlottesville as "the

South Street Warehouse" — located near the Downtown Mall and next to the South Street Restaurant. The next year, Matthews would write a long, lyrical song called "Warehouse." The words express his great affection for the place: "Maybe things won't be better than they have been / Here in the warehouse / At the warehouse / How I love to stay here."

Lydia Conder, a designer and the owner of C'ville's Gallery Neo, moved into the pink warehouse, 100 South Street, in 1990. In earlier days, the building had been used to store fruits and vegetables; when Conder arrived, it housed a few apartments, the offices of the Charlottesville *Observer*, and an antique shop owned by the landlord, Roulhac Toledano, of New Orleans. Roulhac maintained a residence on the third floor, which also contained a library: here Conder settled in. The room was splendidly furnished with rare antiques and lined with 12,000 books.

During her first week in residence, Conder met Matthews. She was sitting on the front stoop early one evening reading Charles Bukowski poetry aloud with a friend. "Some girls showed up in a red pickup blasting 2 Live Crew and things got racy, so I went inside and upstairs. Dave Matthews soon followed. He spied my guitar leaning against a chair and picked it up. I asked if he played. He said, 'A little.' He played 'All Along the Watchtower' and then 'I'll Back You Up.' I was transported. It was the greatest thing I ever heard in my own apartment — one of those small moments you never forget. We brushed our teeth together and became real friends after that, and I saw him almost every day, since he was hanging out with my adjoining neighbor Ross Hoffman, who, in those days, was Dave's spiritual mentor. They hung out on Ross's bed, working on the songs and discussing the possibilities of starting a band."

Hoffman took an active interest in Matthews. First he became Dave's supportive friend, and later his "personal manager." As he promoted Matthews' musical talents to everyone he met, Hoffman also began to be impressed with Matthews' acting ability. Saxman-flutist Richard Hardy remembers Hoffman saying: "You've got to see Dave act. He's a great actor." Hardy also recalls Hoffman's admiration for Dave's musical ability: "Ross listened to Dave's songs and said, 'Let's see what we can do and get these on tape.'" The quest to make a good Matthews demo was initiated.

During this time, Matthews began acting in various theatrical projects with a company called Offstage Theater. Offstage was known for its innovative, site-specific pieces, producing their shows in such alternative venues as restaurants, bars, parks, and on the Downtown Mall. They even produced a site-specific series of one-act plays in an apartment on the third floor of the pink warehouse.

Although outside the Charlottesville area Matthews' acting skills remain virtually unknown, those locals who did attend one of his theatrical performances continue to rave about what a great actor he is. "Fantastic," "phenomenal," and "incredible" is standard terminology in discussions of his acting prowess. John D'earth concurs: "He's a really gifted actor. Beyond that, he's got an actor's improv ability. He's a delightful and gifted person." In September of 1990, Matthews appeared in a one-act play called *Just Say No* by San Francisco playwright Barney Strauss Jr. He played a wily used-car salesman. The show was produced at Tandem School; the cast also included John Quinn and Kylie Suture. In a related *Observer* story published in October — one that detailed a television presentation of the performance — Matthews was described simply as a "local actor" named David Matthews.

Matthews quit tending bar at Miller's sometime in late 1990 or early 1991. He became very disciplined, and spent many evenings writing songs. From 7 o'clock until 11 o'clock every night he worked on his tunes in his mother's basement, making them better and better, focusing on nuance and subtlety. Hoffman continued to provide Matthews with motivational input and songwriting critiques, and he also helped to finance the demos and to chronicle Matthews' slowly expanding repertoire of original compositions.

After recording his first demo in November of 1990, and after successfully pursuing Beauford, Moore, Lessard, and Tinsley to do additional demo recording work in early

HAWES COLEMAN SPENCER

Dave plays a used-car salesman in
Just Say No, September 1990

1991, Matthews could have easily let his fledgling acting career fall by the wayside. But he did not forsake the theater that year, even after the Dave Matthews Band played their first gigs in April and May of 1991. Victor Cabas, an adjunct professor at Hampden-Sydney College and UVA as well as a Delta Blues guitarist and singer, appeared in

THE **LATE** SHOW
LIVE ARTS THEATRE ENSEMBLE
COFFEEHOUSE III

Mysterious Feats and Dancing Fools in:

Speakeasy...

...THE RAGS OF RAGTIME

Compiled and Edited by: Francine Sackett. Written Contributions: Fran Sackett John Quinn, Doug Grissom, Tom Coash, Lisa Newman, Dan Scott, Joel Jones, Row Halpin

Directed by: Francine Sackett
Hosted by: Tom Morgan with Musical Performances by Kate Scott and Dave Matthews

Dave played several roles in this 1991 production

Dave's sister Jane at Trax
LOU BARON/PORTICO PUBLICATIONS LTD.

Speakeasy: The Rags of Ragtime with Matthews, produced under the banner of Live Arts Theatre Ensemble Coffeehouse III. Cabas played Ernest Hemingway, and appeared under his stage name, Bryon Nemo. He recollects the experience vividly; Matthews, particularly, made an impression on him. "Dave's a great guy. I remember him standing on a table in a scene with an impish look. He stole the scene. He stole every scene he was in. He gave himself to it completely, with energy and joy. He could get into a pure artistic state." Matthews played several roles in the show; in the program he's listed as "George / Stanley / Brother Righteous Intramural Chairman." Explains Cabas, "Dave played a frat brother, Brother Righteous Intramural Chairman. He was hilarious. That's when he got up on the table. He also played a romantic lead in the play."

Dave performed opposite an ingenue named Berkley Ingram, and they gave eight to ten performances in the early summer of 1991. The show was directed by Francine Sackett, and written by eight people: Sackett, John Quinn, Doug Grissom, Tom Coash, Lisa Newman, Dan Scott, Joel

Jones, and Row Halpin. The playbill cover bore this information, as well: "Musical Performances by Kate Scott and Dave Matthews."

On a number of occasions, Matthews has mentioned his love of acting. In 1994, he told the C-VILLE *Weekly*, "Five years ago, I was very into being an actor or painter" (Chenoweth). During a 1996 interview, he used a theater analogy to describe what it's like to give a live concert: "The live thing is like a play almost. It's kind of improvisational theater, and you give it everything you have." Few readers realized that Matthews knew what he was talking about — that he actually had been a working actor.

Theater allusions also appear in the lyrics of "The Song That Jane Likes," a song cowritten with a C'ville musician named Mark Roebuck, formerly of the band the Deal. It is generally known that the song is lovingly named in honor of Jane Matthews, Dave's younger sister, whom he calls his "soulmate." At home, Jane made repeated requests to hear the melody of the song, long before it had lyrics (Wertheimer). Matthews has refused to ascribe meaning to the lyrics publicly; however, references to his days on the stage are embedded there: "And in plays to write the wire in / I'll come back again / Torching time talking rhymes in." In another age, plays written in verse were standard fare; the works of Shakespeare and Molière come readily to mind. And wires were used to shift scenery in centuries past. The word *stage* even appears in the song. Twists on the words *plays* and *play* occur six times in the lyrics.

Coincidence? Not likely. This song is one of the first two that Matthews ever wrote. It appeared on the initial November 1990 demo, not long after Dave joined Offstage Theater. Perhaps "The Song That Jane Likes" offers hope to fans of his acting that he will return to the theater someday. Playful beginnings, indeed, for the multifaceted David Matthews.

2
EVERYBODY'S FREE

The contemporary Charlottesville music scene has a long pedigree that could probably fill an entire book of its own. R.E.M. used to play the C'ville frat-house party circuit in the 1980s; the town has been home to many bands through the years. A partial list of former local groups that are either defunct or have moved on include: Johnny Sportcoat and the Casuals, Skip Castro, the Deal, Cosmology, Secrets, Grub, Cactus Pie, the Hogwaller Ramblers, Happy Flowers, Matchbook Poets, and Pavement.

Three members of the Dave Matthews Band were active in this scene well before Matthews showed up in 1986. By that time, Carter Beauford, Leroi Moore, and Boyd Tinsley had performed in different well-received bands. The much younger Lessard was still in school, and was not yet living in C'ville. The backgrounds of these four musicians — and in some cases, their allegiances to each other — are a big part of the reason the Dave Matthews Band formed. Some of the guys wanted to play together, some had already played together, and some had known each other for years.

One musician who had direct connections to Moore, Beauford, and, eventually, Lessard was trumpeter John D'earth. With Dawn Thompson and Robert Jospe, he had come to Charlottesville from New York in 1981 as core members of the band Cosmology. (Dawn and John were married in C'ville in 1986.) Cosmology's move to C'ville would prove pivotal. Its impact on the local music scene and the future members of DMB can be demonstrated by looking at the many groups that were formed as a result of Cosmology's relocation from Manhattan: D'earth and Thompson formed the Charlottesville Swing Orchestra, along with Leroi Moore, in 1982; D'earth also played in the fusion jazz band Secrets (which lasted from 1984 to 1990), whose drummer was Carter Beauford; D'earth started the John D'earth Quintet, which would play at Miller's on Thursdays, and which also listed Leroi Moore as a founding member; Jospe would join Tim Reynolds in the band TR3; Thompson would form Code Magenta with Greg Howard in 1990, later to be joined by Leroi Moore. Of their move, D'earth recalls: "We came down here to play our music. The atmosphere was conducive to that."

When not performing, D'earth would conduct the UVA Jazz Ensemble; he also taught music at the Tandem School. Here, Stefan Lessard became his student.

According to D'earth, he and Dawn Thompson "met Ross and Holly Hoffman right away. We got involved with their recording studio. We even started a record company together." D'earth found Hoffman to be "an incredibly sympathetic person, a great guy to work with. He was tremendously encouraging." Jospe, Thompson, and D'earth helped to attract an influx of outstanding guest artists. The C'ville music mix benefited greatly from the flow of fresh ideas, as well as the opportunities for collective writing and for improvisation, that they played a role in initiating.

D'earth and Thompson met Leroi Moore around 1982; Moore became a founding member of the Charlottesville Swing Orchestra, which is still active, and of the John D'earth Quintet. Also, since 1992, D'earth has toured steadily with pianist Bruce Hornsby. D'earth feels that "Leroi Moore is unique. He needs more credit than he gets. He's basically a self-directed musician who's incredibly talented. When there's pressure to show off your chops, he always tries to get to the center of the music. I have such respect for his playing."

Leroi Moore was born in Durham, North Carolina, on September 7, 1961, and raised in Charlottesville. He was attracted to music at an early age, and credits his mother, Roxie Moore, with being his first musical influence. His father was Albert P. Moore. His childhood memories include a "cheap, little old Magnus" organ. Moore reflects: "My mother played the piano, but at that time we couldn't afford one. She liked to play hymns" (Granados). In 1974, Moore started playing the alto saxophone in his junior-high band. Shortly thereafter, he switched from alto to baritone sax. He took up the tenor saxophone, too.

In the same middle-class Charlottesville neighborhood where Moore resided, another budding musician was coming into his own: Moore's good friend Carter Beauford lived on the same street. "We kind of grew up musically together," says Beauford (Colapinto). Moore began listening to rock and R & B groups; Earth, Wind & Fire was a favorite. Then one of his school-band directors pointed him towards Charlie Parker. It was a watershed event in his musical development. After that, he sought out the recordings of Phil Woods, Benny Maupin, and Herbie Hancock.

Moore played some football in high school. He graduated in 1979, and went on to college, but he only remained there for a semester. He enrolled in James Madison University in Virginia, and focused on the tenor saxophone. He started listening to Sonny Rollins and John Coltrane — more jazz masters. Then he learned to play the soprano sax. Moore now has an incredible ability to switch horns for nearly every DMB song; he currently tours with 10 instruments. To those striving to make it as a musician, Moore offers this recommendation: "Pretty much the most important thing you can do is just . . . practice. Play as much as you can" (Granados).

For the next 10 years, Moore played the C'ville-Richmond jazz circuit, frequently with the groups that were anchored by D'earth and Thompson; they would often perform at Miller's. It was at those Miller's jazz gigs that Matthews bonded with Moore, who agreed to play on a demo of Matthews' originals in early 1991. Moore names Beauford as the person he first gigged with; they linked up naturally "because we sort of grew up together. I've known him almost all my life" (Granados). Moore began to play the flute. He also worked at the Census Bureau and the UVA Hospital ("Predictions"). Moore gave private music lessons to beginners around C'ville, as well (Niesslein, "Dave Matthews").

Richard Hardy, a saxman and flutist, formerly of C'ville, who also sat in with the Charlottesville Swing Orchestra (and whose name is misspelled throughout Internet chronologies of the band), says of Moore: "He's one of the very best at his best. He's responsible for lots of arranging, along with Dave. A lot of his arrangements were instrumental in making the songs so interesting." Hardy also played with Moore — and DMB — at various times. "I played alto and flute to his tenor and soprano in 1991 and 1992." Hardy still knows DMB tunes inside and out. He adds, jokingly: "If 'Roi ever got sick, I could still step in." Moore, Hardy feels, "is truly a genius. He's a very intelligent guy. I can't say enough about him. Loyal and honest as the day is long. He honors friendship on a very deep level." Greg Howard joins the list of fellow musicians who willingly attest to Moore's extraordinary character and artistry: "Unlike many highly successful musicians, Leroi's attitude about music and his friends hasn't changed. He's grounded in the desire to create good music."

Moore has a reputation for being an intensely private person. One of the reasons he performs with sunglasses is that they help him to battle stage fright. He suffers so much that at times he doesn't even open his eyes onstage. But Moore doesn't see this fear of performing as, necessarily, a bad thing; it keeps you in top form, he insists, and infuses you with adrenaline and energy (Granados). An "artist and a craftsman" are what Moore desires to be. "I want to be like a carpenter who can build the Taj Mahal or an outhouse, and if they're both sound and solid then one is as good as the other" (Bailey, part 2).

Moore's lifelong friendship with Carter Beauford was probably another reason that the band coalesced in the way it did. The two obviously had a desire to continue playing together. In 1990, they'd been performing in a jazz trio with Jeff Decker that took the stage Sunday nights at yet another C'ville restaurant-bar, Tokyo Rose.

Drummer-vocalist Carter Beauford (pronounced BO-ford) was born on November 2, 1957. His parents were Roland E.

Beauford and Anne E. Beauford. His first musical influence was his father, a jazz trumpet player. When Carter was young, he was eager to learn all about the pop stars of the day — the Beatles, the Dave Clark Five, James Brown, and the Flames — but his father told him, "If you want to play the drums, these are the cats," and encouraged him to get into Max Roach, Buddy Rich, Elvin Jones, Gene Krupa, Cozy Cole, and Louie Bellson. He also introduced him to Gussie Smith, Duke Ellington, Ella Fitzgerald, Miles Davis, and John Coltrane (Cornish).

Beauford's "jazz attitude" was thereby launched. As his mother instructed him in the art of correct table manners, he discovered he was naturally ambidextrous (William F. Miller, "Carter Beauford"). When Carter was nine or ten, his father took him to hear Louie Bellson; that performance made a lasting stylistic impression on him. His dad also escorted him to a Buddy Rich concert: "I didn't know what the hell it was about, but I knew that Buddy Rich was the coolest looking dude. It just blew me away. . . ." (Cornish).

Roland Beauford urged his son to play an instrument — any kind at all. "He thought that was something that kids should get into and learn about," Carter remarks. "I feel the same way. Kids should get into the arts. It's a happening thing" (William F. Miller, "Carter Beauford"). Carter did sense his calling at a very young age; he began playing when he was three years old (Bailey, part 1). He fell in love with the drums and longed to explore new territory, to do things other drummers hadn't attempted. He is self-taught: "My dad was a jazz trumpeter, so I studied indirectly through him just from listening to him play with his band and hearing him put on the records" (Cornish). Carter played his first gig when he was just nine — something of a prodigy — and gigged with musicians in their twenties and thirties.

"I think [a local jazz ensemble] hired me because I was a bit of an attraction — the 'kid drummer who could play' kind of thing." They performed a lot of modern jazz selections, including pieces by Herbie Hancock and Miles Davis — music Beauford listened to at home on a regular basis.

At his audition, the group asked him to play along with the song "Autumn Leaves." Carter stunned them by performing it nearly "note for note." He snared the job and played with the group throughout his junior-high and high-school years (William F. Miller, "Carter Beauford"). Anne Beauford, Carter's mother, confides, "As a kid we knew he had drums in his soul" (Scully). Perhaps Beauford's experiences as a jazz wunderkind enabled him to empathize with high-school bass prodigy Stefan Lessard when the two hooked up in 1991.

Beauford feels that formal training is great but hands-on experience is irreplaceable; you'll never know about making music until you actually test yourself before an audience. He suggests that novice musicians study the masters — like John Coltrane or Miles Davis — if they want to learn how to develop their own voice on an instrument: "Go back to the days of old. . . . Whether you like it or not, you will learn something" (Cornish). Beauford goes on to name Steve Gadd, Dennis Chambers, Tony Williams, Stewart Copeland, Vinnie Colaiuta, Marvin "Smitty" Smith, Dave Weckl, and Will Kennedy (of the Yellow Jackets) as contemporary drummers whose work he admires.

As a student at the Shenandoah Conservatory in Winchester, Virginia, Carter became close friends with Billy

Drummond, a New York jazz drummer. They practiced together every day, and Beauford learned a lot from him; he even examined Drummond's posture. Playing before a mirror, he studied his appearance behind the drum kit. His confidence mounted.

In the end, however, Beauford opted to study occupational therapy at Shenandoah, not music. He still couldn't read music. He earned a degree in occupational therapy and became a teacher (William F. Miller, "Carter Beauford"). For twelve years, he taught at various elementary and high schools in Albemarle County, Winchester, and Winston-Salem, North Carolina (Bailey, part 1). When he quit teaching to play music full-time, his mother wasn't at all pleased, but his father backed him up. He understood that Carter had a calling: "He knew down deep I was a musician," Carter explains (William F. Miller, "Carter Beauford"). Beauford joined Moore once again and played with him in other groups.

There were even a few country and disco bands that benefited from Beauford's skills. He was actually fired a few times because of his daring style. Those who merely wanted a timekeeper for disco hits were incapable of appreciating him. They wanted a drummer to "play it like the record": "Musically, I learned nothing from disco," he states (Cornish). Carter went through a tough period while touring with a jazz band; they lived in a dilapidated 1974 van for a while (William F. Miller, "Carter Beauford").

From 1984 to 1990, Beauford played in the fusion band Secrets, with John D'earth; they covered the Virginia jazz circuit. Matthews first caught Beauford when he was playing with Secrets in 1986. "He would sail with that band," says Dave, "and audiences would just be awed by his playing. I can honestly say I was overwhelmed" (William F. Miller, "Matthews"). The band put out an album titled *Secrets*.

With the album under his belt, Beauford was able to land a job on a television show based in Washington, DC. *BET on Jazz*, on the Black Entertainment Network, was a vehicle for pianist Ramsey Lewis, and Beauford appeared on the show for four years. It was an excellent opportunity: he had occasion to play with the likes of Roy Hargrove and Maceo

Parker. Beauford also performed with noted jazz guitarists Larry Coryell and John Abercrombie. He spent some time in Los Angeles. By January of 1991, he had again installed himself in C'ville, where he picked up the occasional gig; he drove to Washington regularly to do bet *on Jazz*. Around the time DMB started to play some gigs, Beauford left the show.

Carter has other interests, as well. He can play the guitar. He is also the divorced father of a daughter, Breanna Simone Beauford, of whom he is very proud: "She is my everything" (Bailey 1993). Many DMB fans have commented on Beauford's joyful countenance and glowing smile; he often performs with a "permagrin."

Although a number of people have sung harmonies with DMB at different points (Kristin Asbury, Shannon Worrell, and Peter Griesar, to name a few), most DMB fans have just

heard Beauford's vocal harmonizing. It's impressive to see him play drums and sing at the same time. Comments Matthews: "People don't talk much about Carter's singing, but he's good. If I could get everyone else in the band to sing like him we could be like the Bee Gees" (William F. Miller, "Matthews"). Matthews teases Beauford — on Carter's birthday in 1993, Dave made cracks about his age to the audience during a show. Beauford is, in fact, the oldest member of DMB and probably the most experienced.

The rhythm section of DMB is composed of two wunderkinds — one the oldest member of the group and the other the youngest. Both had fathers who were musicians. Bassist Stefan Kahil Lessard (pronounced Les-SARD) is the youngest member of the Dave Matthews Band. Born in southern California on June 4, 1974, he spent his very early years traveling: he had journeyed from California to Rhode Island and then back to Anaheim by the time he was two. Lessard's parents are both extremely musical. His father, Ron, who still performs, has a BA in music composition from the Berklee College of Music in Boston. Ron Lessard's instrument? The bass. The name Lessard has a French-Canadian pedigree; the family is also part Mohawk. Stefan's mother, although of British and American heritage, had a recording career in Spain in the 1960s; the company she signed with, a division of Columbia Records, was also associated with Julio Iglesias. She recorded under the name Jackie, which was shortened from her birth name of Jacqueline. One of her hits rose to number 16 on the Spanish charts. In the 1980s, her name was changed to Janaki, a name given to her by a Native American tribe. Janaki, Ron says, was always singing to Stefan in the womb. "She has a wonderful voice, an angelic voice."

Ron graduated from Berklee in 1976, when Stefan was two. He explains that his son grew up hearing lots of different kinds of music, especially jazz. "There was always music playing in our environment. It was part of who we were," Ron explains. Ron Lessard was employed by various music-related companies throughout the 1970s and 1980s. In addition to playing music and writing songs, he worked for Fender, Gibson, and Ovation. He likes to talk about

Stefan's early musical abilities: "Even at a young age, his sense of timing was incredible."

The Lessard family grew. Stefan has two younger sisters, Ambha and Bhuva. The clan embraced vegetarianism and a holistic, healthy, natural lifestyle, which included yoga. In Rhode Island they occupied a mobile home, and when they returned to Anaheim they moved into a condo. Contrary to what was suggested in a 1996 *Rolling Stone* article, the Lessards were not involved in a nomadic hippie lifestyle involving drug use. "There was one time when we crossed the country in a green tortoise bus," says Ron. "Some of the people on the bus were old hippies. But we weren't into that." Ron believes that this is what his son was referring to when he made a comment to *Rolling Stone* about remembering "a bunch of hippie potheads" (Colapinto).

In 1984, Ron and Janaki became followers of Swami Satchidananda, who had established Yogaville, an ashram an hour's drive from Charlottesville. Singer-songwriter Carole King was involved in the ashram. The Lessards moved to Yogaville and took up residence in a house. There, Stefan quickly developed a love of nature and a passion for music. In an MTV online interview, he credited "Mary Carol, my very first music teacher," with being a primary musical influence. "She's probably the biggest," Stefan added, "but after that . . . Colin Moulding of XTC and also Jaco Pastorius." Ron clarifies that Stefan studied violin with Mary Carol in Virginia.

Later that year, the Lessard family picked up and went to Richmond, where they remained for three years. From there they went to Madison, Wisconsin, and stayed from 1987 through early 1989. Ron Lessard had a huge music store to run in Madison, but the family had begun to pine for Virginia. They finally made their way back to the Charlottesville area in 1989. Purchasing a vast new mobile home in an idyllic setting on 25 acres of land, they reestablished themselves.

Stefan entered the Tandem School, a small private institution with a progressive learning philosophy that was founded in Charlottesville in the early 1970s. Tandem endeavors to tailor its curriculum to the individual interests

of its students. At Tandem, in his junior year, Stefan came under the tutelage of John D'earth. D'earth and Lessard helped to form a jazz-band class that met at 9 A.M. — an early call for most musicians. D'earth set aside his trumpet to play drums on these occasions.

D'earth fondly remembers Lessard's participation in the class. "His vibe at that age was like a 30-year-old's. He was so focused and completely serious — having a great time but serious. We . . . played five to ten songs [per class]. Stefan wrote for the band and so did some of the other students." The class formed a band named the Yabanci Jazzites. To young musicians, D'earth imparts this advice: "Listen to the classics, like Charles Mingus and Charlie Parker. In order to play music, you have to exercise your ears. If you love bass, try to pick out the bass lines in songs."

Ron Lessard also attests to his son's discipline and talent. He marvels at Stefan's focus: "He definitely showed an early discipline to learn the fundamentals of music. If we'd sit down to watch television on the couch, 15 minutes into a show Stefan would say, 'Well, I think I'll go practice.' Or he'd say he was going to bed. Two hours later, he'd still be practicing the bass." Ron takes no credit for helping to develop Stefan's talent, despite the fact that they had both chosen the same instrument. He points out that his son's first bass teachers were Mike D'Antoni and Pete Spaar, and that Stefan also took master classes with Mark Johnson. Stefan never faltered: in Ron's words, he "didn't say that music is what he wanted to do. He said it's what I'm *going* to do."

Ron Lessard also stresses that his son is a whole person, a man of many interests, not just music. Stefan used to skateboard, as well as draw and paint. "He's a great artist." Furthermore, he displays an active interest in horticulture — "He's always telling me about planting things" — and knows his way around a kitchen (his dad declares he's an excellent cook).

In 1990, the Yabanci Jazzites continued to create music at Tandem, but the group had suffered a personnel exodus. D'earth recalls: "The next year, most of the people dropped out. But Stefan hung in there with a class of beginners.

Before, we'd get through eight songs. Now we'd be lucky to get through one. Yet he was really encouraging to the other people. He has an amazing spirit. For a young guy, he exemplifies the vibe of an old soul. He's a very wise person in himself." Matthews agrees: "Stefan is the youngest but he acts like a wise old man, an Obi Wan Kenobe" (Provencher, "Matthews").

"I've learned a lot from him," reflects Ron, who is also convinced that his son is an old soul. "He's very wise and very loving about all aspects of life. I'm proud of Stefan, musically — of course, that's really understood. He has genius qualities musically. But as a whole person — how really caring and loving he is towards everyone — it's amazing. He's very easygoing. And the most impressive thing is, look at where he could be going with his life, so young, at his age. Instead, he has it all together."

Stefan credits the Miller's milieu as being his true launchpad into the world of jazz: "My music teacher [D'earth] was a jazz trumpet player, who played at a bar, Miller's, where Dave bartended. The rest of the guys played there, too. I was starting off on bass and was interested in jazz, so they let me sit in" (Catlin, "From Frat Houses"). Ron, who used to own a C'ville musical-instrument store named Stardust Music, recalls yet another fascinating fact about his son: from the time he turned 16, Stefan has worked continuously as a musician, whether sitting in with John D'earth at Miller's or playing with DMB.

Lessard's taste in music differs significantly from that of DMB's other members; for one thing, he's a lot younger than they are. He's into reggae, jazz, and alternative rock. "Like, I was a huge Nirvana fan," he says, "and no one else even understood anything about that. I was trying to get Dave to scream on his songs and stuff." Lessard remembers that when he met Matthews, Dave was doing a rendition of Dylan's "All Along the Watchtower," but apart from that, Dave's repertoire consisted merely of four original compositions at the time the band got together (Catlin, "From Frat Houses").

As DMB's reputation was taking off, during his senior year, Stefan dropped out of Tandem. "I have a really tough

43

time turning down gigs," he reveals, "and it got to a point where we were playing so much that I couldn't go to class" (Bailey, part 1). He did get his General Equivalency Diploma, and was accepted into the music program at Virginia Commonwealth University for jazz performance while still a high-school junior, but he only attended for 10 days in August of 1991. His father recalls: "We left the decision up to him. Since he was part of the band from day one, he didn't want to leave in the middle of their first success. He thought the band was starting to sound so good. He figured he could always return to school at another point, since he was so young. He wanted to stick with the band." Obviously, Stefan's instincts about DMB's potential for success were correct.

The experience of simultaneously surviving the teenage years and developing into an internationally recognized musician is one that few can share. "I feel like I've grown up with this band," says Stefan. "It's been my college" (Catlin, "From Frat Houses"). Ron Lessard believes that his son has navigated these treacherous waters admirably, *and* contributed an enormous amount to the musical development of DMB. "He's helped with a lot of the arranging and songwriting. He and Dave work on songs together. His playing is egoless. He and Carter are incredibly tight as a rhythm section."

Violinist Boyd Tinsley was the last to sign on. Born in Charlottesville on May 16, 1964 to George Franklin and Helen Carter Tinsley, Boyd Calvin Tinsley grew up, in the same neighborhood as Beauford and Moore (Bledsoe), with a brother, Bruce, and two sisters, Bertha and Betty. He attended C'ville's Walker Middle School, and dreamed of becoming a rock star — a guitar-playing rock star. "I was in sixth grade and had signed up to take a course in music expecting to take up the guitar," Tinsley recollects. "But lo and behold, it turned out to be a string orchestra class" (Fields). His passion for the violin heated up quickly. Although only twelve at the time, Tinsley believes he got off to a late start: "Most people start when they are about 4 or 5 years old. But I excelled fairly rapidly. I had good teachers, so I didn't get discouraged" (Blackwell, "Backstage").

The Boyd Tinsley Band

At Charlottesville High School, Boyd received classical training. "I never really played fiddle. All my experience in music was classical up until the time I finished high school" (Fields). For a while, he seriously considered becoming a classical violinist. He studied with violinist Kevin Lawrence. A concert pianist who had heard him play suggested that he go to Baltimore for the summer and study with Baltimore Symphony Concert Master Isador Saslav, who also taught at the Peabody Conservatory. Saslav, in turn, tried to persuade Tinsley to enter Baltimore's Performing Arts High School, but Boyd felt unprepared to take such a huge step: "I knew it would be intensive practicing and studying all the time, and I really don't think I was mature enough as a person to make that kind of commitment. I really didn't know if this is what I wanted and to make that kind of decision, something I knew I had to be absolutely sure about, I basically decided I didn't want to pursue it anymore. I was sort of scared out of it" (Fields).

Putting the violin aside for a year, Tinsley enrolled at UVA in 1982. As a brother at Sigma Nu fraternity, he attended a series of all-night music fests called "Coffeehouses," and describes what he heard there: "Lots of brothers were doing Bob Dylan covers . . . Neil Young covers . . . Grateful Dead" (Colapinto). Then came the brainstorm: What about a rock band with a violinist as a lead musician? "The thought kind of clicked . . ." (Fields). Slowly, things began to fall into place. That wild idea began to seem possible. Guitar-playing friends invited him to jam sessions.

At first he didn't know how to improvise. "I said, 'What? I need sheet music!' " But as he played, he began to develop an improv style. "It was really cool, like a whole new world being born. . . . I realized I can make any kind of music I want with this instrument!" (Bledsoe). There were few electric violinist models for Tinsley to emulate: Papa John Creach, who sometimes sat in with Jefferson Airplane; jazz violinist Jean-Luc Ponty, who played for a bit with Frank Zappa; and jazz violinist Stephane Grappelli.* It was two years before Tinsley "really got the hang" of improvisational style. "I guess it just took time for me to realize that this instrument was part of me and all I had to do was trust myself" (Fields).

Tinsley and his wife, Emily, have a daughter named Abigail. He takes an active interest in politics and current events. Graduating from UVA with a degree in history, Boyd soon realized that it was music, after all, that could offer him a viable career path.

In the summer of 1987, he began working with Harry Faulkner, a rhythm guitarist. Faulkner and Tinsley formed the acoustic duo Down Boy Down: "We were trying to think of what to call ourselves and Harry kind of came up with the name off the top of his head" (Fields). Tinsley and Faulkner wrote songs and performed them in a variety of C'ville venues. The duo became a trio when bass player Brian Wagoner, a friend and fellow UVA student, came on board. The Boyd Tinsley Band was born. They started playing gigs at Sigma Nu Coffeehouses and several clubs.

47

---

* Other jazz violinists who made an impact earlier in the twentieth century include: Stuff Smith, Eddie South, Joe Venuti, and Svend Asmussen.

On the 1996 MTV DMB special, *Crashing the Quarter*, Matthews talks about seeing Tinsley perform for the first time: "I went and I saw Boyd and Boyd was by himself in a fraternity house in a fraternity party with a violin. He wasn't just by himself. I mean, he had a violin and he was on the stage, if you were watching him. But by himself, playing — he had all this weird delay stuff. It blew my mind."

After getting off to a false start with one drummer, Tinsley spoke to his friend Andrew "Drex" Weaver, a student in Boston. Weaver, Tinsley says, "kind of jokingly said, 'Boyd, I'm coming back and I'm going to play drums in your band.'" At first, both considered the idea a gag, but Weaver did finally move to C'ville and take charge of the drum kit for the Boyd Tinsley Band (Fields). Down Boy Down continued to play every Sunday at the Blue Ridge Brewing Company.

For four years, the Boyd Tinsley Band experimented with different sounds, performing both original material and cover versions. Boyd sang, played violin, and wrote songs, as did the group's other members. In time, the Boyd Tinsley Band accumulated more than 40 original compositions in its performance roster. The group toured East Coast colleges and clubs from Pennsylvania to Alabama (Blackwell, "Backstage").

In early 1991, Tinsley was asked to play on the Matthews demo with Beauford, Lessard, and Moore: the song they were to do was "Tripping Billies." In the summer of 1991, Boyd guested with DMB, then a quartet, at Eastern Standard a few times — as his touring schedule permitted. He found himself performing with three different musical entities at the same time: Down Boy Down, the Boyd Tinsley Band, and the Dave Matthews Band. It was not until much later that Tinsley became a full-time member of DMB — in mid-1992. In fact, another musician would join DMB on a "permanent" basis before Tinsley did: keyboardist Peter Griesar. And a rotating series of musicians would sit in with the band throughout 1991 and 1992; such flexible arrangements typified the openness of the C'ville music scene; there were lots of solid musicians-at-large.

Matthews once elaborated on the myriad Miller's inter-

From left to right: Carter Beauford, Dave Matthews,
Boyd Tinsley, Stefan Lessard, Leroi Moore

sections — and the kind of rehearsal schedules they engendered: "The club where I worked at was very laid back. It was a very cool place. . . . I couldn't have worked at a place that was loud and had drunk people screaming. We all met there and Carter, Stefan, and Leroi had their afternoons free, so we worked on recording some of the songs I had written. We just really clicked" (Niesel).

Luckily, all four musicians were free in early 1991 — in the afternoons, at least — to start rehearsing songs that were destined to become the first in the Dave Matthews Band catalog of originals. Those tunes would eventually be worth millions. But, of course, nobody knew it at the time.

3
CELEBRATING & RELATING

A time of trial and incubation. That's what the first few months of 1991 became for DMB. Beauford describes their first rehearsal: "It started out as a three-piece thing with Dave and Leroi . . . working on some of Dave's songs. He only had four songs at the time. . . . And it didn't work out with the three of us" (Cornish). Matthews' memories of the occasion were equally grim: "The first time we played together . . . we were awful. Not just kind of bad, I mean heinously bad. We tried a couple of different songs and they were all terrible. . . . Sometimes it amazes me we ever had a second rehearsal" (Deck).

But they were not prepared to give up so soon. Instead, they arrived at this solution: Stefan Lessard. Beauford reveals: "We managed to get a few things happenin' . . . you know . . . with the songs, but we needed a bass player. That was the bottom line" (Cornish). Lessard joined them; he'd played with Beauford and Moore before (Chenoweth). Matthews, Beauford, Lessard, and Moore spent their afternoons trying things out; at first, they just had the demo in their sights, but they sounded so great together that they decided to continue as a live band. Hoffman continued to encourage all of Matthews' endeavors, and the two remained close (Fox, "Dave on the Stand?"). The quartet rehearsed in Beauford's basement, and then later in Matthews' basement.

Tinsley practiced with them, too. Matthews explains: "I guess we wanted one song, 'Tripping Billies,' we thought would sound neat — we were doing a demo and we thought it would be interesting to have a violin so we called him up and asked him. And Boyd just kind of felt — he really liked the songs and he really liked our band . . ." (Silverman).

They experimented relentlessly with a host of sounds and arrangements. They were searching for a musical direction. Recalls Matthews: "This started taking up all of our time. It's ridiculous to suggest I even had a clue what I was doing. I had three songs, four songs I wanted to record" (Mark Brown, "Coming In"). By the time they had embarked on their fourth rehearsal, things had improved greatly (Deck). The work had become stimulating; everyone was getting along well. "We were in our basements, slapping out these tunes," comments Dave. "We realized quite quickly that there was something very cool here" (Passy). They were ready to venture out of the basement. Says Matthews: "At the same time we made the tape, we started to play some gigs. And people reacted really positively right away. . . . While making the tape, we discovered how much we liked to play together" (Stout, "Dave Matthews").

Their first gig was at an Earth Day celebration in April of 1991. Two hundred people had congregated at the site. Matthews remembers that DMB was "the last band and there weren't too many people left 'cause it was getting chilly. But, all the people that were there were dancing, so we were pretty psyched. And then Boyd played with us that time, and we just sort of kept playing" (Silverman). It's evident that Matthews was surprised by the reaction the band met with that night: The crowd had "never heard us before, but by the end they were all dancing. None of us expected to have people get up and start dancing and celebrating" (Allan, "Herky-Jerky").

It was Moore who would be credited with inadvertently naming the band. He told a club manager simply to write "Dave Matthews" on the poster announcing one of their early-1991 gigs. It would be fun: the audience would be surprised, and, with any luck, delighted, to see an entire band — not just a solo performer — take the stage. But instead of following Moore's instructions to the letter, the manager wrote: "Dave Matthews Band" (Trott, "20"). Dave

51

elaborates: "We called this place and said, just put down Dave Matthews and a band will be there. But she felt that wouldn't be fair, so she wrote down 'band' at the end of the name, and the name stuck" (Chenoweth).

Of course, Matthews now bemoans this, because it put him front and center: "In fact, we should change our name to The Band That Used to Be Called The Dave Matthews Band But Isn't Anymore Because It Was Wrongly Named to Begin With" (Johnson). One insider says another possible name that was kicked around at the time of the band's formation was Dumela, but no one could summon up any real enthusiasm for it. Once the name Dave Matthews Band clicked, it became impossible to change from a marketing standpoint; it had already become their identity. When word-of-mouth took over — and it did so quickly — that was that.

Lydia Conder decided to throw an elegant party on the roof of the pink warehouse on Saturday, May 11, 1991. She asked Dave's brand-new band to provide some of the entertainment. "At that time," says Conder, "the newly composed band consisted of Dave, Carter, Leroi, and Stefan. They agreed, and [drummer] Ian Moore's jazz band, the Thin Men, agreed to open. Stefan Lessard was, at that time, a member of both Dave's band and Ian's, playing stand-up bass in the Thin Men and the electric bass with Dave." Party details? There was a keg of beer in a clawfoot bathtub and a roll-your-own-sushi buffet on the library table. The vista from the rooftop was panoramic — Charlottesville and the mountains that border Monticello. The soirée got underway at 9:30 P.M. A light fog enveloped the city that night, and the lights on the Downtown Mall twinkled in the distance.

"Dave showed up around 11 or so," continues Conder. "He was wearing those plaid flannel pajama pants he always wears. I think there were only about seven or eight people there at the time, but then, maybe an hour later, there were a lot of people — in my apartment, in the hallways, and mainly on the roof. Almost none of them had ever heard Dave Matthews before and it was like that first experience in my apartment when we met, only multiplied out among all my many party guests. It was a great success." Many people danced. Lydia passed a guitar case around and collected $80 for the band. For years afterward, Conder was known in C'ville as "the person who threw that party on the roof of that pink building on South Street where Dave Matthews played."

After the Earth Day show and Conder's party, the band began to play regular gigs at Eastern Standard, a tiny venue (although it's since been expanded) on the Downtown Mall. David Wellbeloved recalls raucous open-mike nights at Eastern Standard during the summer of 1991. "It was a place where the rowdy, not-very-good musicians went to play. It was a pretty fun scene." On Eastern Standard's stage, most musicians would try to hone their acts in order to move uptown one block, to the more prestigious Miller's.

Eastern Standard gave DMB its first weekly gig, on Tuesday nights. Mark Roebuck, formerly of the band the Deal and cowriter of "The Song That Jane Likes," managed a shift at the venue, and it was him who got the quartet hired. Unfortunately, it cost him his own job; this still rankles Matthews: "The guy who had the idea for us to play there got the shaft. We had a small crowd, but we had a pretty intense reaction from the beginning" (Blackwell, "Dave Matthews"). The Dave Matthews Band slowly developed a following. Wellbeloved witnessed those early Eastern Standard gigs: "The only people who saw them at first were friends who'd come in from Miller's, down the street . . . sometimes as few as a dozen people. Primarily, Boyd wasn't there. It was just four of them then: Dave, Leroi, Carter, and Stefan."

Victor Cabas became a devotee of the Eastern Standard Tuesday-night summer gigs. "It was the best music I've ever heard. When they were raw and jamming with each other, they made the most fantastic music." The weekly shows got under way just after Matthews and Cabas had appeared in the Live Arts production of *Speakeasy: The Rags of Ragtime* together. Hoffman kept trying to find the band other gigs as well; he would be seen around C'ville "lavishing praise and motivating the fledgling singer at

Main Street Grill," a venue (since closed) located near Trax (Fox, "Dave on the Stand?").

Hawes Spencer, editor and publisher of C-VILLE *Weekly*, owned by Portico Publications, talks about hearing DMB buzz for the first time: "I was familiar with Matthews from the play *Just Say No*. He was a great actor and I knew who he was because he worked at Miller's. When I heard he had a band, I thought, 'So what?' And I thought he had a lot of nerve to put his name on a band. This was mid-1991. Then later in the year, I started to hear: 'No, Hawes. These guys are really good. You've got to come see them.' So I did. And they were! I remember hearing 'Satellite' and 'Tripping Billies' then. Some of the ballads were really beautiful." C-VILLE *Weekly* would feature DMB or Matthews alone on many covers over the coming years.

It was time to get serious. In the summer of 1991, Charles Newman signed on as manager of DMB; Newman was also a Miller's regular. Matthews reconstructs this period: "The first year was tough. We went through a rough stage. We all had to do other things to support ourselves. We couldn't tour because we had to work. Stefan was in school and Boyd had his other band. Finally, we said we just have to make enough money so we can tour" (Blackwell, "Dave Matthews").

Despite these frustrations, Dave was on a creative high: from mid-1991 to early 1992, he wrote an array of songs. On the Internet, fans claim that as many as 17 new compositions surfaced before October 10, 1991. In fact, for many months, the band played about nine long, jamming, anthem-length numbers. They also experimented with covers, like John Prine's "Angel from Montgomery," Paul Simon's "Me and Julio down by the Schoolyard," and Daniel Lanois' "The Maker."

By February of 1992, there would be approximately 15 original songs in DMB's repertoire. Many of them would appear on their first three CDs. Some would become radio hits several years later; "Satellite," "Ants Marching," "What Would You Say," and "Tripping Billies" arose from this phase of DMB's development. The stalwart DMB concert anthem "Dancing Nancies" was also written at this time. Matthews has sole songwriting credit for almost all

Peter Greisar

HAWES COLEMAN SPENCER

Peter Greisar, 1997

JAN FOX/PORTICO PRODUCTIONS LTD.

of these tunes; for most of 1991, he remained the band's chief songwriter, receiving occasional coaching from Hoffman. But as time went on, this, too, would change. By October 1991, the band had introduced one of Tinsley's originals, "True Reflections," into the mix. Through the years, as the band matured, songs were created by the group as a whole, often, according to Beauford, during soundchecks (William F. Miller, "Carter Beauford").

In August 1991, keyboardist Peter Griesar was asked to join the Dave Matthews Band. His hiring was yet another one of those magical Miller's things. For one week every August, Steve Tharp, the owner of Miller's, closes down for inventory and refurbishing. Griesar, who had tended bar at the establishment since 1989, was laying tile on the club's kitchen floor while Matthews, Beauford, Moore, and Lessard took advantage of the down time to use Miller's as a rehearsal space. Inspired by what he could hear from his kitchen work area, Griesar got out his harmonica and started jamming with the foursome. After a few tunes, Carter said, "You should play with us!" Griesar immediately accepted the invitation.

Peter Griesar was born on March 19, 1969, in Manhattan and raised in New York City. He attended Dobb's Ferry High School. If performing is genetically encoded, then Griesar got it from both sides: his dad was a lawyer; his mother was an opera singer/performer who later became a storyteller, as well. Griesar has a brother and a sister, Katie, who is currently a member of a Portland, Oregon, band called Waltzing Mice.

During his high-school years, he played trumpet and trombone and sang with the school chorus. He "borrowed" a keyboard from the school to play at home — a Moog Opus 3. Griesar rationalized: "Being in a band was a way to get out of classes." Moving to Charlottesville in 1987, he entered UVA. "To be honest, I don't know why I went to college. I didn't have the most exciting academic year my first year. I ended up in trouble with the school and on probation." After taking a stab at summer school, he dropped out in the fall of 1988. He went to work in Colorado at Club Med, Copper Mountain, running the kitchens.

Trax

HAWES COLEMAN SPENCER

Tuesdays at Trax

HAWES COLEMAN SPENCER

In 1989, Griesar moved back to C'ville. Through a friend, he secured a job at Miller's on the lunch shift. Matthews was already there working as sandwich boy-bartender, and the two became good friends. Griesar soon found that as well as serving drinks, his job description included waiting tables. "It [was] a fascinating job. Miller's was such a serendipitous thing for me. I got to meet all the musicians of Charlottesville." At Miller's, Griesar also became acquainted with John D'earth: "He's a stupendous person, and a mentor to a lot of people in this town." Griesar met Ross Hoffman through D'earth, and eventually connected with other C'ville music-scene elders: Leroi Moore, Tim Reynolds, Johnny Gilmore, and Houston Ross, to name a few.

From 1989 to 1990, Griesar played with both Gilmore and Ross; today, he's full of praise for them. The two, asserts Griesar, form a "great rhythm section. [Drummer] Johnny Gilmore was the heartbeat of the scene for a long time. Houston Ross is the baddest funk bassist I ever did hear. He has the hugest heart." Gilmore actually sat in with DMB in 1992, and Ross followed suit on March 3, 1993.

Fans still shout out requests for "People, People" during DMB shows, a song Griesar penned in 1990. "It was a song I tracked down on a sequencer. I worked on it a couple of times. This was before I joined the band. Dave came over a few times then and heard it." Griesar is one of the three people who share songwriting credit (music and lyrics) for the Grammy Award-winning DMB song "So Much to Say"; the others are Tinsley and Matthews. He remembers working out the song's compelling harmonies in 1992 in Hoffman's apartment. "The harmonies came up just literally from singing and playing along, and goofing up, for two or three hours one time."

Griesar's philosophy as DMB keyboardist was "to be as much rhythm section as possible, to hold down the rhythm section." It's easy to pick out his contribution to the band's overall sound if you listen to DMB's early tapes: "A lot of lines I played are now done by other people." In C'ville music circles, Peter Griesar is renowned for his flair for arranging pop tunes. During his tenure with DMB, he always tried to maintain a sensitivity to the conception of the group as "a stage full of lead instruments."

Peter well remembers the band's procedure for rehearsing new songs: it was, in a word, a free-for-all. "We would all help with the arrangements." Every member of the band readily acknowledges that arranging was largely a joint venture. In fact, in the liner notes for *Remember Two Things*, the first DMB indie CD — it came out in 1993, after Griesar had quit — the entire band is given credit for arrangements, and special thanks are directed to Griesar for his contributions and inspirations.

Many early DMB songs, due to Griesar's instrumentation, sound quite different from the band's subsequent efforts. "Dancing Nancies," for instance, used to fade out, leaving the listener with the sensation of, perhaps, having heard a carnival merry-go-round winding down. The effect was created in performance. Griesar recalls "just playing it one night and not really thinking about it."

Peter joined DMB in time to hit the road. The group played its first out-of-state gig in September 1991 — a Colorado club date. Sax player Richard Hardy had arranged the booking through his friend John Axford, who had invested in the refurbishing of an old venue called the Road House located south of Denver, near Sedalia. Hardy, who accompanied the band, paints this vivid picture of their long haul: "We had two vehicles. We were crunched in like sardines and we drove like bats out of hell to get there in time. At one point, we were so tired that we had to pull over in the middle of the day at a rest stop in Kansas. That was a funny scene when everyone was asleep. If I'd taken a picture, it would show the humble beginnings of DMB — everyone asleep with their mouths open." They had one huge truck and a car. Along for the trip were manager Charles Newman, Hardy, Moore, Lessard, Matthews, Beauford, Griesar, roadie Anse Clinnard, Fenton Williams, and possibly one other crew member.

How could they have known that this, DMB's first out-of-town date, would end up as a double disappointment — for the band and for the Road House's owner? The band opened and closed the club. It was a two-night stand. Hardy explains: "They didn't have enough money to advertise and the sound system was terrible." Furthermore, "The venue was in the middle of nowhere." The band made $1,000 for the gig — it's amazing they were paid at all — and the Road House was immediately shut down.

Absorbing the blow, the band returned to C'ville and picked up right where they had left off. They played a few more times at Miller's; but now the dynamic had begun to change. During DMB gigs, wherever they might be in C'ville, the venues would become insanely crowded. The band's popularity, in a local context, was soaring. Matthews emphasizes: "We played everything, everywhere we could in Charlottesville" (Silverman). Newman cites DMB's heightening profile as one reason that Coran Capshaw — C'ville entrepreneur, rock promoter, and owner of Trax — booked the band into the much larger club. There were a few, sporadic gigs at Trax in the late summer and early fall of 1991; on October 22, 1991, the group debuted "Ants Marching" — then named "No New Directions." In November of 1991, they initiated a series of weekly, soon-to-be-legendary gigs at Trax that would continue for years. This cavernous venue was located about ten minutes away from the Downtown Mall and was closer than Miller's was to UVA. Its name alludes to the club's proximity to the town's railroad tracks.

Trax is sort of L-shaped. Fans of DMB who've never been there often try to picture its interior when they first listen to the early performance tapes that were recorded at Trax. As you enter the long tavern area, with its towering barn-like ceiling, you see the soundboard on the left. Straight ahead, you spot the stage, which is raised about three feet off the floor. It's a typical proscenium, 30 to 40 feet deep; a dark curtain serves as a backdrop, and it is illuminated by stage lights. Next, you notice that a large collection of pictures and posters decorates the dark-beamed upper walls. Rustic pillars line the main dance area, about every fifteen feet; some sections of the floor are covered with a dark matting. You then catch sight of a bar area; a video arcade and a number of pool tables occupy an extension to the left of the bar. Signed publicity shots adorn the walls in this wing. Bar stools are scattered about. Near the rear of

the bar, at the backstage entrance, you see that a sign has been installed warning that passes are required for those hoping to penetrate any further. The air is constantly saturated with cigarette smoke. In 1997, there was a framed DMB *Under the Table and Dreaming* poster hanging close to the Trax stage, in a position of honor.

As any musician who has played the club knows, Trax essentially is a warehouse. The acoustics are poor. David Wellbeloved, who has often played there, notes: "Without 200 people, it can feel pretty empty." Trax was one of the two venues Capshaw owned at that time — the Flood Zone in Richmond was the other one. These venues would help catapult DMB to fame by providing them with a live-wire audience — a blend of college students and townies.

Capshaw had managed other C'ville-based rock groups before 1991, including Paris Match, which featured Shannon Worrell and Dennis Guiman. He loved the Grateful Dead, and had attended about 400 of their shows (Colapinto). According to local sources, Capshaw was actively looking for another band to manage. As a club owner, he had the connections and the background in music promotion to launch a band. And he really wanted to launch a band. Capshaw is a complicated figure. Known in C'ville as a man who should not be crossed, he has also been described as a sweetheart. Some venture to say that, with his curly gray hair, he faintly resembles Bob Dylan.

Observers report that Capshaw actually stayed inside his Trax office, working, during most of DMB's first gig in that venue; he did emerge at one point, though, for about ten minutes, to gauge the crowd's response. It was positive. Capshaw later told C-VILLE *Weekly*: "Not everybody gets this band when they first hear it. I always thought it was good, and then at one show, I was just suddenly like, 'Hold on a second. This is important'" (Bailey "On the Road . . . part 1").

Impresario Capshaw eventually replaced Newman as the band's manager. It was ironic, since it was Newman who had convinced Capshaw to book them in the first place. Capshaw's clubs could hold about 900 people, and DMB's audience soon swelled to hundreds of people a night.

The band was given regular weekly slots: Trax on Tuesdays in late 1991, and the Flood Zone on Wednesdays in the spring of 1992. They opened for other, larger acts (like Drivin' n' Cryin') at the Flood Zone starting in January of 1992, and by the spring had built up enough momentum for a regular Richmond gig. In order to fill these clubs, DMB had to draw both townies and students. University of Virginia students — especially sorority girls — would flock in droves to Trax beginning in the late fall of 1991. Capshaw banked on it, and his calculated risk paid off. University of Richmond students would jam the Flood Zone in 1992.

The creative climate of the C'ville townie milieu during DMB's formative period was charged, intricate, and symbiotic. Symbiotic is a key characteristic here, according to some insiders. There truly was a spirit of shared artistry and inspiration; it pervaded the local music scene and the realms of the other arts, too. Some Charlottesville scenesters speak of the period between 1991 and 1994 with a great deal of nostalgia, as if it were a sort of golden age that was destined to implode. But whatever spin you put on it, one thing is evident: the richness and openness of the C'ville arts scene during the early 1990s had a direct and positive effect on DMB.

Artists were everywhere. World-renowned painter Steve Keene (the creator of many album covers) was working as a dishwasher at Eastern Standard; now-deceased musician Haines Fullerton, cowriter of "#34," was a bartender at the same club; and Dave Matthews could usually be found hanging out at Miller's. A bar named Fellini's began to draw an artsy clientele in 1992. Every Sunday night in the summer of 1992, a band called the Hogwaller Ramblers played there. Like DMB, the Ramblers had gotten off the ground in 1991. According to arts provocateur Matthew Farrell, the scene at Fellini's emblematized the general artistic spirit of the time: "Everyone would be there. You'd walk in on a Sunday night and you'd find maybe ten writers, fifteen musicians, five playwrights, actors, everyone. It was the densest culturati imaginable. And they all believed in staying here rather than going to a place like New York, because there's a certain community and humanity to life here. Everyone played music with everyone. Everyone wrote songs and books and wrote plays for each other — just generated this tremendous amount of material." Matthews dropped by frequently.

Musician Cristan Keighley, who, like Matthews, moved to C'ville in 1986, recalls: "There was so much going on then. It was one of those alchemical times, with the right people there feeding off each other — the way vibrant music inspires more photographers and painters — and you draw from one another. So much revolved around drinking. There was so much drinking going on at Miller's. It reminded me of stories of Paris in the 1920s . . . the salon-café society." Keighley tended bar at Trax in 1992, when DMB played their Tuesday-night gigs.

David Wellbeloved, who, along with Rick Jones, David Goldstein, Dan Sebring, and, eventually, Jamie Dyer, would become the Hogwaller Ramblers, describes the atmosphere at Fellini's as "transcendent. It was magic. I have never experienced anything quite that unique. It was a rustic, intimate kind of room that sounded shitty, so everyone had to sit up close to everyone else. People would sing along. Sometimes we'd make up songs on the spot. And everybody knew everybody." Matthews sat in with the Ramblers a few times in the fall of 1991; he liked to jam with them outside on the Downtown Mall.

The C'ville private-party scene was cooking, as well. Although wild bashes are a standard occurrence in most American college towns, C'ville, thanks to UVA, was in a class of its own. At one point during the 1980s, *Playboy* magazine ranked UVA the number-one party school in the country. In an effort to rid itself of this rowdy reputation by association, C'ville passed laws that enabled it to raise the legal drinking age in its jurisdiction and tightened campus-party rules. The university did its bit, as well, elevating admission standards; after all, UVA aspired to be "the Harvard of the South." Many venues — and, consequently, the local music community — were seriously affected by these initiatives. The club scene withered — and in light of this, DMB's long and successful engagement at Trax is all the more impressive.

Down but not beaten, by 1992 C'ville was seeing a resurgence in both college bashes and artsy soirees. One C'villean named Roman threw megaparties — as many as 300 people would attend — and always made sure to include revelers of different social stratas. Roman's lavish functions got under way at 10 P.M., and they would last until dawn. Held on nontraditional party nights like Sundays or Tuesdays, the parties generally conformed to this winning formula: supply good wines; serve delicacies prepared by talented young chefs; invite an unorthodox mix of people — throw in old professors, young ingenues, pretty sorority girls, and some downtown mallrats; stir it up. At these often-formal bacchanals, sexual boundaries were occasionally explored and traversed. Small wonder that invitees would juggle vacation times or work schedules in order to attend. Members of DMB, their management, and their crew were familiar faces at these festive gatherings. So were Matthews' sister Jane and her longtime love, Temple Farrell. A vital release for the creative energies of the C'ville talent pool, the parties were also a forum for the exchange of ideas. And they were a lot of fun.

Guitarist Haines Fullerton was another C'ville fixture who had a direct influence on Matthews and, subsequently, DMB. Originally from Minnesota, Fullerton lived for a while in Memphis before coming to UVA in 1977. Known simply as "Haines" to many, Fullerton was part of the band the Deal, as was Mark Roebuck. Both musicians cowrote two different DMB tunes. The Deal, which formed when all its members graduated from UVA, had a regional hit, and they released an album, called *Brave New World*, on an indie label in 1987. They broke up in 1988 (Fox, "Well Known").

As a bartender at Eastern Standard, Tokyo Rose, and Trax in the early 1990s, Fullerton became known throughout C'ville as a humble, kind, yet complex person with extraordinary musical gifts. Shannon Worrell, who worked with Fullerton on her 1994 release *Three Wishes*, remarks: "He facilitated lots of good things between people. . . . What Haines could do is make people put their egos aside. Kristin [Asbury] and I even started playing together because of

Haines" (Fox, "Well Known"). Worrell and Asbury then became the group Monsoon (with Lauren Hoffman), and eventually formed September 67. As September 67, they came out with a CD in 1996 entitled *Lucky Shoe*.

Some people suggest that Fullerton taught Matthews a lot about playing the guitar. Others imply that it was Matthews who got Fullerton playing again around 1991 after Fullerton's long, self-imposed exile from the music scene. Either way, Fullerton, Matthews, and Worrell were spotted playing guitar together in a park one block from Miller's during this period, so it's clear that Fullerton was playing again, and playing around Matthews. Wellbeloved encapsulated Fullerton's impact on the entire music community like this: "Haines had an influence on everyone's playing who ever played with him. He could musically articulate. You couldn't sit down with him and not come away a changed musician. It was almost mystical. He had a huge influence in this town on many people."

Matthews developed a great deal of affection for Fullerton, and would often play for him. The admiration was mutual. Victor Cabas recalls a late evening at Tokyo Rose in the fall of 1991, during which Fullerton played a live tape of DMB for him and detailed it nuance by nuance, lyric by lyric. "He went through every song of Dave's," says Cabas, "and explained it to me. He really understood the poetry of it. He said, 'Dave's gonna be big. He's going to go global.' Haines never said things like that and he said it with such utter conviction."

Newman had given different live 1991 DMB tapes to Fullerton and Cabas. The two traded those tapes that night. Fullerton and Cabas were on the vanguard. Frenzied tape trading was to become an aspect of the DMB phenomenon that would draw in fans across the world. In fact, it was not long after the group formed in 1991 that DMB members decided to allow fans to tape their concerts by plugging tape decks directly into the band's soundboard (Scharnhorst). This important decision would prove to be a crucial marketing tactic: the band received invaluable free publicity as college students distributed these "approved" bootlegs to their friends across America — at their own expense.

HAWES COLEMAN SPENCER

Trax, January 1992

HAWES COLEMAN SPENCER

In their acknowledgments for their first CD, *Remember Two Things*, Matthews and the band thanked Fullerton; they would also give him shared songwriting credit for "#34," a track on their second CD.

Guitar player extraordinaire Tim Reynolds was another C'ville musician who would have a powerful effect on the music of the Dave Matthews Band. Internet rumors often fly about Reynolds: cyberfans are convinced that he will join DMB permanently because he played on the first four studio CDs, the first live double CD, and the EP and toured annually with Matthews as an acoustic duo. Reynolds' ties to Matthews go back to 1987; he was Matthews' first musical ally in C'ville (Bessman). "We played more hard rock then," recollects Reynolds. "We did it for fun. I had a band that was doing its own thing. [Matthews] eventually got his own band together. Some smart people helped pick the line-up, so they immediately started going places" (Rosenberg).

Nine years older than Matthews, Reynolds started playing in C'ville in 1981. Born in Weisbaden, West Germany, he grew up in America. He first performed as a child in a Pentecostal church. "My dad wouldn't let me do anything else, and I wanted to play music so bad [and] it was the only place he'd let me do it." Enraptured congregations had heard him play electric bass countless times before his high-school graduation. At the ripe old age of 18, Reynolds ran away. He was gone for two weeks, and when he returned home, he and his father sought a compromise: "I had to get into his head I wouldn't be Mr. Church Music Guy" (Rosenberg). It worked. Tim eventually became interested in Buddhism; his father became supportive of his music. Reynolds began playing in rock bands and took up the electric guitar and the sitar, among other instruments. His band, TR3, formed in 1984. Its members were Robert Jospe (formerly of Cosmology and his own band, Inner Rhythm), Charlie Kilpatrick, and Warren Richardson.

For Reynolds, excellent musicianship involves emotion. In 1988, he was overheard complimenting another musician at Miller's: "You sounded great last night, you meant every note you played" (Becker, "Reynolds"). It's a standard that Reynolds continuously strives for — emotional connection. He also writes songs. For well over a decade, he had a Monday-night gig at Miller's. In 1993, he released a CD, *Stream*, produced by Greg Howard.

In 1992, Reynolds and Matthews would instigate a tradition: they would play acoustic gigs as a duo. Matthews recalls how it all came about. Reynolds, he says, is "a phenomenal guitar player and we performed together four years ago [1992] but never toured. So we billed it 'Dave Matthews and Tim Reynolds' to make sure people knew it was just the two of us. We did 3-hour shows and it was great, great fun" (Bessman). Matthews has often referred to Reynolds as his guitar hero.

During one Dave and Tim acoustic show in 1996, Matthews said, "I've known this man for about 10 years, and the first time I sang in public it was with Timmy. And the first time I ever got my heart broken by someone who can play so fuckin' awesomely, it was Timmy." Matthews clearly feels that Reynolds' musical contributions are important to DMB's music. "He's an integral part — he makes everything wider and deeper, and longer and louder and quieter" (G. Brown, "Chance"). John D'earth echoes Dave: "Tim is a huge force in all of this — a rare person — sui generis. He pursues his thing with religious fervor."

As 1991 drew to a close, Matthews, Beauford, Moore, Lessard, and Griesar had been playing gigs together for several months, building momentum and garnering acclaim. The artistic community of C'ville now harbored many supporters of the new group, many kindred spirits. And soon its configuration would alter again. Whenever Boyd Tinsley was in Charlottesville, he would, as one scribe put it, play "with one of the hottest new local groups, The Dave Matthews Band" (Blackwell, "Backstage"). On Thursday, April 30, 1992, the Boyd Tinsley Band played their final gig; ironically, it was at Trax. On Saturday, May 2, 1992, "Robin Hitchcock with the Dave Matthews Band" was the billing at the same establishment. By mid-1992, DMB was popular enough to draw crowds at Trax twice a week; a year before, they'd played Lydia Conder's rooftop party for $80. The contrast was not lost on Tinsley: he decided to commit solely to DMB.

4
SLOW BUT SPEEDING

The Charlottesville press, galvanized by DMB's surge in popularity, began running stories on the band in 1992. In January, the *Daily Progress* dubbed DMB "one of the hottest new local groups" (Blackwell, "Backstage"). C-VILLE *Weekly* ran its first cover piece on them in February, and it contained the prophetic question: "Is the Dave Matthews Band the next big thing?" (Deck). The *Observer* profiled them in its summer 1992 Our Town section under the headline "Local Band Begins Rock 'n' Roll Ascent" (Becker). In early September, the *Daily Progress* ran a story called "Matthews to Headline Benefit," in which Matthews was identified by C'villean arts impressario Thane Kerner as "obviously the biggest current draw from Charlottesville" (Jones). Kerner also told Hawes Spencer of C-VILLE *Weekly* that DMB would become famous.

How did it happen? And so quickly? According to people who saw them at Trax, the answer is a combination of factors: the extraordinary, charismatic performances of the band members as they meshed into a whole; the open taping policy; the music's dance beat; and the truly unique nature of the band's originals. Each member of the sextet quickly became a local celebrity, attracting a fervent, almost cult-like following. From late 1991 through early 1992, their gigs consisted of either opening up for bigger acts or doing a stint themselves — at no charge. By the end of spring 1992, they were charging five dollars a person for shows that would often last three hours. They also started to play frat houses.

The Boyd Tinsley Band dissolved. Matthews describes it as the end of an era, remarking: "[Tinsley] sort of stepped across from his band to ours" (Silverman).

The Dave Matthews Band made its first television appearance on Adelphia Channel 10 on Wednesday, April 29, 1992, at 7:00 P.M.; the performance was rebroadcast on Thursday, April 30, and Friday, May 1. A poster announcing the event had a big picture of Thomas Jefferson on it and was emblazoned with the words "He's Back . . . And He's Pissed." In addition to DMB, the program included a short film called *Godzilla the Errant Abyssinian* and *Power Lunch*, a Joel Jones/Offstage Theater production. The poster copy also reads "Let's Get Lost on Adelphia Channel 10."

Around this time, Mindy Peskin, then aged 17, started to attend the weekly DMB shows at Trax and some of the band's gigs at the Flood Zone; at first, she had to sneak in using someone else's ID because she was underage. She describes the Flood Zone circa 1992: "It used to be a two-story venue with a bar in the back, both upstairs and down, and a large, wooden open floor that leads to the stage. Really, it used to be a warehouse." The stage was raised about four feet off the ground. Peskin continues: "There are two stairwells, one next to the bar and for the public, the other just left of the stage, for the band or Flood Zone help. Upstairs, there's the same rear-end bar that was shaped like a U then, with a large open space directly overlooking the first floor." There was a foosball table and a pool table upstairs, as well. The third floor was used, primarily, as a backstage area, and it housed the club's offices. "The backstage area was actually a bit gross — old, beat-up furniture, tiny bathrooms and poor lighting."

Mindy gradually became familiar with the musicians, and eventually became good friends with them: "It was my constant attendance that introduced me to the band." First, she got to know Leroi Moore and Coran Capshaw. Later, she connected with Carter Beauford. "That May [1992], I called Coran and after a long conversation of compliments and critiques of the band, I hired them to play at my high-school graduation party at the Flood Zone." The thought of having DMB as your high-school-graduation party band is mind-boggling to most fans; it was quite a coup for Peskin.

It happened on June 1, 1992. The entire event was documented. Recalls Peskin: "They played a full show from 9 to 12, with a half hour set break or so. Basically it was just like any other night at the Flood Zone at that time. There were about 100 people and the band generally treated it like a normal evening, but with many more UVA and Charlottesville references, of course! It was casual attire and quite an evening. I only wish I had started [audio] taping them then instead of in July. I do have a videotape of the show and despite my poor filmwork, it is still one of my favorite home videos."

That summer, Peskin saw DMB perform about four times a week throughout Virginia. They played their weekly shows in Charlottesville and Richmond, plus a lot of outdoor festivals and Friday after Five gigs. Peskin always felt they would make it big. "I started taping shows in July and realized as the weeks went by that the crowds were growing, the band was putting out new tunes each week, and that the whole scene was getting bigger and bigger extremely quickly."

Roy Thigpen attended UVA from 1990 to 1993, and saw the band at least 20 times at Trax between 1991 and 1992. He reminisces: "The crowd was almost exclusively a UVA crowd with the male/female ratio being usually high — with more girls than guys. Frankly, I was going there since they seemed to attract so many girls. The crowd was generally respectful. I mean, all we had to do was jam to the music! I have memories of grooving at Trax to 'Tripping Billies' and 'Granny.' The most lasting memory I have is hearing Dave play 'All along the Watchtower.' That song has a powerful meaning to me, and hearing a Dylan song/ Hendrix cover not only played but actually *improved* impressed the hell out of me."

Thigpen shares more of his impressions of the shows. "As is the case with most college students, I was occasionally drunk when I went to see them. Dave used to talk a lot between songs but was hardly coherent. I think he did this on purpose to mess with our minds. The power of the Dave

Matthews Band music is that it seems to generate a real palatable, positive energy in the audience. They play songs that can be considered pop, country, jazz, hard rock and roll, and even kind of funky. They are impossible to fit into one category. This is what makes them so great in my eyes. I will always admire the creativity, innovation, and sheer musicianship of the Dave Matthews Band."

Uncertain, at that point, whether DMB was destined to make it big, Thigpen and his friends actually thought two other groups, Modern Logic and Indecision, might go all the way to the top. These groups have since disappeared. Thigpen notes that thinking about DMB makes him nostalgic for his college days; it's a fond association.

Cristan Keighley, whose background includes graphic design, theater, and sound production in addition to music, was a bartender at Trax. He can well remember how frenzied the scene came to be: "It was maddening on Dave nights. You'd have to get hundreds of people in and out the door. I'd serve $700 worth of beer single-handedly."

But working at Trax did have its benefits. During rehearsal time, Keighley was able to hear the band play privately. "The band would come in at 3 or 4 in the afternoon and use it as a decompression chamber. I would pull up a chair and just listen. Stefan and Carter would start playing some rhythm. Dave would strum quietly and Boyd and Leroi would solo on top of it. I knew I was listening to an expression of their talents that few would ever hear." Keighley has known Matthews since the summer of 1992, and has been to many social gatherings that DMB members also attended. He thinks the three secrets of the band's success with the college crowd are: "You could dance to them, sing to them" and "Coran marketed the hell out of them."

In 1992, Matthews spoke about the band's gigs at Trax: "It's kind of an inspiration to play here on Tuesdays. . . . There's a kind of a twisted celebration going on. . . . People seem to impose some kind of understanding on us — it's strange and it's gratifying" (Becker, "Local Band"). As he would continue to do for years, Matthews also credited his talented fellow band members with supplying the charisma in their live performances.

Matthews also explained his use of irony and his uniting of opposites in the songwriting process: "I got in the habit of trying to mix different emotions in the same song . . . a militant aggression and a sweet song, mix the two together, one part that inspires a fury and one part that inspires a relief" (Becker, "Local Band"). Often, he elaborated, he would write lyrics on the spot as he performed. "One song, 'Warehouse,' didn't even have real words until two weeks ago. We had been playing the song for a few months, and each time the words were just some gibberish I made up on the spot every night. In that case, the tune was so good we just had to do the song whether it had real words or not" (Deck). Or perhaps they were just in need of material.

In fact, some insiders report that songwriting pressure was being exerted on Matthews during this period. Rumor has it that some band members were eager for Matthews to come up with yet more originals — or at least work on more covers. They didn't feel that their repertory was large enough; there weren't enough songs on the set list. And so Hoffman and Matthews went away for a couple of weeks in the spring of 1992 and returned with about eight more finished Dave Matthews songs.

Then events took a peculiar twist. By the middle of May, Hoffman and Matthews had lost touch because Matthews was so often performing or on the road. Both seemed to feel that their professional association had ended. On May 13, 1992, Matthews signed an agreement that ensured Hoffman 7.5 percent of Matthews' songwriting revenues. This remuneration would serve to acknowledge Hoffman's contribution to Matthews' songwriting development (Fox, "Dave on the Stand?"). In addition to providing artistic input, Hoffman had been filing for copyright on Matthews' tunes, and generally making sure the songs were legally protected.

By the summer of 1992, while continuing to fulfill their weekly gigs, DMB had also begun to play East Coast venues in Nags Head, North Carolina; Washington, DC; Philadelphia; and New York City. They'd opened for Blues Traveler, the BoDeans, and the Connells. The local press also reported at this time that record-company scouts were sniffing around DMB. All this had happened within roughly one year of their formation (Becker, "Local Band").

In September 1992, Matthews dissected the band's potent concert magic for a C'ville *Daily Progress* interviewer: "The combination of us is, I guess, very appealing in a live performance. We couldn't have predicted it . . . we don't plan out what we are going to do onstage or the energy onstage. If you just take everyone's part and break it up and put it by itself, it really doesn't have too much to it. But when it is all put together, it is part of something. Like the dancers or the people that are watching, they are taking part in the total music that is going on" (Jones).

Matthews' own fancy footwork was often admired by adoring throngs of girls at these early shows. "I don't know about the footwork," Dave muses. "That's more of an affliction . . . I get embarrassed because it looks like I'm doing the Charleston. . . . It doesn't always happen. See, if it was consistent, then it'd be cool. But instead, they stay still and just bop up and down like anybody's feet. Then all of a sudden there's this complete spaz that takes place. My knees start bending in strange directions and I'm like 'What's happening to me?'" (Allan, "The Dave Matthews Band").

On the subject of delegating responsibility, Matthews says — in the same 1992 interview — that he prefers to let others handle contracts, tour dates, and the future. Capshaw, he explains, manages the group, "booking gigs and handling schedules." Hoffman is identified as Matthews' personal manager (Jones). By the end of that summer, Hoffman and Matthews had obviously patched things up again.

Matthews offers more insight into his hands-off attitude towards the business end of things: "You can delegate just about everything. What I want to do is sing, play guitar and write songs. I don't want to know about anything else. I don't want to know how much money I'm getting paid. If any decisions that would concern the band come up, then [the managers] would ask us" (Burtner, "Money Side").

On September 30, 1992, the band performed at the Flood Zone in Richmond with percussionist Miguel Valdez. Griesar loved playing with Valdez: "He was an incredible percussionist, the best I ever recorded with. It was because he was an incredible listener. He added so much energy and joy to the music." Beauford singles out Valdez as a figure who had a huge effect on his own music: "Miguel . . . used to be the percussionist in our band, but he passed away. . . . He was phenomenal. He gave me all sorts of ideas for patterns and different ways to look at rhythm" (William F. Miller, "Carter Beauford"). Valdez died of hepatitis in 1993. The band dedicated the song "#34," on *Under the Table and Dreaming*, to his memory.

That fall, Mindy Peskin enrolled in UVA and maintained her contact with DMB. "I started spending weekends away from school with them, traveling down south to places like Charleston, South Carolina, where the crowds were equally as big and excited."

The band's early policy of open taping fed that enthusiasm wherever they played. Joshua Nicholas Tolson, who was born in Charlottesville and eventually moved to Richmond, was one of the first DMB "tapers." He says that DMB was "the first band that I saw live before I'd heard any recordings of them. I was 18 in 1992, and I could not get into all the clubs. The DMB shows at the Flood Zone and Trax were two of the few places people who were under 21 could go." Tolson visited some friends who went to Hampden-Sydney College in Farmville, Virginia, which is the only all-male college in the nation. "They [DMB] were playing in the basement of one of my friends' fraternities — Sigma Nu. 'True Reflections' was the song. I'd heard a million bands before but this was different. People were more into it. They had six people, and sax and violin, before From Good Homes and Agents of Good Roots. Once we caught on they were playing Trax and Flood Zone — I was living in Richmond — as early as I can remember I was bringing my home tape deck into the shows and setting up into the soundboard. Back then, you could show up at 10:30 or 11:00. Dave would be there doing solo tunes. You could grab a table. You could sit on the stage and talk to Dave. You could give him some input before the show on what you'd want him to play. There were so few people there."

On another occasion, Tolson saw Matthews and Reynolds play at the Memphis Bar and Grill. Sitting just three feet away, Tolson was practically toasting the musicians. "Dave would talk about his boxers and how his butt itched. There was a lot more interaction at that time." Tolson also recalls that during a performance at the Flood Zone, Matthews, prompted by a television that had been switched on in the background, suddenly revealed that he loved the *Tonight Show* — "It's my favorite show!" It was a quirky yet typical admission for Matthews to make during a concert. This sort of spontaneous display of humor, wit, and personality on Dave's part would become an element of the performance band's persona. Everyone wanted to hear what he would say next.

During the early days of DMB tape circulation, a cultural phenomenon called "Davespeak" actually developed. Fans would not only clamor for DMB music, but they would also eagerly anticipate whatever wild and cryptic bon mots Matthews would utter between songs. His comic-improv sensibilities were honed; he became highly quotable, and his words would affect a generation. Today on the Internet, hundreds of web sites are devoted to keeping up with the latest Davespeak. You can download it and read it whenever you're in a bad mood or need a good laugh.

Tolson also recalls that Matthews would frequently come out and solo before playing with the entire band. "He would practice things he'd been doing at home." Tolson says he enjoyed hearing a version of "Say Goodbye" that Matthews appeared to compose spontaneously, and also remarks that he liked the original lyrics of "After Her" more than those of "Satellite," the hit song that it became — it was no longer a sweet love song after the words were revised. "Dave is one of the best love-song writers out there because he sings from the heart. He has such an emotional style. You can see it in his face."

Between 1992 and 1994, Tolson personally taped at least 30 shows. He got to know the now-famous DMB soundman Jeff "Bagby" Thomas, who was "almost a part of the band. Dave would talk to him as much as he'd talk to Boyd onstage." Dave Matthews Band legend has it that it was

Thomas who named many of the songs. Tolson enjoyed the whole taping scene. "It was a really good time. You met great people. You'd show up early for a spot on the board. For the first year, you could always get a spot on the board." After that, it became more difficult.

Tolson believes he was among the first tapers to record DMB digitally. It was on March 17, 1993, at the Flood Zone. "I got a minidisc recorder. I asked Bagby, 'Is it still cool to hook this up?'" Tolson was granted permission.

All of Tolson's friends thought that DMB would break through to the national market. "We'd talk about how big the band was going to get and how you'd better see them like this, now." He remembers paying six dollars for a ticket to see them perform for a crowd of 800 or less.

A photographer as well as an Internet savant, Tolson — equipped with his camera — first hung out backstage with DMB at Van Riper's Music Festival in 1992. After taking some photos of Beauford, Tolson got to socialize with him at an Ivy, Virginia, gathering. "We were in my friend Mike's basement with Carter for two hours, talking about nothing in particular. This was a few houses down from Carter's. It was my favorite moment in my career of liking the DMB. Carter offered to make me a cheese omelette!"

The following week, at the Flood Zone, Tolson was able to deliver the pictures he'd taken directly to Beauford. He also had several backstage conversations with Matthews at various points: "Once he got a really short haircut and we joked about it." Tolson also watched Moore play pool at Trax. Now Tolson runs a DMB web site that gets at least 50 hits a day. He admits that following DMB was addicting — as so many other fans find out. "I don't know why it was. They were just so different. They didn't have a poppy sound. Dave's voice is like a different instrument. They also sounded different than other bands at the time . . . Big Head Todd and the Monsters, and Aquarium Rescue Unit. I think DMB is just genuine. They were meant to play. Carter is also a big factor. He's not just a rhythm section. His rhythm along with Dave's rhythm guitar really sent me along. The flute and the sax. . . . The violin spoke to some of us in the south — it connects to our roots. Another thing was you could hear the same song and each week it'd be totally different. They'd always try new things, new intros."

Matthews told MTV Online questioners that tape trading "was the best free promotion we've come across." Other bands have benefited from taper culture, which is addicting in and of itself. The Grateful Dead was the original taper band. Many bands have loosened their policies and followed suit, aiming for the kind of success the Dead achieved. Blues Traveler and a lesser-known group named moe. allow taping. Other bands — like Phish — even have special taper seating sections at their shows and special taper tickets. Tape trading is a hobby, and should not be confused with bootlegging. In tape trading, no money is exchanged. Often, the sound quality is poor, but the tapes serve as documents of ephemeral live performances. Musical historians "recognize the value of preserving live performances that represent the rawer essence of an artist's evolution" (Bothner). That's the taper's credo. Bootleggers, however, have no such scruples. They sell recordings of live shows for profit to indie record companies; these are then mass-marketed, often at a price of $60 a pop. Bootlegging is illegal. Tape trading is not. This distinction became very important for DMB fans in 1997.

The Grateful Dead always had an open taping policy. Their motto, in the words of a Dead spokesman, was: "We're not in the record business, we're in the music business" (Bothner). This proved to be one of the Dead's great marketing decisions; it propelled them to an even greater popularity. It whetted their fans' appetites not only for their recordings, but also for their incredible live performances.

Drummer Vinnie Amico of the band moe. described their taper-culture fan base: "It just happened because we tour so much and we do a lot of improvisational long jams so it kind of picks up that fan base. Which is a good crowd to have. They follow you around, they tape your shows, they give the tapes to people in California or Vancouver or Ottawa or wherever. We have this big Internet thing happening, with tape trading and information through the network" (Saxberg). This is exactly what happened to early DMB fans. Fueled by the tapes that fell into their hands, their desire to hear the band play whenever and wherever possible — to follow them around and tape their shows themselves — grew and grew.

Some people have a difficult time understanding this addicting hobby; then they hear the live tapes for the first time. They can't help but want to hear more. When it comes to a band you really love, taping is a passionate and entirely justifiable pursuit. Trading for show tapes you don't have becomes all-consuming. Going on taper runs — following a band on tour — is financially draining and swallows up a lot of time, but tapers are up to the challenge. Some save their money throughout the year so that they can hit the road for summer or winter tours, while others take temporary jobs as they travel. A few manage to make huge investments in recording equipment: as one taper explains, "it makes you feel close to the music." The Dave Matthews Band eventually began receiving letters from parents, pleading with Dave to send their children home from tours and taper runs (Provencher, "Matthews Band"). The Pied Piper effect had kicked in.

The band was smart to decide on an open taping policy at the very beginning. This would allow their fan base to grow exponentially, and at an astonishing rate. Griesar recalls seeing the taper-culture results as DMB toured in 1992. "We went to North Carolina — playing for the first time at UNC. I couldn't believe it because there was a jeep ahead of us blaring our music. We had a loyal and huge fan base already. It made it possible to make money as a band. People knew us, loved us, couldn't get enough of us." Matthews concurs: "We'd go to another college in another state and the kids would already know the music. It was very gratifying that people would go out of their way to spread the word" (Scharnhorst).

By 1992, the taper-culture methodology of spreading DMB's music at a grass-roots level via the band's college-age fan base was in full play along the East Coast. Another key element of this plan was the regional frat-house circuit. In fact, these two components worked together: college-age tapers

would feed tapes directly into the frat-house scene, increasing demand for DMB and expanding their live following.

Capshaw had expertise in booking and promotion; he had firm ideas of how to maximize the band's money-making potential. Matthews says: "That's how we did it, we went to Athens [Georgia] and we played in fraternities. And then after we played in fraternities a few times and it looked like people were coming not only for the party but for us, then we switched to the Georgia Theater, and then other people could come, besides that. So then a different town to do the same thing — play fraternities and then once you're established in that, then stop playing fraternities, and start playing just clubs, where you can be guaranteed money 'cause people will come" (Silverman). Obviously, the plan worked well.

Griesar remembers playing those frat-house gigs, which he found tremendously beneficial to the band's musical development. "We'd all be there, psychically in tune. We'd do three set gigs, starting at 11 P.M. and ending at four in the morning. It was really good for us to run out of material, and then continue to play — jamming, accenting things. That made for an incredible level of musical communication."

The band's early touring experiences were physically demanding, as Matthews recollects: "That was a tough time, and there were many points at which you just knew you were on the edge of leaving the scene. So it wasn't candy and cream and peaches and fun. There was a hell of a lot of hard work, driving every day, playing six days a week. It was a workout" ("Dave Matthews Band Is Thriving"). Matthews also vividly recalls some of the atmospheric conditions of the smaller places they were booked into. "It got pretty damned humid in those little clubs that we played. We'd go out of tune a little" (Considine). All that time band members spent together as road warriors also took its toll; Matthews admits: "If we'd been in a van for another six months, I don't know if we'd still be a band" (Cadigan).

Beauford, too, has clear memories of the early days. "We've had some rough times together. . . . We really started from the bottom. We scratched and clawed our way up, and I think we all remember what it was like when we didn't have anything" (William F. Miller, "Carter Beauford").

By November 17, 1992, the band's set list for their weekly Trax gig had expanded to: "Granny," "Cry Freedom," "Recently," "Pay for What You Get," "Halloween," "Typical Situation," "Jimi Thing," "The Song That Jane Likes," "Lie in Our Graves," "Help Myself," "Satellite," "Tripping Billies," "Lover Lay Down," "One Sweet World," "I'll Back You Up," "Warehouse," "Angel from Montgomery," "True Reflections," "Me and Julio down by the Schoolyard," and "Two Step." By 1997, only the original tunes "Granny," "True Reflections," and "Halloween" had not been made into studio recordings; a live version of "Halloween" was included on the 1994 EP.

During a Wednesday-night Flood Zone show held on November 25, 1992, just before Thanksgiving, Matthews invited the crowd to a special event. It would become an annual DMB tradition that was perpetuated for years. "Thank you very much for coming," Dave began. "Oh, by the way, we're having a huge party on New Year's Eve, so if any of you are in town, y'all gotta come down. We're gonna be over at the Omni here in Richmond. It's gonna be a huge party, that is, if you all come. Boyd's gonna be doing a brand-new dance from his forefathers in Egypt and Northern Africa — other parts of Northern Africa. I'm going to be doing an Irish-jig dance that's been handed down from father to son, father to son, father to son. And when it got to me, father to daughter — until the operation. And I learned how to do it, too. So that's all at the party on New Year's Eve at the Omni. I'm gonna say it a few times. The Omni — New Year's Eve."

The band would ring in the New Year at Virginia gigs for the next five years. Around this time, DMB started to work actively on the idea of making an independent CD, and to court record companies.

5
REQUESTING SOME ENLIGHTENMENT

To sell an independent CD or attract the interest of a record company, most bands need to have lots of original songs. By the end of 1992, DMB did. They had roughly 30 tunes. This core creative canon, which would be repeated over and over again in live performance with some minor set-list variation, became the cornerstone of DMB's musical catalog and a key source of its popularity.

It took the band three CDs (and five years) to get most of this 1991–92 material recorded and released, but few realized this; while the general record-buying public thought that their 1996 release, *Crash*, contained all-new material, hardcore DMB fans knew (via the taper culture and from what they had heard at live shows) that six of the release's twelve songs hailed from the band's first full year together: "So Much to Say," "Two Step," "Tripping Billies," "Cry Freedom," "Drive In, Drive Out," and "Lie in Our Graves."

This unusual approach to issuing material should have been seriously assessed by professional music critics, yet most members of the national and international music press, as they attempted to examine the specifics of DMB's core repertoire, found themselves unable to categorize the band's music. Matthews himself acknowledged this critical phenomenon when asked how DMB's music could best be described; he replied "con-fusion" ("Dave Matthews Band Eases").

It's true that some critics have discussed DMB's musicianship and their original material with intelligence and a firm knowledge of the specifics. But many others have given these things only a cursory, narrow examination in the context of short, general CD reviews or limited — albeit positive — reports on their concert performances. None have traced the roots of the band's repertoire to this 1991–92 period.

Other press responses to them have just been baffling. In the band's national media coverage, curious associations have occurred. For example, throughout 1996, *Rolling Stone* displayed a penchant for repeatedly lumping DMB and Hootie and the Blowfish together. On its May 16, 1996, cover, which featured David Duchovny and Gillian Anderson of television's *X-Files* rolled sexily together in a sheet, DMB's name appeared in a column under that of Hootie and the Blowfish. But it turned out that DMB was simply reviewed inside the issue — there was no reason for their name to be on the cover at all.

In mid-1996, then-*Rolling Stone* writer Jim DeRogatis was told to write a review dismissing both Hootie and the Blowfish and DMB — to "get to the root of why all this stuff sucked." That was the actual assignment. DeRogatis strongly dislikes both groups, so he had no problem with it. He hoped to include a thorough trashing of the Spin Doctors, as well. Then DeRogatis was charged (the word came down from editor-in-chief Jann Wenner) to write a positive review of Hootie and company, but to maintain the negative focus on DMB (and the Spin Doctors). His original piece was published in the June 12, 1996, issue of the *San Francisco Weekly*; a cleaned-up version came out later in *Rolling Stone*. The *San Francisco Weekly* version included a bonus: a one-sentence slam of jam bands that specifically mentioned DMB. Both DeRogatis and the *Rolling Stone* editor who had actually assigned the negative reviews subsequently lost their jobs in what they termed the *Rolling Stone* "Hootiegate" incident (Green).

In the *Rolling Stone* of December 12, 1996, a feature appeared entitled "The Raging Optimism and Multiple Personalities of Dave Matthews" (reprinted in full in this book). The writer of that feature, John Colapinto, asks Matthews about DMB's connection to Hootie and the Blowfish, and the question seems to come out of the blue. Perhaps, again, it was an editorially mandated query. Fans of DMB are mystified by this linkage. Certainly the music of the two bands sounds nothing alike. Matthews deftly responds to Colapinto by saying nice things about Hootie and the Blowfish; he comments that they once "played on the same circuit." In 1995, during an MTV Online interview, DMB was asked if they knew Hootie and the Blowfish. Matthews answered: "We played with them once last summer."

To compare all the bands that have ever played the same tour circuit — or opened for one another — would be to take a tremendously broad approach to music criticism. Ultimately, it would be an absurd exercise. Surely this is not the basis for the year of *Rolling Stone* coverage that aligned the two bands. Perhaps comedienne-actress Janeane Garofalo reads *Rolling Stone*. In a stand-up routine she performed circa 1996, she made a derisive comment linking the music of Hootie and the Blowfish and DMB and their fans. Her performance still crops up occasionally as a rerun on the Comedy Central cable channel.

If region is the common denominator of the two bands — and this is implied by critics, editors, and stand-up-comedy performers alike — then most people from Charlottesville would insist that a geography lesson is in order. Hootie and the Blowfish are not even from Virginia, let alone C'ville (they're from the Carolinas). Some DMB fans suggest the strange linkage is simply this: both bands are racially integrated and from the South.

Other national magazines and newspapers have attempted to identify a "C'ville sound" in their coverage of DMB. *Time* ran a story in 1995 declaring that Charlottesville was poised to become the next Seattle due to DMB's success (Bellafante). Many Charlottesville natives find this notion ridiculous — it's just another lame attempt to reduce and categorize. C'ville musicians clearly do not have a single sound.

Hawes Spencer of C-VILLE *Weekly* talks about the reaction of his staff to the idea: "We made fun of it. There must be UVA people working at *Time*. There's no single music scene or Charlottesville sound. That's a misnomer."

Shannon Worrell's take on the concept is this: "I don't know why there've been so many bands from here. There's nothing really cool about Charlottesville, you know what I mean? I mean it's a beautiful place and all, but you can't, you know, strike a pose or whatever. Most people don't so much hang out as hibernate" (Provencher, "Telling Rock").

And Matthews? He has stated that although there is a lot of music in C'ville, the effect has not been the creation of an identifiable local sound: in fact, the *lack* of a concrete scene/sound allowed DMB to mature more naturally; "It helped us develop a sound our fans found acceptable" (Grant).

* * *

So, if we stop trying to categorize and really look at DMB's instrumentation, it becomes obvious that this is one factor that sets them apart musically from most other popular bands. After all, this group performed with a symphony before they ever became MTV superstars. With Tinsley's acoustic and electric violins, Moore's 10 different instruments (saxes, horns, flutes, and whistles), Beauford's incredibly extensive drum kit, Lessard's electric and upright bass, and Matthews' acoustic guitar and lead vocals, DMB comes up with arrangements that are unique in the world of rock music.

Matthews describes their general musicianship: "The guys in the band have such diverse tastes and all of them are so capable of moving away from whatever our musical center is. They can stretch things out much further" (Johnson). He also explains that the blend of their talents and instrumentation is the key to their music: "It's the combination of us, the personality that's created when we're all together, not the personalities individually" (Cadigan).

Peter Griesar thinks that the subtle refinement of Matthews' original songs helps to distinguish the band's sound. "When people ask me how to write songs, I tell them to work on them over and over again until what might seem simple to you becomes complex to fresh listeners, full of nuance and subtlety." And Tim Reynolds observes: "Dave has all this stuff that works because you haven't heard it before. . . . There are little subtleties he's developed when you start listening, a unique rhythm and singing style" (G. Brown, "Chance").

John D'earth identifies that same subtlety — and "swing" — in Dave's guitar playing. "Miles Davis said that 'swing' is all about placement — it's where you put a note, where it's placed that matters. Dave's guitar playing is like Miles Davis's playing. The hookup is so subtle and exact. It's also about what he wouldn't do. Dave's got a beautiful sense of space and architecture. The music is deep and profound. Dave's really a poet. Traditionally, poetry was always sung. Dave's a Dionysian type, like Dylan Thomas. It just pours out of him. It's a piece of who he is. This is who he is. It's out of his own soul and being."

Matthews credits the entire band with playing "so much from the heart. The sound of the band came from that . . . and it really is how we all play with each other" (Cadigan). As lead vocalist, Matthews is modest about his vocal contributions to the overall sound of the band. "I just sing the way that feels normal," he confides. "Sometimes I think I sound a little bit like the Lollipop Guild, but that's ok" ("Dave Matthews Band Is Thriving"). He always tries to convey emotions when he sings — not just lyrics. He also uses his voice as an instrument. "Mainly, it was just me and the guitar, which is where I started to use my voice to do what a lot of people might have gotten the guitar to do" (Trott, "20").

Matthews expounds on DMB's one-of-a-kind, signature sound: "I know the reason we sound like we do has to do with the instruments and the people playing them. What ties the songs together are the characters that are dealing with them. But I do struggle at times not to repeat ourselves" (Snider).

* * *

There is an obvious correlation between biography and the content of many Matthews songs, especially those from the band's early, richly productive period: 1990–92. Dave bravely chronicles the events of his life in his music. In so doing, he is participating in the long-standing tradition of importing poetry into popular songwriting. He is also perpetuating the "folk" tradition of storytelling, to which he was exposed in his youth. While an entire academic study could easily be devoted to a theoretical examination of DMB's sophisticated musicianship and composing techniques (in fact, some music professors now incorporate DMB as text in theory classes), an informal look at biographical elements connected to the band's first 30 tunes yields a different perspective on the musical development of the Dave Matthews Band. It brings us more directly into the realm of the personal. There is a compelling connection between real life and creative impulse in the 1991–92 period (and beyond).

Matthews (and eventually the band as a songwriting unit) used numbers to designate the order in which the songs were written. Sometimes the numbers simply became the titles, as with the later songs, "#34," "#36," "#40," and "#41," providing clues for DMB archivists as to when and why the songs were written, and what actual events were springboards for their creation.

These 30 early songs address family, love, relationship frustration, politics, Jesus (and other religious luminaries), death, the idea of carpe diem, drugs, and suicide — in short, a wide spectrum of human experience and emotion.

"The Song That Jane Likes," dedicated to Matthews' sister, has theatrical allusions imbedded in its lyrics — a nod to Dave's acting days. The music was cowritten with Mark Roebuck, and, evidently, it was finished before the lyrics were. For this reason, Matthews has said that "I'll Back You Up" was the first song he ever completed.

The latter tune, a love song, Matthews wrote for his ex-girlfriend, Julia Grey, whom he had met in South Africa. Grey later moved to Charlottesville, after Matthews did. She was also interested in the theater. One fall during this period, Grey appeared in a Live Arts production of *Speed-the-Plow* by David Mamet. Her program bio reads: "JULIA GREY (Karen) has been confined to the library for four years [at university] . . . and has decided to experiment with Reel Life. Hence, for the past two years she has been continent-hopping, learning to get by on pennies and centimes, and has landed (feet first) in the lively village of C'ville. As with most visitors to this town, her stay has been longer than first anticipated — but she has lingered long enough to become (thankfully) appropriated into the local art scene. This is her first major role ever and hopefully not the last."

Matthews has mentioned during many shows that he asked his longtime girlfriend to marry him three times, but that she always turned him down. In a show he did with Tim Reynolds, he got more specific: "I dated this girl for about seven years and I asked her to marry me. I asked her to marry me three times. . . . I had to ask three times, because each time I asked she said no. . . . It turned out to be good, though, because now we're really great friends." Young women in the audience audibly gasp at this revelation; they can't imagine anyone turning Dave down.

He mentioned Julia by name during the February 2, 1996, University of New Hampshire Matthews-Reynolds show in the context of his by-now infamous Road To Zimbabwe story. She was with Matthews on that eventful trip. Grey eventually returned to South Africa. Matthews told a local newspaper that "I'll Back You Up" was written for a woman who had moved back to that country (Sanmini-atelli).

"Recently" is another upbeat song about lovers and courtship that Matthews has said was written about good times in South Africa. Like "I'll Back You Up" and "The Song That Jane Likes," it's on the original November 1990 demo engineered by Greg Howard. The tune seems to be in keeping with Matthews' optimistic mood about love in 1990 — hopeful and "looking forward to much more."

The 1992 song "Halloween," as Matthews has often explained in concert, was written as an embittered retort to "a woman who turned him down" — perhaps Grey. Rejection, anger, and pain well out of it; the song details the breakup of a relationship. It hurts Matthews to sing this tune because there's so much screaming in it. The repeated lines "Don't walk away / Love / Love / Love," and the screaming, invoke the deep, painful emotions that come at the nightmarish end of a love affair — as well as that sense of having lost control over how that ending unfolds. An early version of the lyrics also included these lines: "Out of town she came / eyes open and staring up at me."

"Halloween" wouldn't debut until October 31, 1992; its name seems to have been derived more from the date of its debut than its content. Perhaps there is a happy irony for Matthews in it, however. He reveals that he met his next girlfriend, Ashley Harper, that same Halloween: ". . . I haven't dressed up for Halloween since four years ago ['92]. But that's where I met my girlfriend. I was just painted, a freak. That's more of a costume for me than the moon or an ape" (G. Brown, "Happy Hippie"). (See the articles by Colapinto and Bailey in this book for more on Matthews and Harper.)

Matthews told America Online interviewers that he writes all his songs for his family. In the tabulature book for *Under the Table and Dreaming*, Matthews comments on "The Best of What's Around": "Thanks to bad days and hard times, we notice the sweet nectar." It's certainly a song about making the best of one's circumstances — of making lemonade out of lemons, to use a common phrase.

"The Song That Jane Likes," "I'll Back You Up," "Recently," and "The Best of What's Around" were the only cuts on the November 1990 demo, according to Greg Howard. The family ties, the South African connections, and the Grey inspiration: all were important elements of Matthews' life at the time, and each was woven into the songs he was writing.

"Cry Freedom," Matthews' 1991 song about South Africa's protests and politics, initiated a thematic vein in his work that he would return to frequently. And the band, collectively, embraced the theme of South African politics: two years later, DMB performed a song about the tragedy of Chris Hani, a man who, at the time of his brutal murder in April 1993, "was arguably South Africa's most popular black leader after Nelson Mandela." Hani's death "threatened to plunge the country into anarchy and derail the first all-race elections the following year" ("Killer").

The original lyrics of the song, called "#36" — it debuted on April 18, 1993, at a Brown's Island, Virginia, concert — referred directly to Hani's murder ("two men slice and dice each other up in his place"), and mourned the leader by chanting his name over and over in the chorus. More than a year later, on October 21, 1994, Matthews introduced the song during a show with these words: "I guess last year, sometime last year, Chris Hani, I don't know if you're familiar with him but he, uh, he was the . . . leader of the military wing of the ANC and was fighting for a little bit of liberation in South Africa, and he walked outside, I guess, after breakfast one morning and caught a bullet in the side of his head, and he died soon after that. So, anyway, on that day, after hearing that bad news, we came up with this kinda happy groove, and the song's kinda about love and huggin' and kissin' and dancin' and gettin' babies, and makin' babies, and makin' love." Clearly, his South African experiences had a major impact on Matthews' songwriting — and subsequently that of the band, now a writing collective.

"One Sweet World," another early-1991 tune, is a humanitarian plea for peace, an attempt to make us honor the common roots of our humanity. Matthews has often complained about the divisiveness of government and the negative effect of self-serving politicians. This song, with its beautiful instrumentation, asks us to unite for a higher purpose and to get along — because we're part of "one sweet world."

The song that would become the band's first hit single, in 1994, was actually written in 1991. Matthews has quipped in concert that "What Would You Say" is about Charlottesville. In the sheet music/guitar tabulature book for *Under the Table and Dreaming*, the cryptic line Matthews uses to explain the song reads: "A dog, a stuffed monkey and a television with 400 channels." The lyrics point to the ironies of life. Here, also, we see the inception of the carpe diem theme, which can be traced through most DMB songs from this era. It all starts with the line "Everyone goes in the end."

"Seek Up," another Matthews-penned, richly textured, complex tune from this time, alludes to death. Here Matthews warns: "Soon we will all find our lives swept away." The song also explores the emotional push/pull, yin/yang energy of a relationship: "You seek up an emotion and your cup is overflowing / You seek up an emotion, sometimes your well is dry."

Another major carpe diem-infused song is "Tripping Billies," with its cheery "Eat, drink, and be merry, for tomorrow we die" chorus. Matthews interprets the title like this: "Well, see, you've got billy goats. A herd of billy goats. Tripping goats. Hillbillies on acid, maybe that's another possibility. Maybe there's a party and maybe everybody's venturing into the shadowy corners of their mind, and maybe someone at the party is upset about what they find in the recesses of their mind. And other people say, 'Look we're at a party, you should enjoy things, forget about those dark, little corners in your head' " (Mervis, "Crashing"). He has also said that the tune was about a beach party in South Africa involving hallucinogens (Marzullo and Leta).

"Lie in Our Graves," which debuted almost one year after the band's first gig, is another "seize the day before you die" song. Lyricist Matthews talks about the importance of embracing what life has to offer: "When I step into the light /

My arms are open wide." The song ends with "I can't believe that we would lie in our graves / Dreaming of things that we might have been." The lyrics also playfully invoke the Bobby Darin hit "Splish Splash." Matthews, Beauford, Lessard, Moore, and Tinsley all receive song-writing credit: "Lie in Our Graves" may be the first product of the DMB collaborative writing experience. On June 23, 1996, Matthews introduced the song by saying, "Hey, this is a song that sings about the hopes that when we all get to the end of our lives that we'll feel, we'll feel pretty good about what we did, so don't compromise yourself."*

Why all these death references? Because of his father's premature passing, Matthews had come to terms with the preciousness of life at a very early age. Perhaps there's a correlation. Many of his songs reflect his philosophical struggle with loss as part of the ongoing process of life. In his lyrics, Matthews always points out that death could be right around the corner; he implores his audience to appreciate life's joys while they can.

In a song that became a concert favorite, "Dancing Nancies," Matthews poses the soul-searching question: "Could I have been someone other than me?" Throughout the years, he has introduced the song in a variety of interesting ways, but at a June 19, 1996, show held in Deer Creek, Indiana, he went so far as to explain the song's South African genesis. He thought of it while he was ambling through South Africa, circa late 1991, early 1992. Starting out in Port Elizabeth, he covered a lot of ground: "It was a long fucking way. Well, I was actually hitchhiking, which you can do sometimes there, and be successful. And I was unfortunately not successful, and I walked my skinny chicken legs off, and I thought to myself . . . I thought to myself, what the fuck am I going to do with my life?

---

* Another 1991 song, "Mother's Night," which deals with death and world politics, is attributed to Matthews on various Internet web sites. It's rumored to have been discovered on a tape owned by one of his relatives. Apparently, the song was never performed by DMB — only by Dave as a solo. The song contains the lyric line "Just step out into the light."

Walking around in the middle of Africa with nothing to do? What am I going to do? What am I going to do? I said, well, hey, I could be an accountant, I could be an explorer, I could be myself, could I be . . . somebody else . . . ?"

There has been much talk about "Warehouse" as a tribute to the attics of grandparents. This concept was prompted by DMB's *Under the Table and Dreaming* guitar tab book and Matthews' single pithy line of explanation: "Have you ever been in your grandparents' attic?" However, Matthews' South Street warehouse days (as described by Lydia Conder) seem to be a more realistic source for the inspiration and setting of the song. The tune is highly symbolic; the warehouse becomes a metaphor for the ups and downs of life. Certainly, Matthews experienced both in the course of his own adventures at the pink warehouse — while playing on the rooftop or rehearsing in Hoffman's apartment. Interestingly, both Trax and the Flood Zone can also be described as "warehouses."

Because of its title, "Granny," a 1992 song about love, has often evoked in its listeners a greater sentiment for grandparents than has "Warehouse." "Hello, how are you doing today? / I hope this finds you feeling healthy" does sound like something one would say in greeting a grandparent, but the ensuing lyrics are clearly about the trials and tribulations of romantic love. Rumor has it that back in 1992 Matthews hoped the song would become the band's first single; supposedly he could imagine masses chanting the catchy chorus, "Love! Baby!" But, mysteriously, "Granny" would not even be included on any of the band's first three studio CDs.

Other 1992 crowd faves — like "Spotlight" and "Blue Water Baboon Farm" — disappeared abruptly from the band's repertoire and were never recorded in the studio. Because the DMB canon of this era was performed almost ritualistically at weekly gigs, when a tune suddenly vanished, its absence was diligently noted by fans and responded to with the same level of excitement that met the introduction of a new song. When asked about the disappearance of "Spotlight," Matthews expressed worry that the lyrics of the song, a parody of a life of fame, might be misinterpreted now that DMB was famous. He also claims to have forgotten how to play it.

One song that Dave did say was written for a relative was "Satellite." He revealed to MTV Onliners that he wrote it for his mother. However, the tune was initially called "After Her," and the lyrics had a very different tone when it was first played in 1991: "In my life never before have I, lover, so adored / Her eyes, her hair, everything she says." The song ended with these lines: "With biggest steps I'm running / after her I will run / After her." The melody remained identical. So "Satellite" was, at first, it seems, a love song. It might have been inspired by Julia Grey; but, for whatever reasons, the beautiful ballad was soon rewritten to be a song "for Dave's mom." Matthews now coyly tells people that he forgot the words to "After Her" so he had to rewrite the tune, and it became "Satellite."

In fact, Matthews often tells people that he's forgotten songs. Whether he really has or not (and most rock stars are not forced to defend their set-list selections like this), it only spurs DMB fans into action. They constantly conspire to slip him tapes of such songs as "Spotlight," "Blue Water," "After Her," or even "#40," eager to remind him of the chords or words to these classics. This is probably the only nonfinancial drawback of an open taping policy: should you want to forget a song, or just leave it alone for a while, your fans will produce a live tape to jar your memory.

The 1997 Grammy-winning "So Much to Say," written by Tinsley, Matthews, and Griesar, debuted around February 13, 1992. C'ville insiders speculate that the song probably originated with Tinsley. The lyrics are alliterative and metaphoric; Matthews, Tinsley, and Griesar share lyric and music credit. The tune is, Matthews confides, about the struggle everyone undertakes to become an individual, to break out of "treading trodden trails for a long, long time": "It's something that we learn when we're children and trusting and naive. Everything seems so simple, until we find out, well, not necessarily find out, we just become actors and actresses, trying to portray ourselves the best possible way we can. Sometimes it's natural, and sometimes we can just be ourselves and it's enough. But other times it seems we have to do ourselves better" (Roland). The music originally had more of a calypso feel, but, without keyboards or Griesar, the song metamorphosed into a straight rock tune.

"Ants Marching" protests being compelled to live the life of a drone. One of the few Matthews compositions with alternating G and D chords, the song was at first (in 1991) called "No New Directions." Both titles sum up its theme. Matthews told an America Online interviewer that the band wanted something louder, so he rewrote it. The tune ends with this uplifting thought: "Lights down, you up and die." Again, the familiar Matthews philosophy — enjoy life; it's so precious — is invoked; Dave entreats the audience to make something of their lives before they bite the big one.

This completes the early set of merry, upbeat-sounding, enjoy-life-because-death-looms songs, which includes "What Would You Say," "Tripping Billies," "Lie in Our Graves," and "Drive in, Drive Out." The ironic tension these tunes create between the upbeat sound of their music and the fatalistic mood of their lyrics would become a hallmark of the Dave Matthews Band.

"Christmas Song" is an earnest, beautiful ballad about Jesus; Matthews has often introduced it as a song about a guy he admires a lot. It is obviously seasonally inspired, and this is likely a vestige of Matthews' Quaker upbringing. Not many rock stars functioning outside the religious-rock milieu write songs professing a fondness for Jesus; neither do they present their audiences with such blunt lyrics as "When Jesus Christ was nailed to his tree / He said 'Oh Daddy-O, this is how it all soon will be.'"

"Minarets" contains lyrics addressed to "Santa Maria virgin child." Played first in October 1991 at the Flood Zone, it was originally called "Screaming from the Minarets," a phrase that becomes a refrain in the song. (A minaret is a slender turret connected to a mosque, and is commonly associated with the Islamic religion.) Another political protest song about the senseless wars that have been sparked by religious differences — in this case, Christians versus

Muslims — the song is a thematic mix of religiosity and politics.

Matthews' love of poetry is tied to politics in the song "Typical Situation," also deriving from the fall of 1991. It was written in direct response to Robert Dederick's political diatribe "a prayer in the Pentagon." Here Matthews addresses the complex issue of global plurality, and laments the idea that individuals must conform or be locked away: "We can't do a thing about it." He connected to Dederick's writing so closely that he felt inspired to answer it creatively — and thereby joined a long poetic tradition.

Current events informed the 1992 tune "Help Myself," previously titled both "Dangerous Hours" and "Desperate Hours." It chronicles a violent murder in its first verse. The song is also a thematic precursor to the 1996 DMB hit "Too Much." "Help Myself" is about amassing things you don't need — "big house, big yard" — without much regard for those who have less than they require. Matthews intones sarcastically, "Every once in a while / To help the helpless comes into style." The song eloquently profiles the position of the haves versus the have-nots in society. Continuing a trend, Matthews inserts lines about death's imminence, and again gives voice to his ongoing concerns about social injustice and selfishness.

"Lover Lay Down" is another gorgeously melodic ballad about true love. It's about someone who, Matthews sings, was "leading me all around in circles." One can only speculate as to who might have inspired him to pen the tune in early 1992: "So much we have dreamed / And you were so much younger / Hard to explain that we are stronger." But it was obviously someone he had known and loved for a long time — when they'd both been younger.

"Drive In, Drive Out" profiles an on-again, off-again relationship that won't end but clearly isn't satisfying: "I'm over this arrangement around here." It expresses the frustration of love and foreshadows the death knell: "Sooner or later we're done / Sooner or later I'm gone because, because / Sooner or later we're gone." Although earlier lyrics had different moods for the verses, the chorus and basic instrumental lines remained constant from inception. Matthews has said he wrote it specifically to showcase Beauford's talents; Carter drums out the ending into spectacular 6/8 time. Describing the process he used, Matthews says: "When I came up with that, I knew that it was a Carter song, and I wrote that very end bit knowing how Carter would make that happen. I knew that he would turn that into this 6/8 madness, because I'd heard him do it before" (Considine).

Like "Drive In, Drive Out," "Two Step," also from this productive 1992 era, romantically details the pleasure of having a special lover, only to acknowledge that "life is short but sweet for certain" — another of Dave's pervasive death references — and, poignantly, that there are "Things we cannot change." Matthews has said that "Two Step" is "about a love affair that takes place in the middle of great world upheaval. It's romantic and mysterious at the same time" (Bessman). He has often referred to it as one of his favorite songs.

Along with "I'll Back You Up" and "After Her" (before it morphed into "Satellite"), "Lover Lay Down" completes a trio of ballads expressing the joys of love. "Granny" alludes to pain and cleansing with its use of the rain/tears metaphor. "Seek Up," "Drive In, Drive Out," and "Two Step" detail the ragged periods of fighting, making up, and the ensuing feelings of ambivalence. "Halloween" completes the arc, examining love's downside, the pain of the end. These songs seem to trace the various stages of a romantic relationship. Was the Matthews-Grey liaison the inspiration for any part of this musical saga of love's highs and lows? Perhaps there were other sources of inspiration, as well.

Boyd Tinsley's "True Reflections" debuted in 1991. As he does on DMB's John Prine cover, "Angel from Montgomery," here Tinsley sings lead. In Tinsley's own words, "True Reflections" is "a very personal song that kind of just came out of me, you know." He points out that the tune is a "nice counterpoint to Dave's songs which are sometimes a little more difficult to figure out" (Bailey, "On the Road . . . part 2"). The song also points a finger at hypocrites —

"Now that you've seen your true reflections / What on earth are you gonna do?" — and challenges them to "Find some inspiration" buried deep within, to mend their shallow ways.

"Jimi Thing" and "Rhyme and Reason," circa late fall 1992, are drug songs with opposite endings. Like "Tripping Billies," "Jimi Thing" is about a positive drug experience; Matthews has said that it's one of DMB's two "hippie" songs. In 1995, the upbeat and catchy "Jimi Thing" was considered for release as a single, but its nine-minute-plus duration took it out of the running for commercial radio airplay. "Rhyme and Reason" is a complaint about a pain in the brain that won't stop "until I'm six feet underground." Here is yet another death reference in a 1991–92 Matthews song, only this time the persona is suicidal. In "Rhyme and Reason," mention is also made of a "needle to the vein" — an allusion to heroin. Matthews has often introed this song by saying it's about "too much of nothing."

"Pay for What You Get," which Matthews amusingly introduced at DMB's November 25, 1992, Richmond show as being about Freebird, was seriously explicated by Matthews in the *Under the Table and Dreaming* tablature book: "I spend a lot of time thinking about what I don't have and how I can get it. When I succeed in attaining it, often it comes with things I didn't expect." The infighting and conflict involved in being in a successful local band with aspirations of going global were beginning, by 1992, to take their toll on Matthews. "Pay for What You Get" is also about a woman who left in the midst of this growing chaos: "Everybody asks me how she's doing since she went away / I say I couldn't tell you, I'm okay."

The word *Grey* would again manifest itself in Matthew's life in 1993. That year, Dave launched his own music publishing company, and called it Colden Grey Ltd. The name was publicly identified as a veiled death allusion: the words sound just like "cold and grey."

Of course, as Matthews himself would be the first to admit, the ultimate interpretation of DMB's music is up to each individual listener. There is no right or wrong. Matthews invited America Online DMB fans in 1996 to

"Interpret as you wish . . . that's the fun." It's important to know — from a biographical standpoint as well as a musical one — that religious, psychological, social, and political issues, as well as events in Matthews' personal life, did directly affect the creation of the first 30 songs of the Dave Matthews Band. Beauford, Griesar, Lessard, Moore, and Tinsley obviously made major contributions as well.

The band's lineup of original compositions developed more slowly after 1992. This was due to several factors, the two most crucial being Capshaw officially signing on as the band's manager in early 1993, and DMB signing a record contract with RCA on November 1, 1993.

6
THE THRILL OF IT ALL

The band's fame continued to grow. Matthews modestly characterized the phenomenon: "It really is not our doing. It's that we happened to fall together in a way that thrills us and that thrills people, too" (Jones).

Coran Capshaw, who'd wanted a management contract with Matthews — and the entire band — for a greater part of 1992, was pleased when it finally happened: he signed an official artist-manager agreement that went into effect around February 3, 1993. The contract was actually with Matthews. Dave's side of the deal was negotiated in January 1993 by Chris Sabec — a recent graduate of the University of Georgia Law School. Sabec had met Matthews at a show, and even though Sabec had no previous experience in entertainment law, Matthews had selected the young lawyer to be his personal attorney. Capshaw's side of the deal was handled by lawyer Philip Goodpasture, and he was given a 20 percent cut of the band's income — up to $40,000 a month — and 15 percent after that figure had been reached, financial terms that would prove especially profitable in the coming years. Hoffman was contractually allotted 25 percent of Capshaw's gross as part of this contract (Fox, "Dave on the Stand?"). Now Matthews had a manager, Capshaw, and a "key man," Hoffman. Matthews also gave Capshaw his power of attorney. Capshaw and Hoffman began working together, running Red Light Management with the help of office manager Jane Tower (Fox, "Legal Thang").

The ensuing years would bring confusion over the specific business relationship between Matthews, Capshaw, and Hoffman. As the band became more famous, the financial responsibilities, and the delegation of various duties, became highly complex. Eventually, this confusion would result in a legal dispute centered on Colden Grey.

In late March 1993, DMB underwent a personnel shakeup. Griesar quit the band. His reasons? "I don't remember why I quit. I forgot. You lose touch with what it was, due to talking about it so much." Griesar knew the band was going to be big and he believed in their music. The idea of an indie CD had been in the works for a while, but Griesar had taken on other obligations. He'd bought a house and with it came a mortgage.

Griesar's last show has widely been reported as the Tuesday, March 23, 1993, Big League Chew show at Trax, which Matthews kicked off by promising the crowd a "thrill a minute, thrill a minute." Performance highlights that night included a beautiful, nameless song that would later be labeled "Heathcliff's Haiku Warriors" (Matthews played it solo) and "#34" with words. The layered "#34," written in 9/8 time with a major-seventh sound, is credited to Matthews, Beauford, Moore, and Haines Fullerton. Its lyrics (which have since disappeared) contained these lines: "Lean on me / I'll lean on you / And we'll be okay."

Whether that March 23, 1993, show was really his last, Griesar isn't sure, but he did play that night, because Matthews introduced him during the performance. "Whenever it was, my equipment fried in the middle of the last encore," Griesar says. He thinks that some of the shows attributed to him on web sites were actually played by keyboardist Doug Wanamaker, yet another musician who sat in with DMB. "Around the end of March," comments Griesar, "they took him on the road." Griesar's departure was abrupt; he reported his decision to Hoffman and Matthews: "The next night I played my last show at Trax. I didn't really have much of a chance to say goodbye. Off like a rocket. I only saw Dave once in the first year after I quit."

Griesar's departure affected the band's sound, yet many feel he left an indelible musical imprint on DMB. David

Wellbeloved says that "Peter Griesar was so, so key to the development of the band. His contributions are as important as anybody's. Peter solidified their sound in a way you can still hear in their songs." Griesar rehearsed and performed about 35 originals and many covers with the band before his exit.

By April 15, 1993, DMB was opening for Toad the Wet Sprocket at William and Mary Hall in Williamsburg, Virginia. John Athayde ("Bobo"), known to many in the Internet community as a major DMB expert — he owns over 150 hours of DMB live audiotapes — saw the band for the very first time that night. He was a high-school sophomore in 1993, and explains, "We were all like, 'Who's this Dave Matthews guy? Probably some acoustic folky guy doing bad Dylan covers.' Well, it was a guy, with a band, doing Dylan, but it blew us all out of the water. The only song we knew that whole night was 'All Along the Watchtower.' Unless you had an older sibling at UVA or Virginia Commonwealth University or University of Richmond, chances are you'd never heard of them. I had friends that left after Dave played because they said, 'That's the best band you'll see tonight.'" Athayde paid $14 for his ticket to that show. Of course, as have most DMB fans, he saw the band many more times after that first experience. Athayde felt that the Richmond arts scene was and is, he remarks, more varied than C'ville's: "It's bigger and it's the capital of Virginia. There are tons of clubs. C'ville has a lot of jazz but Richmond is more diverse."

During the summer of 1993, Mindy Peskin needed a job. Beauford suggested that she start working for the band, since she spent so much time hanging out with them anyway. Capshaw hired her to help organize local C'ville events and to do computer/organizational work for DMB. "I started out helping with the itineraries," Peskin says, "which included compiling information from directions to the venue, to contacts, to hotel accommodations."

Bama Rags was formed in 1993, and quickly became a success. The name, as Matthews once quipped in an online interview, was an inside joke and preferable to "swaddling clothes." And sell clothes they did. Bama Rags became a powerful DMB merchandising entity. Capshaw used the model of the Grateful Dead for this part of the band's business plan, and to this day, DMB owns their own merchandising. It has proven to be quite lucrative — so lucrative that some fans have joked that DMB really stands for "Dave Merchandising Band." The band hired a local company, Blue Ridge Graphics, to print their logo on T-shirts and baseball caps. Alex Stultz was the merchandising coordinator for Bama Rags at the time; he toured with the band, bringing along a portable T-shirt stand.

Meanwhile, Peskin diligently compiled the band's initial mailing list of fans who wanted DMB's touring schedule and newsletter. "Starting from scratch, I ended up loading in thousands of names of people from all over the world." Peskin regrets that the mailing list fell by the wayside, replaced by the official DMB web site operated by Red Light Management, "because there are many people out there starving for information on the band."

The band's hectic 1993 touring schedule became the focus of a two-part feature in C-VILLE *Weekly*, written by Jim Bailey, who spent a week on the road with the band in June 1993. (The feature is reprinted in this book.) Day after day, DMB and entourage traveled in their vans, set up their equipment, grabbed some food, played gigs late into the night, enjoyed a little downtime, and started all over again the next morning — spacey and out of cigarettes. Many of the people mentioned as DMB support personnel in Bailey's article have now been with the band for years: Fenton Williams, Jeff Bagby Thomas, and Alex Stultz, to name a few. Loyalty to the band on the part of support staff and techs (roadies) has been strong from the start, paralleling the devotional zeal of the fans.

Bailey's article captures the band at a transitional stage. They play an afternoon debutante party in Lawrenceville, Georgia; during the same week, they move up a notch in status to play for a crowd of close to 700 at the Georgia Theater in Athens. One point that Bailey makes is that DMB was extremely popular in other parts of the South. This might have come as a surprise to Virginia fans, who were blithely bopping to the band in C'ville and Richmond, taking DMB's weekly presence at local clubs for granted.

"Say Goodbye" debuted on July 6, 1993, at Trax under the title "Any Noise/Anti-Noise." On this night, Greg Howard sat in with the band, temporarily replacing Lessard. Written by Matthews, the tune implores a friend to become a lover just for the night. "But tomorrow go back to your man / I'm back to my world / And we're back to being friends." Whatever the genesis of the song was, considering the band's crazy schedule at that time, it's not hard to imagine an incident that might provoke such a request. This song would be released three years later on the CD *Crash*.

The summer schedule included a couple of gigs at the Wetlands in New York, a one-night stand in Chicago, and another stint at the Georgia Theater. These were on top of all the Richmond-C'ville weekly shows. Matthews and Reynolds also played a frat-house gig with Shannon Worrell on July 26, 1993. Throughout this period, DMB played the material that would later appear on their first release, *Remember Two Things*, which was recorded on A-Dat digital recorders ("The Dave Matthews Band," MTV Online Interviews).

The good times rolled on in C'ville. Cristan Keighley has fond memories of partying with Matthews and crew member Fenton Williams during the summer of 1993. Matthews, Williams, and some others went over to Keighley's house after hanging out at the Main Street Grill. Cristan recalls jumping on a trampoline with Dave until all hours of the night and enjoying his impersonation of a gibbon.

Rumors had begun to circulate around C'ville that Matthews' acting career was again on the rise. Scenesters say he'd been approached to star in an independent movie with a budget of a million dollars. The financing fell through; it was never made.

On October 16, 1993, John Athayde saw DMB at Lake Matoaka, near William and Mary College in Williamsburg, Virginia. "It was a cool hippie festival," he says. That same month, the band also played several South Carolina and Alabama gigs. In one four-month period in 1993, DMB performed in seven states and the District of Columbia.

One of the things Matthews wanted most at this point in the band's career was a major record deal. Capshaw had declared that it was part of his plan to delay signing with a label until the time was right: "A lot of bands believe the goal is to get a recording contract right away. We wanted to build a fan base and then recording companies would come to us" (Burtner, "Money Side"). Insiders report, however, that when those companies did begin to manifest some interest, the potential deals just kept falling through — as they did with A & M, for example. At the time, Matthews divulged: "We are listening to two different offers and leaning towards signing with one" (Blackwell, "Two Things"). The band signed with BMG/RCA on November 1, 1993. Most fans think that the success of their indie CD *Remember Two Things* led BMG/RCA to DMB. Actually, the band signed with the big record company before the indie CD was even released.

Hoffman, as Matthews' key man, negotiated the deal, working closely with Chris Sabec (Fox, "Legal Thang"). The process that led up to it was complicated. A subsidiary of BMG, RCA, needed to find a new band it could take to the top. Its discovery of DMB was, in fact, another happy by-product of the taper culture. John Brody, an intern for Los Angeles-based RCA executive Bruce Flohr, brought a live DMB tape to work one day in 1993. Flohr, then a senior A & R development director for RCA's West Coast division, was enthusiastic. Evidently, he's not easily impressed. He remarked in 1994 that "Most demo tapes that come across my desk are brought in here by lawyers and managers. That's why most are crap" (Burtner, "Money Side"). Flohr called Peter Robinson, his New York counterpart, to tell him about DMB. Amazingly, Robinson had already made plans to see the band that night at Wetlands in Manhattan. Robinson attended the gig and loved DMB.

At that time, RCA Records was under the guidance of Joe Galante, who has since returned to Nashville to lead the label's country division. Galante went to see the band, too, and recalls, "It was 2:30 in the morning when [Matthews] went on. He hit the stage, and it was magic. The kids were singing along, people were dancing, the band was incredible, and there's just a personality they had. I hadn't seen something like that since maybe R.E.M." Signing DMB, Galante adds, was "the easiest decision I ever made in my life" (Roland).

The buzz around Charlottesville in October of 1993 was that DMB was about to sign with RCA. *C-VILLE Weekly* tried to verify the rumor, but Capshaw declined to comment (Atkins, "Bottom Line").

Richard Hardy sat in with DMB at Wetlands on or around Halloween. He recalls that on this evening, the general mood was celebratory; the band had turned in a sensational performance. Everyone was thrilled. The RCA contingent caught the wave; says Hardy, "Someone from RCA Records A&R congratulated me afterwards, as if I were in the band!"

A midnight release party for DMB's first CD, *Remember Two Things*, was held at Plan Nine, a music store near UVA, on November 9, 1993. The line, 400 people strong, began forming at 7 P.M. Capshaw elaborates: "This midnight sale idea has only been used for the big bands like Nirvana and Pearl Jam in the past. But Plan Nine treated this as one of those and it turned out to be the biggest yet" ("Remember"). Band members stayed until 5 A.M., autographing CDs and posters. Dan Garner, manager of Plan Nine, also reports that the event was a success: "We have done midnight sales before, but this was the largest crowd we've had . . . bigger than U2, R.E.M., and Pearl Jam. I don't think there was any way I could have estimated it would be this big" ("Remember"). People bought in bulk; one guy alone bought 31 copies. Plan Nine employees speculated that he was a fraternity pledge. Later, on Tuesday night, a party was held at Trax in honor of the release. The band and everyone at Red Light Management/Bama Rags celebrated hard that week.

Remember Two Things boasts some interesting credits. Greg Howard and Tim Reynolds played on the CD. Howard and John D'earth arranged "Recently." The entire project was produced by John Alagia and DMB. All the tracks on the disc were recorded live at Trax, the Flood Zone, and the Muse (located in Nantucket, Massachusetts) — except "Seek Up" and "Minarets."

The band wrote an entire page of thank-yous, included in the CD booklet, to all the people who had helped them. As previously mentioned, there was a special nod to Peter Griesar "for all the musical contributions and inspirations." The crew — named as "Fenton [Williams], Bag the Mallet [Jeff Bagby Thomas], Michael [McDonald], Henry [Luniewski], the angel Elijah [Rock]" — was thanked. Family members as well as other bands and musicians — the Samples, Blues Traveler, Aquarium Rescue Unit, the guys in Down Boy Down, Miguel Valdez, and Conductor Isador Saslav are some highlights — received expressions of DMB's gratitude. Some local writers, like Lawrence Becker, were thanked. Both Mark Roebuck and Haines Fullerton were acknowledged. Jane Tower and Chris Tetzeli, Red Light Management staff members, got nods, as did John D'earth, Tim Reynolds, Charles Newman, Shannon Worrell, and Ashley Harper. Finally, Trax, the Flood Zone, UVA, "and everyone else in the world who we know or don't know," got their due.

On November 17, 1993, Colden Grey Ltd. was formed as a publishing company for Matthews' original compositions. Rather than splitting the profits with a music publishing company, Hoffman had suggested to Dave that he publish his own material. Matthews agreed, and asked Hoffman to run the enterprise, whose mandate would be to handle the rights to 29 Dave Matthews songs. Matthews became the sole shareholder and president of the company, while Hoffman served as secretary-treasurer. Businessman Stirling McIlwaine assisted Hoffman in his quest to collect the royalties (Fox, "Legal Thang").

In another part of the country that year, far from C'ville, yet another fan had become hooked on the band through listening to live tapes. The taper effect had reached beyond the Midwest. Ryan Senter, now a resident of Los Angeles, was living in Colorado at the time. He was 18. It was the first time he had ever been introduced to the concept of tape trading. "Dave really monopolized the bootleg cult. If it wasn't for that, he wouldn't have been as popular as he was in Colorado then, from a bar tape recorded in Virginia."

At first, Senter spread the word about DMB as if to do so was his calling. "It was always cool that it was a band no one had heard of and they were so good. You'd try to talk them up so people would remember the name. Then, when it came to reality, you hoped they'd remember you'd told them about DMB first."

Ironically, Senter later came to resent the growing multitudes of DMB fans. Like so many of the band's early fans, he felt territorial about them. The emotional backlash gained force as DMB's success mounted. "I wanted everyone to hear DMB and once everyone had, I felt something had been taken away from me. Part of it was killed. Now it's everyone's. I got emotional about it. I speak for a lot of people when I say that. I started disliking people for liking them." Senter misses his early DMB concertgoing days, when "you could look at the person next to you and that person would be in the same stage of life and mind. Everyone took it seriously."

Throughout 1993, Senter found DMB's music and the taping process to be addicting. "At one time I was jonesing for the stuff. When *Remember Two Things* came out, it was great. I was happy just to hear that it was out." Senter would go on to have backstage experiences with the band in 1994 and 1996.

The song that was to become "Proudest Monkey" was introduced on December 11, 1993, at a Williamstown, Massachusetts, show. Originally labeled "Route Two/Evolution" by tapers, the tune was inspired by a difficult touring experience. The band had driven through a terrible snowstorm to reach the gig at Williams College in Williamstown. Other bands might have canceled under the circumstances, but DMB persisted, and soon found themselves heading along an alternative course, via Route 2, over a Berkshire mountain. They got lost, and then they got stuck, but they took the stage at 10:30, only two hours late. According to fans who were there, because the show was delayed and the audience had already gathered, there was no official sound check. The band did the music to "Route Two/Evolution" as a six-minute sound-check jam in front of the crowd. Matthews made up words on the spot, singing lines like "can't go any faster, gonna lose my way." Next, they segued into "One Sweet World."

When he revised the lyrics to "Proudest Monkey" — the original music, credited to the band as a whole (Beauford, Lessard, Matthews, Moore, and Tinsley), was retained — Matthews built on the symbol of the monkey. He changed the words to ask, "I wonder do I want the simple, simple life that I once lived in well." The concluding lyrics are "Now I am the proudest monkey you've ever seen / Monkey see monkey do." The arduous trip over the mountain had been a metaphor. Certainly, these lyrics suggest that repetitive performing leads the performer to feel that he's locked into a cycle of limitation, delivering his music by rote.

At the end of 1993, the band was poised to go global; the simple life was gone.

7
BETTER THAN THE BEST

The Dave Matthews Band kicked off 1994 with a January 3 gig at the Variety Playhouse in Atlanta, Georgia. It looked like everything would go swimmingly that year, but appearances were deceptive. As 1994 began, a tragic event rocked the Matthews family.

Dave took the stage for an acoustic show with Tim Reynolds at the Wetlands in New York City on January 19. As their informal gig got underway, Matthews announced: "Anyway, I got in this morning from a seventeen hour flight. . . . I sound like a comedian — 'I was flying in this morning.' . . . But anyway I flew . . . I was in South Africa where I'm from and my family's from. That's a country full of lots of violence and lots of hatred. But it's also full of lots of love and lots of good people. But I was there mourning the very recent murder of my sister. So this evening goes out to her and in her memory." Dave then launched into an achingly mellow version of "Tripping Billies." He was singing for his older sister, Anne.

South Africa was, in fact, the site of the senseless shootings of Dave's sister, Anne, and her husband. Dave has asked that the details not be publicized for the sake of Anne's children, whom he and Jane are now raising in Virginia. Later that year, when the top-selling *Under the Table and Dreaming* came out, the CD was dedicated to the memory of Anne.

Preparations began for DMB's first CD under the RCA/BMG umbrella. The first order of business was to find a producer.

Beauford recalls the search: "We had a few guys in mind, like Hugh Padgham and T-Bone Burnett, but eventually our manager told us about Steve" (William F. Miller, "Carter Beauford"). That "Steve" was the legendary British record producer Steve Lillywhite, whose roster of clients included the Rolling Stones, U2, Peter Gabriel, Morrissey, Talking Heads, David Byrne, Aretha Franklin, XTC, the Pogues, World Party, the La's, Big Country, the Psychedelic Furs, Joan Armatrading, Simple Minds, and Marshall Crenshaw. Lillywhite had also produced the work of his ex-wife, Kirsty MacColl (Mackie). In 1996, upon DMB's recommendation, Lillywhite would also work with Phish on their *Billy Breathes* CD.

Born on March 15, 1955, Lillywhite worked his way up in the UK recording industry — from tea boy to tape op to engineer — finally becoming a producer. His first producing credit was with Siouxsie and the Banshees in the late 1970s. From there, Lillywhite's career took off (Gillen). Now, he works in both the US and England.

Lillywhite finds it hard to describe the duties of a record producer: "What a producer should be able to give to a project is something you can't necessarily define. It's difficult to explain. I mean, you want to notice a production, but in a way, have it not be noticed. You want to bring out exactly the best of what an act has to offer, and just that. And for me, with a well-produced record, the first thing isn't, 'Wow, that's a well-produced record.' You say, 'that's a great record,' and you only discover the production — maybe — after a few listens." He especially enjoys recording artists with strong voices. For a while during the 1980s, his use of drumming was a signature production element (Gillen).

Undermining the stereotype of the abrasive rock-and-roll producer, Lillywhite is actually polite and easygoing; Matthews characterizes him this way: "He's this incredibly serene Brit, very 'Would you please' and 'Would you mind terribly' (Provencher, "Matthews").

As he explains how he selects artists to work with, Lillywhite says, "It depends. Sometimes I work with new bands, sometimes I work with people who already have a

Steve Lillywhite
LISA HAUN/RETNA

reputation. I'll work with anyone who'll send me a tape, really, because you never know what it's going to be like. I look for a voice to start with, for a really good voice. Then songs. Then musicianship." Lillywhite also professes to having no preference for either of these approaches: building records piece by piece, or recording bands live in the studio. He would do both with DMB.

There are no secrets of success when it comes to producing, insists Lillywhite, although his professional track record indicates that if any exist, he's party to them. "It's the only job I've ever had, really. So I feel like I know the job quite well. I just sort of do it, really. I try not to think too much about things, I just take it as it comes and use my instincts to see it through" (Mackie).

Although DMB was impressed with Lillywhite's credentials, band members weren't sure what to expect from him. Would Lillywhite want to mess with their sound? As Beauford explains, any fears they had were short-lived: "He was totally open-arms. He told us 'Look guys, I'm not here to change you or your music. I'm not going to put my concept on your band. I'm just going to make your album sound good. And I guarantee you the record will go platinum.' " The band sensed Lillywhite's sincerity. Indeed, Lillywhite, as Beauford notes, "lived up to everything he said" (William F. Miller, "Carter Beauford").

First takes are actually used sometimes. Lillywhite's belief in the magic they can generate reflects the respect he has for a band's unique sound: "The first take always has something about it, and quite often the second take will not have the same qualities the first take had. You then have to work quite a lot longer" (Mackie).

The band acquired a publicist in January 1994. Ambrosia Healy, who had worked with DMB in Boulder, Colorado, became their press rep. As a publicist for the Fox Theater in Boulder, she had handled the press for acts that played at the venue. After a DMB gig at the Fox drew 400 people, Capshaw asked Healy to work for DMB exclusively. "That band had something special early on," she comments. "They really had word of mouth" (Vannoy). Healy's philosophy is that a band's success is built on press: people read a feature on a group, go to see it, and then become loyal fans. And so Healy got to work calling writers and asking them to do articles on DMB. The band's visibility increased substantially as a result of her efforts.

The band continued to tour throughout February, March, and April. They played constantly — 20 to 25 times a month — doing gigs in Georgia, North Carolina, South Carolina, Missouri, Virginia, Alabama, Tennessee, Kansas, Colorado, Michigan, and Mississippi. The venues they hit varied: clubs and theaters in major cities and college towns. There were no more afternoon debutante parties. All the while, Matthews was grieving deeply, slowly recovering from the shock and trauma of Anne's death. He had to work through his grief while under enormous pressure to perform.

In a February 1994 interview, Matthews extolls the virtues of theater acoustics. Speaking of the Flood Zone, he says: "The sound's good. You can hear the room really well, it's got a real good natural reverb. You can hear what the audience hears. I love theaters in general." He also expresses his love for the Fox in Boulder and the Georgia Theater in Athens. As of early 1994, what was Matthews' favorite venue? Irving Plaza in New York (Matera).

Asked about the band's rehearsal schedule, Matthews mentions a rehearsal hall above the offices of Red Light Management in C'ville, but then adds: "We practice very rarely. We don't practice much at all. We play. The only time we're together is when we're performing." Of course, they were performing nearly every day. Matthews goes on to encapsulate DMB's grass-roots audience-building philosophy again, but this time he seems to be casting a wider net: "To afford traveling and moving around, we started playing fraternity audiences and school functions and that was the audience that originally got to know us. But we get some older people. There's a lot of familiar faces at the Flood Zone" (Matera).

Describing the band's eating habits in the interview, Matthews confesses: "I'm a huge meater. My favorite meat is red dead cows. I love cows so much. I feel bad about it, but I'm a carnivore. Others in the band, Stefan and Boyd, are strict vegetarians. Carter has a taste for fine food. So we don't have a favorite as a group. We're all completely different" (Matera).

At that time, Matthews felt the band's biggest problem was that they were still relatively unknown. "We need more and more. We need to know more people. We don't know enough" (Matera). That problem was solved in 1994. DMB would "know" millions of new faces.

In April, the EP *Recently*, a five-song compilation featuring Dave and Tim doing "Warehouse" and "Dancing Nancies" live, as well as a remix of the whole band doing the title song, was released under the auspices of Bama Rags — not RCA. "Halloween" and "All along the Watchtower" were included on it, too. The CD was only available at DMB shows, through mail order, or at the Plan Nine record store in C'ville. Two nearly naked people, a man and a woman, appeared on the cover; the young woman was a local model, Erin Van der Linde.

John Athayde recalls an especially amazing DMB performance on April 10, 1994, again at Lake Mataoka, Virginia.

It was part of a seven-hour concert that included other bands, among them Fighting Gravity and Everything (E:). The show was sold on a general-admission basis. The sound company showed up two hours late, and this meant the first band's set had to be canceled and subsequent bands had to come on late. Everything (E:), the band that immediately preceded DMB, overplayed their set. A noise ordinance went into effect late at night, and this made the ending of the concert quite dramatic. The police were trying to shut the show down, and DMB said they just had one more song to do. They proceeded, despite the threat of fines and police intervention. Athayde remembers: "They did this mad-ass jam on 'Recently' for half an hour. They had guys from every band on the stage, twelve people, including Doug Wanamaker, a whole mash."

In early May, Dave and Tim played a marathon radio show series for local Charlottesville radio station WJTU. Their first slot, on May 4, aired at 11 P.M. It was advertised in local newspapers as: "Radio according to Tim and Dave. We asked these two guys, who love to play together, about doing a radio show together. We also told them to do whatever they want." Reynolds and Matthews also performed live from the Prism Coffeehouse in C'ville on Saturday, May 7, 1994 — their contribution to the radio marathon's six-hour finale. The duo went on to play other shows throughout 1994.

Later in May 1994, DMB made a pilgrimage to Bearsville studio in Woodstock, New York, to record their first RCA/BMG CD, *Under the Table and Dreaming* with Lillywhite. Many months of preparation culminated in nearly two full months of studio work.

It was a creative time for the band and Lillywhite, but there were lots of problems to be solved. Beauford remembers how Lillywhite helped him the first time they went into the studio. He'd set up his drums in a booth, and it just wasn't working. With Lillywhite's aid, he moved the drums all over the studio, trying them out in every nook and cranny. Neither Beauford nor Lillywhite were satisfied with the acoustics of any of the potential locations. "But then it occurred to Steve," says Carter, "to carry the drums up to a loft above the studio, so we dragged them upstairs and got one of the best sounds I've ever heard in my life! He took the time to experiment and got a killer drum sound" (William F. Miller, "Carter Beauford").

Matthews noted the difference between playing live and studio work while recording at Bearsville, and he translated what he learned into a little nugget of philosophy: "It's an interesting thing, really, because the jam approach allows you to just go with a feeling and to explore, but in the studio you have to be more organized and more aware of what's going on on the record. Which is like a lot of things, really, when you think about it. Everyone's got their hesitation to commit with whatever" (Provencher, "Matthews").

John Popper of Blues Traveler was brought in to guest on one track, "What Would You Say." Tim Reynolds, continuing his recording association with the band, also came up to Bearsville, to play acoustic guitar.

Under the Table and Dreaming has proven to be the most successful CD release to date by DMB: sales figures are four million units and counting.

It was a big year for studio work. *Under the Table and Dreaming* was not the only CD that DMB members would work on in 1994. Matthews and Moore made guest appearances on Shannon Worrell's CD *Three Wishes*. Worrell, a friend of Jane Matthews, thanks Jane and Temple Farrell in the credits. Dave sings backup on a couple of songs, "Eleanor" and "See Jane." Moore plays on "Wondertwins." Tim Reynolds also performs on "Wondertwins" and "Eleanor"; he jams, as well, on two additional tunes. Red Light's Chris Tetzeli was Worrell's manager at the time.

Their grueling tour schedule propelled DMB through July, August, and September. By now, western states had been added. They were booked at the Backstage in Seattle and given more dates at the Fox Theater in Boulder. They also played the Gerald Ford Amphitheater in Vail, Colorado.

Then DMB joined the H.O.R.D.E.: Horizons of Rock Developing Everywhere. Created in 1992 by Blues Traveler and other bands (including the Samples), the H.O.R.D.E. was a live-music experiment, "an alternative to the alternative." Often compared to Lollapalooza, a touring rock show that tries to introduce music fans to different forms of music, the H.O.R.D.E. focused simply on presenting good live music.

A change occurred in C'ville in August, and, as a result, Trax was no more. Capshaw hadn't owned the club for a while. A businessman was now taking it over from its current owner and renaming it Crossroads Concert Hall and Sports Bar. C-VILLE *Weekly* reported that the 16,000-foot complex, including the adjacent club, Max, would shortly undergo a change of hands ("Arts Watch").

John Athayde noticed a change in the crowd when he attended the DMB show at Strawberry Banks in Hampton, Virginia, on August 13, 1994. It came as a huge shock to him. "There was a Clifford Ball [Phish festival] crowd there — an enormous number of people." The show was general admission, and "People were calling out 'What Would You Say' and play 'Ants Marching,'" songs that were soon to become big hits.

In September 1994, Capshaw handed over the band's scheduling to Monterey Peninsula, a California-based booking agency; DMB would continue to get gigs in the western states through this, one of the top booking agencies in the US (Burtner, "Stardom").

Monday, September 26, 1994, was the date of the huge autograph party for the midnight release of *Under the Table and Dreaming*. The title of the CD, a phrase from "Ants Marching," evokes Matthews' childhood, when he would play under a table and daydream about the world of adults (Chenoweth). The extravaganza was held at DMB's old haunt, Trax, now called Crossroads Concert Hall, and the adjoining club, Max. Elaborate preparations were made, and RCA reps were in attendance. Tickets sold out in four hours; more were issued; stormy weather did not diminish the crowds. On the slate were acoustic performances by Dave Matthews and Tim Reynolds, Shannon Worrell, Kristen Asbury, and others. First, the musicians did a set in Crossroads, then they wandered next door to Max for another. Other DMB members strolled around signing copies of the CD. On this subject, Tinsley comments: "Signing autographs is just part of the business for us. Not just part of the business, I enjoy it, we all enjoy it" (Scully).

Even DMB moms were on hand to celebrate. Beauford was accompanied by his mother, Anne. "I think it's going to happen this time," Carter declared that night. "It's been a long time for me — 30 years." Roxie Moore, mother of Leroi, spoke of the pride all the band members' parents felt at their sons' success. "We're just glad they're out of the nest," she joked (Scully).

Record-company brass were effusive in their appraisals of DMB and the band's dedicated following — RCA anticipated that these fans would snap up copies of the CD right away. Greg Linn of RCA remarked: "This is really, really unique, cause very often we're having to start from the beginning. . . . We have 175,000 [CD units] out now, and by next month, we expect to have all 200,000 out there, which is extraordinary for a first album. . . . It took someone like Bruce Springsteen three albums before he broke out, before he got a following like this" (Chenoweth).

Before the Crossroads event, Matthews expounded on why DMB had chosen to sign with RCA: "The level of interest grew and they came to see us — courting us, or maybe like hungry hyenas. They seemed really reasonable. A lot of people have said all they have is Elvis — nothing that really stands out as pop music, but I said, that's great — so there's room for us, and we won't be put on back burners. . . . About eight months went into befriending each other. Other record companies made bigger offers, but the attraction was the time they spent getting to know us. And the dog — Nipper! — the master's voice" (Chenoweth). Far from being put on the back burner, DMB would become one of RCA/BMG's premier acts.

The night of the Crossroads party was a charged one for Jane Matthews. She recounted to a reporter a story about seeing her brother perform at Brown's Island, in Richmond, Virginia. Jane was accompanied by their mother that night, and now remembered Mrs. Matthews' reaction to the Brown's Island scene: "And there was this crowd around him. It was really strange, and it was emotional for her to see him surrounded like that." As for Jane's own response to her brother's fame: "I don't know how I feel. I guess I can't really get a grasp on how really big it is. He's always had a lot of charisma; he's always attracted people in some way. It scares me that people love him so much who don't really know him. I just want him to eat well, and get enough sleep, and I hope he's happy with his music. I'm pretty sure that if he ceases to enjoy it, he'll move on — that's what he always does" (Chenoweth).

Boyd Tinsley, for one, was still stunned by it all. "In fact," he said at the time, "I've been in shock for a year. You hope things will happen, I just had no idea this would happen so quickly. . . . We were just the right people at the right time. Dave is a good songwriter, and we all are good players. It just works, I guess" (Blackwell, "Dave Matthews").

In describing the songs on *Under the Table and Dreaming*, Matthews identified "The Best of What's Around" as a song he wrote before the band got together, and revealed that "#34" was an instrumental tribute to a friend who had died (Blackwell, "Dave Matthews"). He also expressed his belief that the band should be in no hurry to make a video. Although they'd been receiving reels of sample footage from interested directors, the band had more immediate preoccupations. Matthews revealed as well that he'd kept financial control of all of his songs (Chenoweth).

Though increasingly feeling career pressures, Matthews was still, in 1994, writing most of DMB's material. "I guess the biggest challenge is to keep writing songs. I have a fear that the well will run dry. I don't know why, but I feel fairly confident that I don't have much to say. That's a concern of mine — I'm not writing better now than I was three or four years ago" (Chenoweth). And the music-business machinery was growing solid around him. By this time it included Dave Matthews Band, Inc.; Bama Rags; and Colden Grey Ltd. Matthews had begun to develop a sense of DMB companies. "I got on the band for a little ride, and then different people got involved musically, and in other ways, so now if I got off, it would be letting down a lot of people and myself" (Chenoweth). Red Light Management now had 15 employees. Furthermore, DMB was having a positive, trickle-down economic effect on some C'ville businesses. Local outfits had been hired to provide DMB with artwork, graphics, logos, and the clothing the band merchandised (Burtner, "Money Side").

On a personal note, Matthews mentioned missing, as an interviewer phrased it, "his current companion who attends Sweet Briar." He was referring to Ashley Harper (Chenoweth).

The day after the Crossroads party, September 27, 1994, was to be, by mayoral decree, Dave Matthews Band Day. Charlottesville's mayor, David Toscano, explained that this honor was bestowed as the result of the efforts of a DMB promoter who was helping the band to launch their world tour. How do you get a day named in your honor in C'ville? "Basically, you just have to ask," Mayor Toscano admitted. All reasonable requests connected to special events or needs would be considered, he added (Atkins, "Bottom Line"). Press pictures taken on the occasion show Dave humbly accepting a proclamation from the mayor and playing a gig. What a gig it was. Four thousand people gathered at the UVA Amphitheater to help kick off DMB's world tour. The opening band was From Good Homes.

But that gig was a tough one for Matthews. Early in the show, while he was playing guitar, his right wrist buckled. Matthews ended up playing for the rest of the evening with his knuckles. His hand bled profusely, cut to pieces by the steel guitar strings as 4,000 eager fans looked on. Matthews is a trooper: somehow, he got through that performance, but as soon as it ended he was whisked off to the hospital. The problem was diagnosed as a pinched nerve (Marzullo and Leta). However, it would not be the last time he would have a problem with his hand while playing guitar during a show.

Magically, the CD containing the song "#34" debuted on the charts at #34. *Under the Table and Dreaming* hit the charts running and sold 30,000 copies during its first week of release. The people at Plan Nine records were elated for DMB. Dan Garner, Plan Nine's manager, put it into context: "To be in the Top 100 is good. But to be in the Top 40 is up there in another tier. This is pretty phenomenal" (Blackwell, "New Release"). But the band was not on hand to accept the congratulations of their friends and neighbors.

Charlottesville Mayor David J. Toscano proclaims
"Dave Matthews Band Day," September 27, 1994

LOU BARON/PORTICO PRODUCTIONS LTD.

They were on the road again.

Their two-and-a-half-month world tour included a gig at Club Soda in Toronto in October. By November, DMB had made it to Europe. Former C'villean Mindy Peskin was by now continuing her studies in France, and was on hand to witness one of DMB's first European performances. The band had already played one venue in London and another in Amsterdam; Peskin joined them in Holland for the November 3, 1994, show, and was amazed at the size of the audience who'd come to see her hometown band. "I met up with them, plus a lot of friends from Red Light who came over for the week in Amsterdam. The show was packed, mostly with American students who were studying abroad and who'd traveled up to the Netherlands to hear a familiar American band play." Perhaps the American taper effect had penetrated Europe via the network of students such as these.

From late September to December 1994, DMB's US dates were set for some major centers: New York, Los Angeles,

Seattle, San Francisco, Philadelphia, Pittsburgh, Boston, Chicago, Nashville, New Haven, Athens, Richmond, and Providence. According to RCA/BMG publicity material, most of these gigs were sold out, and they were held "at clubs ranging in size from 900 to 5,000 capacity."

The release of "What Would You Say" as a single from *Under the Table and Dreaming* would swell the band's already burgeoning fan base. The Top-40 crowd joined the existing DMB fan club. In October 1994, "What Would You Say" made AAA (Adult Album Alternative) radio history as the "most-added single" ever by a debut artist in that format: "That means more adult album alternative radio stations put the single into airplay rotation in one week than any other single (by a debut artist) in any other week" (Neisslein, "Dave Matthews"). "What would you say / Don't drop the big one / If you a monkey on a string / Well, don't cut my lifeline" would be chanted by millions.

At this point, DMB became a highly visible opening act. Of course, they'd been opening for people since 1991, but now in 1994, their first hit single was out and they were appearing at middle-sized venues in major US cities: they had truly accessed the big time. Since DMB has become a headliner, Dave always introduces to the audience the bands that open for them. For many years, DMB occupied that "on deck" position, and Matthews knows how hard it is to get the crowd's attention in this capacity.

Many bands suffer what's known as "the opening-band syndrome." That's when "The lighting is lousy, the mix is muddled, the set is short, and most of the audience is still looking for a parking spot" (Mehle, "Opening Band"). It's also when lots of people line up at the concession booth and the bathroom. Often, ticket holders fight their way through dense arena crowds, blaze trails through miles of aisles, and sigh with relief when they finally sit down because the headliner still has not taken the stage. "It's only the opening band" is a phrase often muttered by tardy concertgoers, even as they sit before talented musicians who are playing their guts out.

One of the bands that DMB opened for was the Samples. Formed in Boulder, Colorado, in 1987 — long before DMB

— the Samples have had the good fortune to work with many great bands. Ironically, many of the groups that have opened for them have become bigger than they are. Singer-guitarist Sean Kelly of the Samples quips: "We're the Blarney Stone of bands. Open for us, and your career is made." Hootie and the Blowfish and Toad the Wet Sprocket both opened for them (Oland).

Ryan Senter, who had moved to California by 1994, had a chance to hang out with DMB backstage on one leg of their tour. It was during the fall at a Ventura, California, show that had not sold out. Senter was excited to be seated near Tinsley's part of the stage during the performance. "Boyd brings an energy to the entire concert — his whole style, how he gets into it. The coolest thing about Boyd is how he'd just stand in the dark with the violin on his hip. And then he'd be in the spotlight and he'd just explode." After somehow managing to convince a security guard that he was Dave's nephew, Senter went backstage when the show was over. "The first person I saw back there was Boyd, chilling on a couch." Senter spent time with both Matthews and Tinsley that night.

The band made a series of appearances in Southern California in early December 1994. One *Variety* music reviewer saw them on December 6 at a small (its seating capacity is 595) but famous LA rock club on the Sunset Strip — the Whiskey. His review began with this sentence: "Though Virginia's Dave Matthews Band didn't completely live up to the glowing reports from the East Coast, the band did show off its considerable talents, both in musicianship and songwriting, in its LA headlining debut." He then commented: "But as the two-hour show progressed, an obvious confidence emerged and with it the fire and excitement that DMB is known for." Welsh singer David Gray opened for DMB (Augusto).

As of the first week of December, DMB was headlining in LA — a city considered by many to be the rock-music capital of the world. That's a big leap for a band that barely a year earlier had signed their first major record deal. The Whiskey must have brought in a tough crowd the night of December 6: the reviewer mentions the "industry folk whose constant chatter" bothered the opening act. This is typical of LA's jaded entertainment-industry types who are "comped" into shows for free and behave as if respect for the artist is an impossible concept to grasp. Also during December, MTV, VH-I, and the Box added DMB's first video, "What Would You Say," to their rotations. The video was shot in Boulder, Colorado.

The band had performed two new songs during the fall leg of the tour. "Get in Line" premiered in Boston on October 8. From the first "oh yeah" sustained opening notes of the vocal, which jumps fifths and octaves, to the quick underpinnings of the bass and guitar, to the mellow "Please don't hurry . . . Please don't worry" break section, the song is musically exciting and melodic. "Get in Line" was not included on DMB's next CD. However, the other new song, "Let You Down" by Stefan Lessard and Dave Matthews, did eventually make the grade. It debuted in Dallas at the Trees on December 17. This acoustic ballad is about disappointing someone and then asking for their forgiveness.

The band's coup de grace in this amazingly successful year was being picked as one of *Rolling Stone*'s "New Faces of 1994." They were featured, along with fellow "new faces" Offspring, Sheryl Crow, Green Day, and Oasis, in the December 29, 1994 issue; the Dave Matthews Band was represented with one photo and four sentences of description. A blurb from the *Rolling Stone* piece reads: "WHY THE KIDS SEEM TO LIKE 'EM. A shy blend of rock and acoustic folk featuring guitar, violin and saxophone."

The band played their traditional Virginia New Year's Eve gig at the Marriott in Richmond. That night, the set list was comprised of "Two Step," "Best of What's Around," "Granny," "What Would You Say," "Get in Line," "Say Goodbye," "Satellite," "#36," "Ants Marching," "True Reflections," "The Song That Jane Likes," "Dancing Nancies," "Warehouse," "Jimi Thing," "Lie in Our Graves," "Recently," and "Tripping Billies." Except for "#36" and "Get in Line," all the songs were from the 1991–92 era. Referring to the band and audience countdown to 1995, Dave said, "Our timing may not be perfect, but who gives a fuck?" Boyd chimed in, "It's all relative." Dave passed

Jeff "Bagby" Thomas
JACK BAILEY/PORTICO PUBLICATIONS LTD.

out cigars to the audience before the countdown got under way, and then admitted, "I hate fuckin' cigars."

Attention was being lavished on DMB by music-industry honchos. Everyone wanted to emulate or share in the band's artistic and financial success. Coran Capshaw was the mastermind behind DMB's maverick business approach. Band publicist Ambrosia Healy acknowledges the inspiration for his plan: Capshaw "knew how the Grateful Dead's business was set up. The important thing is they have a manager who believes in doing it yourself. Why should you give merchandising up to someone else? It makes good business sense" (Wright).

Most managers do tend to conform; they operate according to the structures and terms dictated by major record companies. Not Capshaw. He utilized the Dead's model for building a fan base; the band's early decision to allow taping was also a nod to the legacy of the Dead. In-house merchandising was a third Dead-derived business element. "Bands bigger than us are contacting us about how we are

At the Grammys, February 26, 1997

handling merchandise," Capshaw announced in 1994. It was Capshaw's idea to insert a catalog of caps and T-shirts into the *Under the Table and Dreaming* CD (Burtner, "Money Side"). Bama Rags published a newsletter every other month throughout 1994 and 1995 that contained info about the band's schedule and promoted its merchandise.

Matthews is often asked directly about DMB's merchandising strategy. He defends it by saying that the band has paid its dues. "For the first three years, we weren't getting any reaction from the industry. We just thought we'd promote ourselves with the bootleg tapes people were making. But of course we weren't making money off them. So we started making the T-shirts and selling them on the road, and it supported us" ("Dave Matthews Band Is Thriving"). Dave has also reframed the explanation of how DMB's fan base was built. "A lot of people think the whole grass roots thing was some marketing decision, like we chose to have a live following first. We toured because that's what we knew how to do. And we worked hard at it. I'm glad things happened the way they did, and we didn't sign a record deal in 1991 or 1992, because I don't know if we'd be the same band we are now" (Riemenschneider).

Matthews contributed a piece to the June 1995 issue of *Musician*, entitled "Building an Audience from the Grassroots," in which he outlines DMB's methodology for interested music professionals. In addition to frat parties and clubs in the Southeast and Northeast, he explains, the band also played resorts: "We wound up playing to people from all over the country and they would in turn spread the word to their respective hometowns. Colorado was also a great market — it's like playing a national resort." Elaborating on DMB's open taping policy, which helped spread word of the band across the country, and the formation of the various DMB companies, Matthews says: "Our managers, Coran Capshaw and Ross Hoffman, helped us organize our growing touring business company. We started a small touring company and a small corporation to control our spending and savings." Most of the crew, Matthews adds, believe in what DMB are doing and have been with them from the start; crew and band have a "shared commitment." Dave goes on to credit the bands DMB has toured with. "With some help from Blues Traveler, Widespread Panic, The Samples, Big Head Todd and the Monsters, and Phish, audiences started growing in the North and West." Matthews concludes, "I think the control we have over our careers is a result of our grassroots footing. In an industry that doesn't know their teeth from a smile or music from money you need more than a 'deal.' " Capshaw sums it up this way: "This is an independent, self-running machine. If for some reason the record company falls off the earth tomorrow, this band will keep going without losing ground" (Burtner, "Money Side").

Detractors seem to come with achievement. The band's financial success has also made them the butt of jokes and complaints. Around this time, for about five minutes on the air, a Detroit radio deejay flogged this pretend product: "Dave Matthews Band Spaghetti Sauce."

Another key to the popular success of DMB's music is its ability to reach beyond a single demographic group. Although DMB was obviously wed to the college crowd from the start, at this particular point in the band's development, early 1995, they began to break through to a wider, national audience. Matthews links this capability to his South African roots: "I guess the one thing I learned from the music there was that it doesn't have to be aimed at a specific person, it doesn't have to appeal to a 13-year-old or a 25-year-old or someone who's 50. Why can't it be aimed at them all?" (Riemenschneider).

The band was becoming a music-industry prototype. Not only were they a popular and critical success, but also their innovative approach to taping, merchandising, and audience building was turning them into icons for the business side of the industry. Starting in 1995 (and continuing today), articles were written about grass-roots bands who wanted to be like DMB. It almost became a standard lead line: journalists would write, "This band is going to be the next Dave Matthews Band" as they introduced yet another unknown rock group with a feature article. Rusted Root was described by *Billboard* in 1995 as following in the footsteps of DMB (Borzillo, "MTV"). Agents of Good Roots (who have now signed with RCA and are managed by Coran Capshaw), the Pat McGee Band, Blessid Union of Souls, Eddie from Ohio, and Why Store were all identified as potential inheritors of the grass-roots success mantle currently worn by DMB. A *Richmond* [Virginia] *Times Dispatch* features writer compared several hometown bands to DMB (Ruggieri). Even RCA began to put out publicity material comparing some of its other bands to DMB in an attempt to help lesser-known acts ride DMB's coattails, despite the fact that their music wasn't of the same genre. *Billboard* ran an article based on a press release that began, "Country band Lonestar and rockers the Dave Matthews Band may not share musical styles, but the RCA acts have traveled similar grass-roots paths to success" (Borzillo, "Lonestar").

Finally (and it seemed to many "overnight"), DMB set a national standard, a benchmark, something to strive for; they were better than the best.

Time jumped on the bandwagon when it announced that C'ville was about to become the next Seattle due to the outstanding achievement of DMB. On January 30, 1995, the magazine reported: "Combining plaintive alterna-rock lyrics with a Graceland-period Paul Simon sound, the Dave Matthews Band has become the rage of college radio. 'Under the Table and Dreaming,' its major-label debut, has also made the quintet an MTV favorite and poised its genteel hometown of Charlottesville, Virginia, to become the next Seattle" (Bellafante). Matthews was described as a hobby painter and "a self-proclaimed mamma's boy." Since the band had made only one video, it seems hyperbolic to allude to them as MTV favorites: they were actually video neophytes. Could *Time*, too, have simply taken RCA press releases and incorporated them uncritically?

Now the band found themselves straddling two worlds: that inhabited by the national press and DMB's new, nationwide audience to whom that press spoke; and their Virginia community. C'ville was still DMB's home, but their touring schedule didn't allow them much time there. The band's songs were being played as bumper music on National Public Radio. Back in Virginia, their tunes were co-opted by a pep band and used to incite basketball fans to cheer. Mary Alice Blackwell, the Charlottesville *Daily Progress* music columnist, even heard a DMB tune blaring from trumpets in a gym at the Central Fidelity Women's Basketball Tournament ("DMB Tunes").

In late January, DMB played up in Phish country — Burlington, Vermont. They did a show at the Memorial Auditorium that featured five songs with Trey Anastasio, Phish's lead guitarist. Anastasio played on renditions of "Jimi Thing," "Recently," "Ants Marching," "Tripping Billies," and a jam.

Early in 1995, DMB and the Richmond Symphony collaborated on a major project. On the nights of February 14 and 15, these two musical enterprises held benefit concerts together at Richmond's Carpenter Center. Dave Matthews Band material was performed, and all proceeds went to Operation Smile — an international project that provides medical care to indigent children — and the William Byrd House in Richmond — a nonprofit social-service agency. John D'earth was enlisted to arrange the scores for the orchestra, even though he'd never done such a thing before. The project was the brainchild of Matthews and Ross Hoffman, and was about two years in the making. D'earth was approached about it in 1994. "I always felt there was so much musical potential in Dave's songs," he remarks. "I wondered if I was qualified to deal with the orchestra." D'earth had to learn how to arrange on the computer. In preparation, he listened to Dave and Tim tapes and DMB tapes, but he knew he couldn't do the job right unless he had direct access to Dave. So Matthews worked with D'earth a couple of times, and D'earth felt he really got some good ideas for him. "I arranged ten songs for the orchestra. I worked ten to twelve hours a day on this for a long time." He sequenced all of Dave's guitar parts. "Every one of the symphony charts was written from his guitar parts. Everything was generated from those."

Richmond symphony conductor George Manahan expressed initial concern that the music would be too simple. D'earth himself didn't know what to expect from his foray into orchestral arrangement. But it turned out well:

Manahan, D'earth, and Hoffman really got into it. "There was a good vibe," says D'earth, adding: "I wrote some difficult music. There was some great bell-tone stuff for French horns in 'Recently.' I wrote out a huge, long jam for the strings in 'Dancing Nancies.'" The set list for the Valentine's Day Richmond Symphony-DMB concert also included "Granny," "Warehouse," "Typical Situation," "Lover Lay Down," "Ants Marching," "Lie in Our Graves," "Pay for What You Get," "Help Myself," "Satellite," "Christmas Song," and "Say Goodbye." On February 15, the only variation was that "#36" replaced "Say Goodbye."

One fan in attendance that first night was John Athayde. He recollects: "No one knew what to expect. The first night, everyone in the audience stayed seated. The second night, I hear, everyone was dancing in the aisles. The scoring was incredible. Dave came out and sat on a stool. When they played 'Warehouse,' with an entire string section, it was a sonic blast. The whole horn section sounded so lush and beautiful. There was no jamming, because of course, you can't jam with an orchestra. The detail in every little part was so great. It was a beautiful experience."

D'earth confirms that the audience got a little bit wilder on the second night. "I was sitting in the front row. I was there to conduct Dave. He'd be jamming and there were 40 girls sweating and dancing all around." Otherwise happy with the project, D'earth wishes they could have had a bit more time to execute it. "I love this band and these guys. My only regret was we didn't have enough time to rehearse. I'd like to do another one."

Not surprisingly, the tapes of these concerts are hot items on the trading circuit. The project was also the genesis for a phrase that crops up regularly in media reports on the band: "the symphonic sounds of the Dave Matthews Band."

Throughout February, DMB continued to attract attention. Mid-month, MTV added the video of "What Would You Say" to Buzz Bin. Stefan and Dave appeared on MTV's *Alternative Nation*, cohosting with veejay Kennedy. The band also made their first appearance in cyberspace, answering questions about Dave's campaign against cheese, Boyd's classical training, Leroi's memories of basketball,

DMB on *Saturday Night Live*, April 15, 1995

and Carter's knowledge of car transmissions. On February 22, 1995, DMB dictated responses to the questions of MTV Online queriers, who lavished praise on all of the band members. When asked what he thought of crowd surfing, Dave replied: "I wouldn't." Stefan answered: "Right on, man. Whatever floats your boat." Matthews also commented on the current political situation in South Africa: "Nelson Mandela is great. He makes all the US presidents I've lived under look like they should be on swing sets with lollipops." The band also informed onliners that they were currently on tour with Big Head Todd and the Monsters, and would be on and off through May 1995.

On February 23 and 24, 1995, DMB played two sold-out shows at the Roseland Ballroom in New York City. They are generally considered to rank among the band's finest sets of back-to-back live performances. The opening-night set list was "Seek Up," "Satellite," "Dancing Nancies," "Lie in Our Graves," "Rhyme and Reason," "Say Goodbye," "Help Myself," "What Would You Say," "Recently"/ "Recently" reprise, "#36," "Ants Marching," "Angel from Montgomery," and the final encore, "Tripping Billies." John Popper of Blues Traveler guested on "Recently."

The Roseland shows started with the band tuning up — it sounded like a charivari — as Dave announced "Back in New York City!" His words echoed throughout the ballroom. Then the band broke into an inspired version of "Seek Up," during which Dave sang: "You seek up an emotion / Sometimes your well is dry, Hey!" It became a concert ritual for diehard DMB fans to shout "Hey!" along with Dave and the band during "Seek Up." Since the song was never officially recorded on a studio album that way, this was clearly another taper culture-loyal audience phenomenon. Lessard's bass work was especially outstanding on the two Roseland versions of "Seek Up."

Before the band launched into "Dancing Nancies," Dave shared some thoughts: "So uh, I know that uh, when s-s-someone quests — when someone comes up to you and says, 'Man, you're all fucked up,' then you uh, you get kinda pissed off. 'Cause you say, ohwuhuuh, 'Listen, man. I'm what I am. I'm uh — I'm what I am. I do my best thing.'

But I said sometimes I — I wonder if uh . . . if maybe when someone tells me I'm all fucked up, if maybe they got a point or something, you know." This is widely accepted as vintage Davespeak. "Dancing Nancies," as well, generated a DMB concert ritual around this time: the initiated now always point towards the ceiling during the "Dancing Nancies" lyric line "Look up at the sky." At Roseland, after "Dancing Nancies," Dave segued right into: "Here's a song called 'Lie in Our Graves.' It's about being dead, yeah."

On February 24, 1995, DMB made their network television debut on CBS, appearing on the *Late Show with David Letterman*. Of course, they performed their hit single "What Would You Say." Since Letterman's show is recorded in the afternoon, the band was also able to do a show that night.

The second night of the Roseland gig, DMB was joined by John Popper again, and Trey Anastasio of Phish. The crowd chanted "Trey, Trey, Trey" before he was plugged into the equipment — not surprising, since Anastasio is king of his own tape-culture realm. That night, DMB again kicked off with "Seek Up." Some highlights of the 14-song set list were "Say Goodbye" with John Popper, "Minarets," "Granny," "All along the Watchtower" with Trey Anastasio, "Two Step," and "Halloween." Part of the Roseland stint was filmed for CNN, which aired the footage in March as part of a major story on DMB and their incredibly devoted fan base.

Under the Table and Dreaming was continuing to work its way to the top of the rock charts. In March it went gold. The band made two more television appearances: *House of Blues* on TBS and *Spring Break Weekend* on MTV. At the end of March, DMB took off to Europe to play a few dates. They were gone about two weeks, and performed gigs in London, Paris, Madrid, Milan, Cologne, Hamburg, Stockholm, and Copenhagen. When they returned to the US, they did not take a break. They just kept touring.

The band debuted two new songs — "#40" and "#41" — on April 5, 1995, at the Academy in New York. The first of these (also known to tapers as "Always"), is a pretty, mellow love song; it was removed from the set lists very quickly, much to the chagrin of the fans. The lyrics make reference to angels, and contain these lines: "I wish that I could crawl inside your mind / And spend some time in there / Hug and hold ya / And mold ya into what I'd like." The song did not find its way onto the band's next release.

Matthews says that "#41," a poignant song with striking vocal octave jumps and sustained falsetto holds, was written around the time he had a parting of ways with longtime friend and business associate Ross Hoffman. "I was thinking about where I come from, and why I wrote songs and what was my inspiration. And how I was now in this situation where those things that I'd done, I so loved, had now suddenly become a source of incredible pain for me. Suddenly, there's all this money and people pulling, asking, 'Where's mine?' The wild dogs come out. The innocence of just wanting to make music was kinda overshadowed by the dark things that come along with money and success. So it's a song about looking back, but at the same time, a song that's still adamantly looking forward and going, 'But I'm still going to carry on, regardless' " (Colapinto). Hoffman's explanation of the events that led to their rupture would be presented in a lawsuit a few months later. The lyrics of "#41" certainly speak of a power struggle and a discovery of self: "I will go in this way / And find my own way out / I won't tell you to stay / But I'm coming to much more / Me." The pressure on the band continued to grow; it seemed as if every day DMB was becoming more famous.

On April 15, 1995, they appeared on NBC's *Saturday Night Live* for the first time. *Under the Table and Dreaming* was skyrocketing — by now it had sold over 700,000 units. *Remember Two Things* had sold 170,000 copies.

By May, DMB had a platinum album — just as Steve Lillywhite had promised they would. They had also completed their second video — for "Ants Marching." The clip was picked up immediately by MTV. In a year and a half, the Dave Matthews Band had made it. But not without strain. And fatigue: they had spent most of that time in the studio or on the road.

8
TAKE THESE CHANCES

The band toured so much that members performed even when they were ill. On May 10, 1995, they played a radio show from Yoshi's in Oakland, California. Matthews began the show by joking, "So now we're on the air, what the people out there can't see is that none of us have clothes on." He then apologized for having a sore throat, saying that "it is the cold and flu season, at least for me." Beauford actually had to sing lead on some songs because Matthews' throat was so far gone, but Dave cheerfully carried on, sipping tea with honey and letting the jokes fly — even irreverently allowing three seconds of silence to elapse, a radio taboo.

The Yoshi's show had a soft, unplugged tone. Beauford played other percussion instruments, not drums. At the end of a "lite" version of "Jimi Thing," the band moved gracefully into a lovely, haunting acoustic song by Matthews, "What Will Become of Me?" The tune had earlier been named "Spilling Out" by tapers. It was not thought of as a complete song, only as an intro or "outro," but the band began to play it separately. Often, Matthews did the tune as a solo; in it he wonders, "What will become of me when I'm all poured out?" The song asks — among other things — what is in store for all of us, at the end. Angels are mentioned in this song, too; by now they had become a fully developed, recurring Matthews metaphor — appearing in "#40," "What Will Become of Me?," and the much-earlier "Warehouse."

Dave looks for munchies in the backstage fridge

Matthews announced at Yoshi's that they would play "Ripping Chillies" as they went into "Tripping Billies." The band premiered a new song called "Don't Burn the Pig" during that broadcast — yet another tune that ironically juxtaposes a soft, beautiful melody with dark lyrics. Lessard's bass really set the tone here. Moore's flute and Tinsley's violin augmented the gentle mix. Later, at a 1996 show, Matthews explained the song's origins: "When I was a little boy, the big men used to take a little pig and see how much of it they could burn before it would die. All the pig could do was . . . [singing] 'scream.' All I can say is [singing] 'Don't burn the pig.'" The chorus is the song's title repeated over and over again. Neither "What Will Become of Me?" nor "Don't Burn the Pig" ended up on *Crash*.

The Dave Matthews Band opened for the Grateful Dead on May 19, 20, and 21, 1995, at the hot and dusty Silver Bowl, located in the desert near Las Vegas. Heralded as a milestone for the band, these shows constituted a massive event that drew 30,000 people per day. C-VILLE *Weekly* ran a special cover and a DMB retrospective to commemorate it. J. Tayloe Emery, a C'ville writer, chronicled DMB's performance during the Saturday, May 20 show: "Dave took off his guitar and began dancing next to Boyd. A smile came over the fiddle player. The sheer amazement of it all — I mean, here was the bartender from Miller's opening up for living legend Jerry Garcia. Leroi Moore hid in the cool shadows and blew his sax . . . Carter and Stefan were holding the song together as Dave and Boyd danced around the stage." Throughout DMB's performance, the crowd was doused with water by men with firehoses. Dave commented to Emery on the experience after it was over: "Amazing. The crowd was the most generous, and the biggest crowd we've ever played to. They really paid attention to us." He then admitted that this was the first Dead show he'd ever attended, and expressed pride that the Dead had requested DMB as their opening act.

This single, three-day stint seemed to cement the link between DMB and the Grateful Dead, at least in the minds of some of the rock press. Because DMB was a live-improv jam band that had modeled its business practices on those of the Dead, there was a legitimate association; however, the similarity did not extend to their music. The DMB-Dead link was further complicated by the fact that publicist Ambrosia Healy's father, Dan, had been the Dead's soundman for many years. Many fans thought that Dan Healy had probably, somehow, helped introduce DMB to the ears of Grateful Dead members. For whatever reason, for the next two years Matthews would be asked by interviewers about DMB and the legacy of the Dead over and over again.

Here are a few highlights from newspapers published within a year of the DMB-Dead gig. The *Tampa Tribune* said that most people think of DMB as "neo-Dead rockers" (Booth). The *Record* (Bergen, New Jersey) asserted: "The most frequent comparison, however, is made between the Dave Matthews Band and the Grateful Dead" ("Influences"). An interviewer for the *Detroit News* told Matthews that *Spin* and *Rolling Stone* were both comparing DMB and the Dead; Matthews replied: "Yeah, I don't understand that. They refer to us, and Blues Traveler, and Phish, as 'children of the Dead' " (Ransom). The *Orange County Register* asked Matthews how he felt about DMB being "pegged" by "numerous rock journalists" as the "leader of the 90's neo-Deadhead horde" (Roos, " 'Crash' Course"). The *Pittsburgh Gazette* commented to Matthews that a *Rolling Stone* reviewer thought "you were all about trying to keep alive the ideals of the Dead" (Mervis, "HORDE"). Later, the *Record* ran a story called "Wish We Were Dead," which posited the theory that hundreds of bands were currently vying to be the next Dead thing in the music biz. The article mentioned DMB, of course, but the writer felt that Phish had to be declared the winner of the contest (Beckerman).

Speaking on behalf of DMB, Matthews has consistently praised the Dead and marveled at the inability of the critics to grasp the musical difference between the two bands. For example, DMB is much more jazz-based than the Dead. Plus, DMB doesn't know the Dead's music very well. "My band as a whole has been to only three Dead shows," revealed Dave in 1997, "and each time was when we played on a bill with them. In fact, I don't think any of us went to see a Dead show before then.* I mean, I was in South Africa; Leroi and Carter were playing jazz; Boyd was in an orchestra somewhere, and Stefan was in elementary school. So because of the road that each of us traveled, we really didn't know that much about those guys. I guess you could say we were blissfully unaware of the whole deal with the Dead — that they were this powerful social event — until we played with them in Vegas a few months before Jerry Garcia died in August 1995. And honestly, that was the first time I experienced that cool, laid-back vibe. But since they didn't give us the baton, I don't know whether we're carrying anything of theirs on, really" (Roos, " 'Crash' Course").

Let there be no question about it: Matthews does like the Dead. "I certainly admire them," he now says, "and have a

---

* It turns out Tinsley had been to one Dead show after all (Allan, "Herky-Jerky").

lot of good friends who have been very into them. . . . You can't ignore their effect on people. With no judgment, I think that they contributed a huge amount of, uh, something . . . to something" (Mervis, "HORDE").

Matthews expanded on the forced link between the two groups and its implications: "Sometimes we're portrayed as some kind of torchbearing thing." Lowering his voice, he added: "Now, we're going to take the mantle and lead the children of the damned, or some such thing. I figure whatever fantasies someone else has, he's welcome to them" ("Influences").

The Dead-related tag, "hippie band," also became tiresome to Dave. He believed that this categorization developed out of DMB's free jam style. The band does improvise all the time in performance, he explained, "so we won't get bored and beat each other up on the bus. We keep the music fresh and improvise as much as we can. But I probably feel more connection to Weather Report and the Yellowjackets and [South African jazz pianist] Abdullah Ibrahim and all sorts of African music. Personally, I think too much is made of the hippie thing overall" (Snider).

Once again, DMB was feeling constrained by the press's attempts to label their music, but none of this pigeonholing had an effect on the band's ever-mounting popularity and musical growth.

*　*　*

From June 21 through July 11, 1995, DMB undertook another world tour, playing festivals in England, Germany, Italy, France, Switzerland, and Denmark. The rock-concert marketing philosophy is a little different in Europe than it is in the US. On the Continent, they don't have opening bands and headliners. They put together a bunch of big names to make festivals; these festivals can draw as many as 10,000 to 20,000 people. The Dave Matthews Band starred at Les Eurockeenes in Montbéliard, France; other acts included Jimmy Page and Robert Plant, Sheryl Crow, Beck, and the Cure. While overseas, Matthews explained: "That's the way festivals work over here. They're not so stiffly [booked] that you have to stick with some clique. . . .

It's funny, but at the same time it's kind of cool. There's a more open view of music" (Shapiro).

Mindy Peskin, who was at that point backpacking in Europe, met up with DMB in Aretzo, Italy (just outside of Florence), and again in Montbéliard. She remembers that about 50 bands played at Les Eurockeenes, and the festival lasted three days. "It was then for the first time that I saw lots of Europeans singing the American lyrics. I realized they weren't my band anymore." Peskin continued on to Switzerland with DMB. "There was some sort of music-industry conference and the sponsors had hired the band for a private party of industry elite. From what I could tell, most of the people were English-speaking (from the US or England), but that could be just the people that I met. Either way, it was a power-packed show and no one left unimpressed."

A touring band has little time for sightseeing. "When you're touring," reflects Matthews, "there's not really a chance to soak up the culture. We'll see a quick flash of Florence. We won't have a chance to see a show because we're doing a show. We won't have a chance to see the museums because we'll be doing a sound check" (Shapiro).

After DMB returned stateside, they played gigs throughout July in Tennessee, Georgia, and North Carolina. On

Monday, July 24, 1995, a special benefit event was held in Charlottesville at Live Arts; all proceeds went to radio station WTJU. That event yielded a compilation CD called *Dear Charlottesville*. The whole thing was put together by Bill Chapman, publisher of C-VILLE *Weekly*, along with musician Paul Wilkinson, and originated with Chapman's desire to do something to help C'ville's "dismal club scene." Shannon Worrell quickly agreed to contribute to the project, and shortly thereafter many other acts signed on. For $10, a ticket holder got admission to the show and a copy of the 14-track CD, which featured virtually all of C'ville's musicians and bands, including DMB — they contributed a recording of "Halloween." Lauren Hoffman, daughter of Ross Hoffman and former bass player for the band Monsoon — which also featured Worrell and Kristin Asbury — played on the CD.* Among the other contributing artists were Baaba Seth, TR3, the Matchbook Poets, and the Fledglings. *Time* had earlier that year implied there was a "C'ville sound." But this CD did not define such a sound; it was conceived to encourage local bands by exposing them to a larger audience and to raise money for a local radio station, which vowed to use the donation — projected to be about $4,000 — to buy new CDs and technical equipment. Plan Nine generously agreed to distribute *Dear Charlottesville* (Atkins, "Dear Dear Charlottesville").

The evening featured four half-hour sets performed by Pro Rock S, Shannon Worrell and Kristin Asbury, Dave by himself, and Operation: Love! Matthews was the *Billboard* superstar of the evening (he was the only Top 40 artist to appear). He told the crowd of 229 that he was honored to be invited, and then did "Typical Situation," "Rhyme and Reason," and four other tunes (Niesslein, "Dear Charlottesville"). It was amazing that he found the time to do it at all; he'd performed a gig the night before in Charlotte, and was scheduled to do another the night after the *Dear Charlottesville* event in Richmond.

---

* Lauren Hoffman, incidentally, would eventually be managed by Charles Newman, DMB's first manager.

Again, DMB played the H.O.R.D.E. at the end of the summer. Stefan acknowledges that it was Blues Traveler that brought DMB into the H.O.R.D.E.: "We knew Blues Traveler. We had opened for them a couple of times, and their sound man used to play a live tape of us during the change-overs on the first year of the H.O.R.D.E." (Catlin, "From Frat Houses"). Those live tapes, then, netted the band yet another benefit: they indirectly brought them a stint in the H.O.R.D.E. that lasted for years.

Touring steadily from July to the first week in October, DMB continued to get great reviews. In one such review of their second headlining gig, published in the August 7, 1995 issue of *Daily Variety*, Matthews was proclaimed to possess "star power." Displaying some of his trademark humility during the show, Dave had said, "I'm a country boy," and this had endeared him to the reviewer — as it has to millions. The *Variety* reviewer got down to specifics: "DMB actually [has] a formula that makes this band's music such an enjoyable listen and guarantees return visits from the enthusiastic throng that packed Universal. The bulk of the Matthews Band's material starts in riffs and bluesy motifs until the melody is resolved in the sweetest pop chords this side of Sting" (Gallo).

In a February 6, 1995 review bearing the headline "Matthews Band Is Poised for Takeoff," the *Boston Globe* called

LARRY SWANK/PORTICO PUBLICATIONS LTD.

DMB "a group that is fast proving to be *the* most original, promising outfit to break from the grassroots, neo-hippie pack." Furthermore: "Boyd Tinsley's Cajun-rustic violin, Leroi Moore's shy R & B sax, Stefan Lessard's funk-fluid bass and Carter Beauford's explosive drums were a weird combination that worked" (Robicheau).

On August 16, 1995, the *Rocky Mountain News* praised DMB's "insistent attachment to melody," and bestowed further kudos for their show at Red Rocks: "Matthews centered the ensemble with his South African-accented vocals and steady hand on guitar while Boyd Tinsley propelled songs to churning climaxes with furious fiddling, then Leroi Moore brought them back down to mellow ground with soulful solos on the saxophone." The reviewer also noted that a shooting star had burst over the gorgeous Red Rocks amphitheater right before "Best of What's Around," making the evening even more spectacular (Mehle, "Dave Matthews").*

An interview with Coran Capshaw was featured in *Amusement Business* in August 1995. He stated that the growing popularity of the band was evidenced in its concert grosses. For the February 23–24 Roseland gig, the band made $124,808. For their March 16–17 shows in Chicago, they pulled in $180,600. On July 23, they were paid $226,761 for a performance in Charlotte, North Carolina. By July 23, they'd surpassed that, earning a total of $233,982 for a Raleigh, North Carolina, gig. In the same *Amusement Business* piece, Bob Kelley, a concert promoter, opined: "They are definitely one of the most exciting new acts of the 90's. You wouldn't believe how the kids get off on them." By the end of July, DMB had sold out 20 of 34 shows. Capshaw generously credited Monterey Peninsula's booking expertise for the growth surge, and added: "We've been fortunate to have support from wide-based, multiformat radio and MTV, beyond the word-of-mouth." He also revealed: "The band has several other albums

---

* This show was selected for DMB's first live double CD, *Live at Red Rocks*, released on October 28, 1997.

worth of material that they perform now on the road and we hope that promoters will want to work with us for a long time to come." Of the kind of crowd the band was then attracting to its concerts, Capshaw had this to say: "Our fan base is a simple, mellow crowd, with no mosh pit. They just come to enjoy the music. We draw a wide age demographic; we don't exclude anyone." The sound production on the 1995 tour was credited to Ultra Sound of San Francisco. The lighting was done by TMS of Omaha. Capshaw continued: "We feel like we have a very production-appropriate show, with sound and lights used only to enhance the music. This is a good band and everything's going well. We certainly don't have any reason to whine" (Waddell, "Dave Matthews").

The band played two major benefit gigs in a six-week period: The Lifebeat Benefit Concert — The Beat Goes On 2 (which raised $500,000 for AIDS research), and Farm Aid. The Lifebeat Benefit aired on August 22 on VH1, while the Farm Aid show was held on October 1, 1995.

The Dave Matthews Band's infamous Internet support coalesced in the last part of 1995. Although there had been some activity on an early list called Minarets, John Athayde recalls that the first solidly established list, a digest called Nancies, began on October 31, 1995. At this point, Athayde started receiving e-mail from fellow DMB fans and began actively trading for the over 150 hours of fan-recorded concert tapes that he currently owns.

When asked about DMB's knowledge of their Internet fan base, Matthews once replied: "I don't spend a lot of time there. I'll go visiting with friends. Most of the conversation about us is there. I love it and I'm honored that people talk about us there because I think it's the last vestige of anarchy. I want to go visit and talk a bit, but I'm sort of self-focused sometimes. I tend to just sit around with my acoustic guitar" (Mervis, "HORDE").

The Nancies became a huge phenomenon on the Internet. It was created to be an alternative to newsgroup discussions (such as those on Usenet) and a replacement for the defunct DMB list, Minarets. Hundreds of people, mostly college students, would (and still do) write and receive up to twenty e-mail missives a day, discussing song interpretations, the history of the band, and the sartorial status of individual band members at DMB's last gig. It was considered bad form to ask questions or make comments about any band member's personal life — this was supposed to be a serious forum for the discussion of DMB's music and live performances.

Participants nationwide felt honor bound to post set lists immediately — as soon as a show was over. Any backstage encounters with band members were reported in detail, especially if they yielded any quotes about DMB's future projects. Reviews of concerts were also offered by Nancies list members. Speculation about which songs would end up on the next CD — and why — was a seminal Nancies topic. One person from Charlottesville told a story about babysitting for Dave's niece and nephew — and other personal encounters she'd had with Matthews through the years. Sometimes, people digressed and good-naturedly asked for Happy Birthday messages to be e-mailed to their loved ones. Other cybercorrespondents would periodically beg the initiated to explain how they had managed to get backstage. Serious tape trading was also a dominant function of the list. Plans were hatched to hand off tapes to Dave of songs he claimed to have forgotten. The band could hardly make a move without someone reporting on it to the entire 'Net group. And it was all done out of love for the band and their music. The band had made another savvy marketing move: Nancies operated on a server run by Red Light Management.

There are other bands with active Internet lists, as well. Phish, for example, reportedly has drawn in more of the Internet community than DMB. But few Internet fan groups would be as meticulous as Nancies members were in their quest to understand and participate in a band's music.

Internet participation is a uniquely 90s phenomenon in the music industry, and it is a truly amazing one. Posting can be done instantaneously; information can be flashed around the globe in seconds. Davespeak goes from Boston to Seattle — or vice versa — in an instant. Web sites can be hit daily. Any plugged-in band has a ready-made fan base at

its fingertips, and such contact can virtually make that band's career.

In 1995, DMB also ventured into writing for movie sound-tracks. Their work was selected for the film *White Man's Burden*; the song used was "Tripping Billies." Originally, the deal was brokered by Triune Music Group on behalf of Dave Matthews. It was later handled by Red Light Management (Fox, "Legal Thang"). The movie was slated for a December 8 release.

But what and who was Triune Music Group? Triune was formed in 1994 to handle the publication of Matthews' music; it consisted of Ross Hoffman, biz whiz Stirling McIlwaine, and attorney Chris Sabec. But Hoffman was removed from Red Light Management and Colden Grey over the course of the summer of 1995. On September 12, 1995, Hoffman and Triune Music Group — an offshoot of Colden Grey — instigated a lawsuit against Coran Capshaw. A 24-page legal document was filed in Richmond Circuit Court. Hoffman accused Capshaw of "trying to squeeze Hoffman's company out of a management and publishing deal" (Zack). The details were confusing; some local journalists initially stated that Hoffman's suit concerned the entire band. In fact, Hoffman's deal had never been to represent DMB: it had always been linked directly to

Matthews, and, subsequently, Capshaw. Headlines in the local papers read, "Lawsuit, Like Stardom, Hits Dave Matthews and Coran Capshaw" (*Observer*) and "Dave on the Stand?" (*C-VILLE Weekly*).

Hoffman and Triune Music Group sought (as stated on page 23 of the document) "compensatory damages on account of Capshaw's conspiracy to injure Triune in its reputation, trade, business or profession in an amount not less than $2,100,112.80." Additionally, compensation for defamation of reputations — business, personal, and professional — was requested in the amount of $2,000,000. Punitive damages of $2,100,000 ("or the maximum amount allowed by law, whichever is greater") were sought. Finally, payment of attorneys' fees and all court costs were requested.

Capshaw was charged by Hoffman and Triune with defamation, breach of contract, conspiracy to injure Triune, and unlawful interference in a business agreement. Hoffman's suit stated (on page 2) that "Between 1990 and 1995, Hoffman personally supervised Dave Matthews' musical career and administered all facets of the publishing of Matthews' music. Hoffman has also been a mentor to Dave Matthews from the very beginning." The suit further alleged (on page 22) that since Hoffman's (and Triune's) removal, Matthews' co-writers were not being paid their share of royalties. Hoffman charged (on page 21) that his ousting had been "motivated by Capshaw's hatred, revenge, personal spite, and ill-will toward Triune and Hoffman, and his desire to make money off the musical career of Dave Matthews and the Dave Matthews Band." The document, of course, became public record as soon as it was filed in Richmond Circuit Court.

Philip Goodpasture, Capshaw's lawyer, maintained that the suit was "meritless." Capshaw, he insisted, was only protecting Matthews' interests, per usual. Triune and Colden Grey had tried to link up. Goodpasture commented, "It was not an advantageous transaction for Dave" (Zack).

This struggle for control over certain aspects of Matthews' musical career, this clash between Matthews' two most trusted advisors, was an acrimonious one: it resulted in the severing of friendships and business partnerships. Ultimately, it was the issue of who should collect Matthews' songwriting royalties — due from Bama Rags (whose shareholders at the time were Beauford, Lessard, Matthews, Moore, and Tinsley) and other music entities — that became the specific point of contention that ended the quasi-partnership of Hoffman and Capshaw.

The events that precipitated Hoffman's removal from Colden Grey and Red Light Management in June and July of 1995 (and the ensuing legal responses) were highly complicated. They took place over a number of years and in several locales. The Hoffman (and Triune) lawsuit alleged (on page 2) that from 1990 through mid-1992, after helping with Matthews' original demos and the shaping of the band, Hoffman had been responsible for administering "all facets of the publishing of Matthews' music." Starting in May 1992, Matthews had agreed to give Hoffman 7.5 percent of his royalties. The suit also claimed that Capshaw had officially become Dave's manager in February 1993, after a contract was negotiated by Sabec, overseen by Hoffman. The negotiations began in late January. In the final artist-manager agreement between Matthews and Capshaw, it was stated (on page 3) that Capshaw would be granted 20 percent of Dave's income, up to $40,000 a month; he was to receive 15 percent after that $40,000 figure was reached. Capshaw was also given Dave's power of attorney. Twenty-five percent of his gross profits Capshaw agreed to hand over to Hoffman, because "Matthews considered Hoffman's services to be essential to the Management Contract." Hoffman was specified as Matthews' "key man," his personal advisor. ("Key man" is a common term in the music industry.) In the latter part of 1993, Hoffman handled DMB's negotiations with RCA, in conjunction with Attorney Sabec, as part of his obligation to Matthews (Fox, "Legal Thang").

Furthermore, on November 17, 1993, Hoffman and Matthews had formed Colden Grey, a company whose precise mandate was to publish Dave's 29 original songs. A few months later, Hoffman, Sabec, and McIlwaine formed Triune. Their purpose was:

1. To collect royalties for Matthews' songs worldwide.
    These included mechanical royalties, ASCAP royal-
    ties, print royalties, and synchronizations.
2. To continue to handle copyrights for Matthews' grow-
    ing list of original compositions.
3. To find any other outlets for Matthews' music that
    they could — film soundtracks, for example — with
    the exception of commercials.

   Triune alleged (on page 5) that it had performed these
services free of charge between May 2, 1994 (the day the
company was established), and January 10, 1995, "in order
to demonstrate to Dave Matthews that it was fully capable
of being his sole and exclusive administrator of music publishing worldwide."
   Triune actually served as a larger replacement for Colden
Grey; it was doing just what Colden Grey had done, except
now that Matthews was so successful and so famous it
took three people to do it. The only vestige of the original
publishing entity was its name: "Colden Grey Ltd." still
appeared on copyrights. That's why all the pre-1995 copyrights listed on DMB CDs bear that name — they had been
filed by Hoffman, via Colden Grey, on behalf of Dave Matthews. Afterward, copyrights were given simply as "Dave
Matthews." On *Under the Table and Dreaming*, all are
listed as Colden Grey Ltd.; on *Crash*, there's a mixture of
both.
   So every time a copy of *Under the Table and Dreaming*
was sold, Triune got 50 cents. Every time a hit from that CD
was played on the air, Triune collected monies on behalf of
Matthews (Fox, "Legal Thang"). Because Triune had no
legal connection to Colden Grey, the triumvirate of Hoffman,
Sabec, and McIlwaine was unable to collect Matthews'
monies from any foreign markets. In other words, an official bond — which could stand up in a court of law — had
to be established between the two companies in the form of
a contract. Chris Sabec flew to Eugene, Oregon, in December 1994 to secure Matthews' approval of this proposed
legal link between Triune and Colden Grey. According to
Sabec, Matthews granted his approval during a two-day car

ride down to Santa Cruz. Matthews, Sabec claimed (on page 7 of the suit), said the deal was "jammin'." Also, Sabec alleged, Matthews had said that Hoffman had always been, and always would be, in charge of and a participant in Matthews' publishing endeavors.

At a dinner at McIlwaine's house in late January 1995, Matthews signed a three-page document giving the go-ahead for the Colden Grey-Triune link-up agreement. Present at the dinner were Hoffman, Sabec, McIlwaine, and Matthews, as well as a few significant others. That night, Matthews also signed a conflict-of-interest waiver: since Sabec was then still Matthews' personal attorney, if he were to continue to represent Matthews *and* act as a partner in this new enterprise, a conflict-of-interest situation could arise. The form Matthews signed was prepared by Sabec's law firm (Fox, "Legal Thang"). According to item 34, "McIlwaine and Sabec told Dave Matthews that he could take the agreements away with him and think about them and bring them back at a later date." Matthews opted not to do so, according to the plaintiffs. Everyone present signed off on the agreements. It was suggested that the documents be shown to Capshaw. Matthews supposedly replied that Capshaw, as manager, had nothing to do with publishing matters (page 10).

Evidently, no one informed Capshaw directly about the Colden Grey-Triune liaison until the early part of 1995 (although there is some dispute over when, exactly, he did learn of it). Throughout the spring, changes occurred swiftly. By June, Matthews had signed an agreement instructing Colden Grey to bring all materials to Capshaw. Triune/Colden Grey was ordered to transfer all operations to Capshaw — effective immediately. Sabec was released as Matthews' attorney.

By July, a takeover based on legal maneuvering had occurred. New attorneys, under the aegis of Capshaw, took control of Colden Grey. But Hoffman (and with him Sabec and McIlwaine) was forced out for good during June and July. As the summer faded, a few months after the Colden Grey takeover, Hoffman and company filed the suit. Dave, it seemed, was not directly involved in the fight at this point. Hoffman had filed suit against Capshaw alone.

Meanwhile, right after this litigious brouhaha erupted, Matthews and Reynolds, and then DMB, went back on the road. "Ants Marching" and "What Would You Say" had both been on the *Billboard* charts all summer. On September 24, 1995, at Swarthmore College in Pennsylvania, "Crash into Me" was first played by Dave and Tim: 18 months before it became a smash hit, this beautiful song of seduction debuted acoustically. Considered by many to be the band's sexiest song, with lyrics like "Hike up your skirt a little more / And show your world to me / In a boy's dream," the tune evokes a powerful mood of slowly building sensuality. It was written by Matthews.

Musically, it continued to be a strong year for the band. Financially, it was their most successful to date. On October 4, 1995, in Woodstock, New York, two more new DMB songs made their way to public ears: "Deed Is Done" and "Too Much." Tim Reynolds sat in. "Too Much" was written by the entire band and would also become a huge hit, and quickly — by May 1996. The song has a funky, upbeat sound and interesting lyrics that point out our greed and wastefulness as a society. We're always taking "too much" of everything — more than we need. Matthews describes the song's theme: "It's where excess has taken over, where your appetite has taken control of the narrator. As opposed to enjoying life, it's devouring life, which seems to be a common theme in the world — certainly in America, where we do just that — eat too much, drink too much, consume too much, and preach too much" (Morse, "Tragedy"). The CD *Crash* would include this song, but not "Deed Is Done."

Back in Richmond Circuit Court where the gavels pound, by October 6, 1995, Capshaw had asked that Colden Grey, and thereby Matthews, be named as a codefendant in the case. In other words, Hoffman and company would be suing both Capshaw and Matthews, if the judge allowed it, even though the suit had not been filed that way. An answer was delivered by November 16: the change was allowed. The suit was centered on a document that Matthews had signed; this was the crux of the case, according to Judge

Randall Johnson, and Matthews was an appropriate co-defendant (Fox, "Dave On the Stand?").

At the same time, there were far more pleasant things going on. Stefan married his longtime girlfriend, Josie. Boyd and his wife, Emily, welcomed their daughter, Abigail, into the world. And DMB went into the studio to record *Crash* in October and November (Bledsoe).

Again, their producer was Steve Lillywhite, and the recording was done at two different sites: the converted barn that holds Bearsville Studios in Woodstock, and Green Street Recording Studios in New York City. Tim Reynolds made another guest appearance on electric and acoustic guitars. Boyd arrived at Bearsville a few days late, due to the birth of his daughter.

Crash was recorded with a completely different mindset than *Under the Table and Dreaming*. According to Matthews, "The first album was a little safer in that we had a list of songs and we just recorded them boom-boom-boom. This one there was much more stopping — let's try fast, let's try slow, let's change the arrangements and words and instrumentation. We weren't afraid of electric guitars, we didn't confine ourselves to acoustic. And we recorded with all of us standing in a circle" (G. Brown, "Happy Hippie").

Matthews also talks about how Lillywhite encouraged them to experiment. "It was a mood in us, and Steve Lillywhite emphasized — to our joy — that we should just forget about the first album and try a different approach. So we recorded it with more of a live feel, in a more relaxed environment" ("Dave Matthews Band Is Thriving"). It was Lillywhite's idea to put "Tripping Billies" on the US release, although it was originally slated for the European version only. Matthews quipped to American onliners: "It's an extra." "Tripping Billies" joined "Ants Marching" on the list of DMB songs that have been released twice — first as a live cut, and second as a studio version.

Moore's use of the baritone sax on "So Much to Say" developed in a funny, spontaneous way. Recounts Matthews: "'Roi borrowed it from a friend and was playing it in the studio on a couple of the tunes we were startin' to record, and producer Steve Lillywhite . . . lost it. He fell in

love with the bari and started insisting the bari be featured everywhere on the album, and we started calling him Steve Bari-white" (Roland).

The *Crash* experience, as Beauford explains, promoted group songwriting: "In fact, a lot of the songs on 'Crash' were written by everybody. We all went into the studio, started jamming, and came up with the ideas. . . . Everything was like 'boom' when we got in the studio, just idea after idea. We created the stuff right on the spot. . . . And this is the reason we feel 'Crash' is the best work we've done so far — it's the *shit*. We are so psyched about it because we were able to go in and create something from the ground up and see it develop. And at the end of the day to have songs that really work is just so satisfying" (William F. Miller, "Carter Beauford").

"Drive In, Drive Out" highlighted Beauford's talents, as Matthews had intended the song to do when he conceived it in 1992. Dave remarks: "[Beauford] knows that kind of time signature. It's second nature to him, whereas it might be a more elusive thing to a lot of drummers. The one thing I think is true is that we rise to the occasion because Carter can establish the foundations and Stefan can establish these chord foundations that are so solid that you could stick the Empire State Building on top of them" (Kelley).

Tinsley had seen Matthews flying over the frets while playing a riff during a sound check earlier in the summer. Boyd says that by the time he made it to Bearsville, a few days after the rest of the band had begun work on *Crash*, "that little riff that Dave played at sound check had become a complete song" (Bledsoe).

The band didn't use a click track as much on *Crash* as they had on their previous effort — which means they recorded most of it live. And they obviously benefited from Lillywhite's love of first takes. In Matthews' words: "There was a lot more spontaneity on this album than on the one before. A lot of the solos were on the first take. It was created in a circle, everyone facing each other. Leroi would have an idea and say 'Hey, try that' and we'd stop the take and give it a try. Stefan could do the same thing, as could anyone. And because we weren't recording everything separately, it made the production a lot faster. It gave us a lot more time to goof off and drink coffee" (Mehle, " 'Crash' Test").

Recreation became a serious pursuit for the band when they were in Bearsville, and it seems to have found its way into their music as a recurring theme. Lillywhite kept challenging everyone to games of ping-pong during downtime, and these matches took on marathon proportions. Fans have often commented that they can hear table-tennis being played in the background of "Lie in Our Graves" (Randall). In 1997, Lillywhite told the DMB newsgroup that during the song's ping-pong track it's possible to distinguish Boyd saying: "Oh no. A microphone!" Still, a lot of work got done. Sixteen songs were recorded for *Crash*, although only twelve made the final cut.

Lessard credits Lillywhite with coming up with the CD's title. "I think the idea to call it 'Crash' was more something going through our producer's mind," says Stefan, "and we decided to go along with him." Stefan goes on to talk about the methods they used to record the CD: "We were put in a room sitting in a circle facing each other and recorded the basic tracks all together. Even the overdubs felt live. It's nice to experiment with different recording techniques, but I think this way was the best way to capture us" (McLennan).

One of Lillywhite's funniest memories was of himself and Dave recording the vocal tracks to "Say Goodbye" late one night. The pair was alone, and Matthews comically directed the opening lyrics to Lillywhite: "So here we are tonight / you and me together."

The song "Crash into Me" evolved musically through the recording sessions at Bearsville. Just by shifting a few guitar notes, Dave improved the song. He explains: "The notes I'm playing are what everybody follows — the kick drum, the bass guitar, even the baritone sax. Originally 'Crash into Me' was straight one-two-three-four, but I found that when I went to a different note on the end of beat three it changed the whole song and really made it move. It goes from C# on one and A on the and of three; on the next line, B is one one and E is on the and of three. The bridge just sits on a D# for a while, right after the line 'in a boy's dream,' and then I make beat one the A. Just that one little turnaround makes the whole song sound so much deeper" (Mettler).

Tim Reynolds, who doubled Dave's guitar lines on *Under the Table and Dreaming*, was given free rein to play anything he wanted on *Crash*. Matthews recalls: "We told him 'Tim, you just do what you like.' He's very good at filling gaps without being too filling" (Mettler).

For "#41," it was Beauford's idea to overdub the sequencing of percussion: congas, wood blocks, then timbales. Although the others were doubtful about the effectiveness of the wood blocks, when they heard the final mix, even Lillywhite was impressed. He asked: "That's hip-hop, isn't it?" Beauford defined it: "Yeah. It's hip-hop reggae rock 'n' roll." "Kind of sums up the Dave Matthews Band in one song," Lillywhite replied (Randall).

In November, attorneys for Matthews and Capshaw released a statement from Dave on the Hoffman-Triune matter: "Mr. Matthews acknowledges the valuable assistance that Ross Hoffman gave to his career. In return for this assistance, Mr. Hoffman has been paid handsomely and continues to receive ongoing compensation. Mr. Matthews regrets that Mr. Hoffman has chosen to bring this suit, as it is damaging to their friendship" (Fox, "Dave on the Stand?"). Dave's attorney, Murray Wright, described the effect this case was having on Matthews. "Dave is a really sweet guy but he has all these friends who want to get a piece of him, and when they do get a piece of him, they just want a bigger piece" (Fox, "Dave Matthews"). A trial date was set for February 1996. The circumstances were dramatic. It was an incredibly distressing time for all parties involved.

The band went on tour as they were putting the finishing touches on *Crash* in New York City. They played shows on the East Coast during December. A big Christmas party was held at the Red Light Management offices in C'ville, and DMB attended. Matthews was blown away: "I don't think we predicted the media success, the industry success, that we've had. . . . I'm amazed in a way, but I feel like it's happened almost without me. We've had 30 people or 100 people working. What's good is that as it grew, it wasn't too overfed; it wasn't too big for itself. I guess that's the luck of not being signed right away. We had a Christmas party and there were all these people there! It leaves me kind of winded, 'cause I never thought — I didn't see myself as being at the center of something that supports so many people" (Wright).

The band did their traditional New Year's Eve gig at Hampton Coliseum, in Hampton, Virginia. It was a two-night affair — December 30 and 31. The second night's show was broadcast live by about 150 radio stations nationwide. Now, all of America could ring in the New Year with DMB.

At the end of 1995, Cristan Keighley had an encounter with Leroi Moore that meant a lot to him. It happened after the December 30 show. Keighley was looking for Capshaw's room in a nearby hotel; a party had been scheduled there. Security guards posted by an elevator stopped him, doubting that Kcighley had clearance to visit Capshaw. As luck would have it, just then Moore stepped out of a nearby elevator. "Leroi put his arms around me and said, 'My man!' He made it obvious I was invited to the party. There were two fans following Leroi, two kids. Moore turned to them and said, 'Hey, get a shot of this. This is from the old days!' and we posed for a picture together."

9
STEP INTO THE LIGHT

Excellent news ushered in 1996. On January 4, it was announced that the Dave Matthews Band had been nominated for two Grammy Awards: "What Would You Say" was up for Best Rock Performance by a Duo or Group with Vocal; the video for the same song was nominated for Best Music Video, Short Form. The band's first studio CD had made a big splash with National Academy of Recording Arts and Sciences voters.

Also, RCA Records announced that over the holidays DMB sales had skyrocketed. One business publication proclaimed: "In the 3 weeks prior to Christmas, they increased their sales by 192 percent, the second highest increase among the Top 50 acts on the Top 200 album chart in *Billboard*. 'Under the Table and Dreaming' is approaching three million in sales" ("Dave Matthews Band Begins"). "Satellite," released in the second week of December, was another big hit on the singles charts for DMB, further enhancing sales; the accompanying video proved to be a success as well.

The band was also named as one of the best acts of 1995 by newspapers across America. For example, the *Omaha World-Herald* named DMB one of the Top Five Acts of 1995, placing them above Blues Traveler, the Rolling Stones, Hootie and the Blowfish, Phish, Green Day, and Foo Fighters (Minge, "1995"). Music-industry trade stats were equally pleasing. While the top 10 rock promoters estimated that US concert impresarios had taken in a mere

$701,983,687 in 1995 — down 10.4 percent from the year before — DMB was singled out as a concert-circuit star, along with the Cranberries. Dave Williams, president of Cellar Door, a concert-promotion firm, stated: "Those were the two most pleasant surprises of our season" (Waddell, "'95's Top 10").

In Richmond, the Triune-Colden Grey $4.1-million lawsuit was settled out of court in January of 1996. Both sides refused to release the exact terms of the settlement.

The precise nature of the business arrangement between Capshaw and Hoffman had remained a point of contention but legal action taken over the holidays had expedited a resolution. Capshaw had requested in November 1995 that the Triune-Matthews contracts be legally voided on the grounds that they created a perilous conflict of interest. Triune quickly fired back a countersuit, charging Capshaw with breach of contract. When the initial lawsuit was settled in January 1996, the conjoining countersuit became moot. Philip Goodpasture declared: "It's over and it's history" (Fox, "Matthews in the Middle").

But was it? "By persuading Matthews to write songs," explained one reporter, "and by helping line up members for the Band in 1991, Hoffman is widely considered to be the Band's creator. He is still receiving the 7.5% cut of publishing royalties that Matthews deeded to him in 1992" (Fox, "Matthews in the Middle"). Triune's assertion that it had operated without compensation between 1994 and 1995 was still being questioned by the Capshaw camp.

Whatever further legal investigations followed, they were not made public. Chris Sabec moved to Los Angeles post-settlement, posthaste. He continued to work for Triune in LA.

Dave and Tim went on tour during the month of February. It was during this tour that fans received upsetting news via Davespeak. During the duo's February 19, 1996, show at the University of New Hampshire, Matthews shook his hand out between playing "Warehouse" and "#41," apparently in pain. He spoke to the crowd: "So, uh, so on this tour, I've got this condition. I'm really excited about it. It's called carpal tunnel syndrome. So, I got it over here in this hand, so I'm really psyched. It makes your fingers feel like they don't belong to you, like they belong to somebody else. Or if you wake up and your arm is asleep, it's kind of like that — that feeling."

Carpal tunnel syndrome is a common, painful condition of the wrist and hand caused by a pinched nerve in the carpal tunnel. The carpal tunnel is the bony channel in the wrist that holds the tendons, blood vessels, and nerves. Repetitive motions of the hand can lead to the pinched nerve, as can arthritis and injury. It's related to RSI, or repetitive strain injury. The symptoms of the syndrome include pain, muscle weakness, and tingling. Anti-inflammatory drugs can be used to treat mild cases, but surgery is required when symptoms are severe. Often, rest will ease the condition ("Carpal Tunnel Syndrome"; "RSI"). This is probably what was affecting Matthews' hand on September 27, 1994, during the Dave Matthews Band Day festivities in C'ville.

Although the fans worried about Dave's carpal tunnel syndrome, Matthews did not let it undermine the University of New Hampshire show. He remained a playful showman throughout; the duo played for hours. Later in the show, Dave again addressed the audience, saying, "First, let me tell you one thing, though. Let me tell ya, rock 'n' roll is fuckin' nuts, rock 'n' roll is nuts. People out there — nuts. Rock 'n' roll, it's — it's nuts." He then informed them that they all had "boogers and crap" to unify them as humans; he said he'd been mentioning that everywhere they'd played. He also threw in a little Captain and Tennille — an a cappella line from "Love Will Keep Us Together."

Internet band rankings were tallied in *Business Wire* during the last week of February. In an article announcing "the ten musical bands that are uppermost in the minds and ears of today's Internet community," rock bands past and present were cited. The top 10, beginning with number 1, were: the Beatles, Pearl Jam, Phish, the Grateful Dead, U2, Pink Floyd, the Rolling Stones, Beastie Boys, DMB, and Led Zeppelin. A spokesman validated the survey: "Cyberspace is fast becoming the most accurate and timely avenue for gauging public interest" ("Beatles"). The acts on this list weren't bad company for DMB, a band that had released its first major studio CD just 15 months before the survey was completed.

The Grammys were held on February 28, 1996, in Los Angeles. Although DMB didn't win, their next CD would put them right back in the running.

In early spring, Matthews returned to South Africa; he played a solo show there on April 8, 1996. Most UVA students didn't know that, however; in C'ville, at UVA, someone pulled off a very successful DMB-related April Fool's Day joke. Posters went up all over the campus promising a free DMB performance, which was to be held in the university amphitheater at 9 P.M. There was even an opening act listed: local band Otis Wants Bread. A hotline number was provided for those who wanted further details, but anyone who phoned got a recorded message saying that the event had been moved indoors due to rain. Publicist Ambrosia Healy commented: "It was a very, very good joke. We

Dave Matthews prank fools hopeful students

By TONY BEELER
Cavalier Daily Staff Writer

The buzz around Grounds yesterday was that local-turned-national phenomenon Dave Matthews would be appearing at the University. Pre-printed concert posters fueled the rumors, and, by evening, students around Grounds had heard about the show.

The catch? Matthews is in South Africa.

Unfortunately, the concert, at which the Dave Matthews Band was to be joined by local group Otis Wants Bread, was an April Fool's Day joke played by still-unknown pranksters.

Posters publicizing the free show stated it was to be held in the amphitheater at 9 p.m. They also listed a telephone number people could call for more information and updates.

Students calling the number heard a message saying it had been moved to the Student Activities Building on Alderman Road because of rain.

Many students initially believed there was going to be a concert but eventually uncovered the joke. Others did not believe the rumors.

DMB publicist Ambrosia Healy was highly impressed with the prank.

"It was a very, very good joke," Healy said. "We thought it was done by Otis Wants Bread and figured that they were marketing geniuses."

Third-year College student and Otis Wants Bread manager Joe Monaghan said the band had no prior knowledge of the joke.

"We would love to find out who did it," Monaghan said. "We appreciate the free advertising."

Neither band had a local appearance scheduled yesterday, according to the DMB concert hotline and Monaghan.

The DMB regularly appeared Tuesday nights at Trax from Sept. 1991 to late 1993. The band played at the amphitheater in September 1994, following the release of their last album, "Under the Table and Dreaming."

A sign sits in Tuttle dorm
DMB did not appear last night

April Fool's Day prank excites hopeful students
Article in *Cavalier Daily*, April 2, 1996

thought it was done by Otis Wants Bread and figured that they were marketing geniuses." The manager for Otis Wants Bread denied any knowledge of the prank, but said the band truly appreciated the free advertising. When the hoax was revealed, there were a lot of disappointed students at UVA (Beeler).

On April 20, DMB did *Saturday Night Live* again, promoting *Crash*. Around that time, Matthews had a discussion with actor-comedian Jim Carrey about the changes fame brings: "I met him the other night, and he said the strangest part is that you sort of stop being a witness to the people around you . . . you lose the watcher, because you become watched, so that's about the most difficult thing. In that sense, it's an unusual place to be where you're not as much of a stranger as you were" (Gatewood). The entire band must have been busy contemplating the perils and predicaments that fame brings: DMB was about to embark on an international publicity blitz.

Most rock stars would probably spend the days before the release of a new CD celebrating and promoting the product. Where was Matthews on Monday, April 29? At a C'ville elementary school teaching third graders. Teacher Thom Lewis had been trying to get Matthews to visit his school and talk about poetry and music since the beginning of the year. Why was Lewis so certain that Matthews would eventually do it? Matthews' niece was a member of his class.

In the course of his hour-long visit, Dave sang songs and answered questions — the kids were allowed to ask him whatever they wanted. Responding to one child's questions, he described a typical day on the road: "Well, I wake up around 1 o'clock in the afternoon." The kids emitted various sounds of admiration, and one piped up: "Just like my dad!" Matthews said he has breakfast, does a sound check, and "Then I phone people for about one hour, and then we play on stage for about three hours, and then after that we meet people. . . ." Another child interjected, "And sign autographs?" Matthews confirmed, "And sign autographs. Then we get on the bus and have pizza, and maybe a couple of beers, and then we sleep on the bus and wake up in the next town" (Sanminiatelli).

His biggest claim to fame, Dave confided to the kids, was being their classmate's uncle; his niece was thrilled by her uncle Dave's comment. Reluctant to discuss his poetry, Matthews, with characteristic modesty, said: "You all write better poetry than I do." He sang three songs to the class: "Ants Marching," "Satellite," and "I'll Back You Up." He told them he wrote "I'll Back You Up" when he was in love, and concluded: "But she lives in Africa. She left me for Africa." He also gave the kids examples of how they could take events from their lives and use them in poetry or songs — just like he does. "I think of things that happened to me in the past week. . . . I just use the things I know." Matthews offered the children a bit of parting advice: "Find something you really love to do, whether it's a fireman, or a scientist, a photographer, a writer" (Sanminiatelli).

That night, April 29, Matthews played an acoustic show at Trax — which, after yet another change in ownership, had reverted to its old name — with Boyd, Stefan, and Tim Reynolds. *Crash* was released on April 30, 1996, and that night DMB played a larger gig at the Classic Amphitheater in Richmond.

Within a week, the ink on the major press reviews was dry, and the reviews of *Crash* ran the gamut. The *Los Angeles Times* managed to identify the band as a "trio," and said "that young Matthews will continue carrying the torch lit by Jerry Garcia"; the *Times* reviewer accorded *Crash* two and a half stars (Scribner). *Entertainment Weekly* said that to rock fans burned out by "Nirvana knockoffs," "the Virginia-based quintet's ear-catching jazz-folk fusion must seem like an entirely new genre . . . it sure sounds fresh." The magazine then asserted: "These boys can play. . . . B+" (Sinclair, " 'Crash' Landing"). *People* gave it a thumbs up in their Picks and Pans section: "As alternative music threatens to become just another bland pop category, the Dave Matthews Band successfully redefines it on its own eclectic terms" (Abrahams). The *New York Daily News* strongly disliked *Crash*. Their review's sub-headline read: "Oddball Group's New Album Is the Scene of Mass Musical Destruction." It accused Matthews of creating "one of the goofiest sounds in America," and called the CD "a virtual hydra's head of sonic horrors" (Farber). However, the *New York Times* loved it, citing musical details such as "rhythmic pizzicati" and Dave's guitar lines ("full of wide leaps and unexpected syncopations"). That review concluded positively: "When the Dave Matthews Band seizes a moment, it's well prepared" (Pareles).

Other assessments fell somewhere in the middle: the *San Diego Union-Tribune* reviewer didn't enjoy the nine-minute version of "Proudest Monkey," but admitted: "Still, there's enough variety and surprise in these 12 songs to propel the patient through 'Crash's' more meandering

moments." He went on to credit Lillywhite "for his deftness in averting instrumental gridlock" (Herbert).

The video of "Too Much" was released. Its imagery highlighted the song's theme, focusing on excess and overeating. Color footage was interspersed with sepia passages. The *Los Angeles Times* pronounced it "too much": "The lines are set to scenes of gluttony that make the Carl's Jr. 'in your face' commercials seem appetizing. Men in wacky, prank-store glasses and bowler hats jerk awkwardly around the set, making this clip unintentionally reminiscent of a cheesy Information Society video" (Ali).

However, varying critical opinions aside, the sales of *Crash* were great. "Too Much" entered the charts in April as a single. By the time the band played *Saturday Night Live*, the song had reached number 10 on *Billboard*'s Modern Rock Tracks. The CD debuted at number 2, according to the *Hollywood Reporter*, with sales of 254,000 in one week; in its first week of sales in 1994, *Under the Table and Dreaming* came nowhere near this figure. The next week, DMB surpassed Hootie and the Blowfish to claim the number-1 spot on the charts; DMB and the Cranberries were number 1 and number 2, respectively, in some markets. The *Boston Globe* found it interesting that DMB had what it took to beat out an Irish group in Boston (Morse, "Hootie"). By May 23, *Crash* was holding at number 5.

Throughout the month of May, DMB toured. They played the New Orleans Jazz and Heritage Festival during the first week, and there they filmed the MTV special *Crashing the Quarter*, which featured the band in concert. It aired on May 16, and featured DMB at its very best — live. After a video segment describing how Dave had met each of the band members, the concert began. Dave announced, "We're the Dave Matthews Band and we're from somewhere in Virginia." They played an hour's worth of songs, and these were interspersed with brief, pretaped interviews with band members. The camera caught the excitement and genius of their live jamming, and the concert footage was buoyant. It was hot onstage. Dave joked about how much he was sweating during the show, and there was some classic Davespeak about "pissing in his pants" — he hadn't, even though it looked like he had. Once again, Dave displayed his comic-improv abilities. The appearance was a triumph for the band in every way.

Next, DMB played various centers in Canada for about a week, and then hopped down to New York to do the Letterman show on May 17. After that, they flew to Europe for dates in Germany and Italy. While still in Europe, Matthews spoke highly of Italy: "I have a real fondness for Italy. Italy is very passionate. And the food here is great. You can go to a restaurant and get a dinner for the price of a Big Mac and it will be good — really good, high to low. I like that" (Shapiro). Matthews also took the time during one transcontinental interview to clarify something about his image on US television: "That's not me; what you see of me on MTV is not real. I didn't get into this business to have my face on MTV or be No. 2 on the charts. All I want to do is play music in front of people. The rest of the stuff can be intoxicating, but it doesn't compare to making music" (Violanti).

Reflecting on the band's reception in Europe, Matthews said: "More people know us, and because more people are familiar, we get better slots. It's the same thing we had to go through in the United States. The culture and languages are different, but basically we're playing in front of new people" (Shapiro).

Lessard agreed with Matthews about the European experience: "We haven't caught on as well over here yet. They look at it like some kind of foreign movie." That June, Lessard also made some important observations about the band's growth, and modestly assessed his own abilities. "We push each other now," he explained, "but it wasn't always like that. Carter had some great teachers, and I never really trained, since I was always playing in a band. I learned mostly on the road. At least now I can play on top of his fills. There used to be times I would just stop playing and let him do his thing." With all their touring and studio experience, did Lessard have a preference for one or the other? "I love recording in studios. As for representing the songs, doing it live is probably better. But for lifestyle purposes, I'd rather be in the studio" (McLennan).

Throughout June, DMB toured domestically, hitting stadiums and amphitheaters in New Jersey, Massachusetts, New York, Connecticut, Pennsylvania, Ohio, Indiana, Illinois, Michigan, and Wisconsin. Ben Harper opened for them on some of these dates. On several occasions, Matthews generously praised Harper to the audience as "the best of what's around."

By the end of June, *Crash* was at number 10 on the *Billboard* charts — one of the top-selling CDs after three months. The band returned to Italy. And Denmark. And Holland. And Germany. And England. In London, in July, they did an unplugged segment at VH-1 studios. During this tour, DMB also had the opportunity to open for Bob Dylan. Leroi, Boyd, and Dave jammed with Dylan's band several times as part of this stint. They played Europe for three weeks, and then came back to the United States to join the H.O.R.D.E. for the third year in a row.

Matthews acknowledged that the band didn't have to play in the H.O.R.D.E. due to their current level of success, but they wanted to support it because it "has played a big part in our careers. We've been a part of it, and we got a lot of help from it. It would be pretty sad if all of a sudden we didn't need it, so we're not going to play it. And anyway, we have a lot of fun doing it" (Riemenschneider). Over the summer, DMB was featured on another MTV show, which was filmed at one of their 14 H.O.R.D.E. dates. The 1996 H.O.R.D.E. was expected to gross around $12 million.

During the week of July 22, "So Much to Say" entered the singles charts at number 22. It spent the rest of the summer climbing those charts and rejuvenating interest in *Crash*.

A sad thing happened near the end of the summer. Aslan Lessard, Stefan and Josie's daughter, died just three weeks after she was born. The band cancelled 11 dates to mourn the terrible tragedy, and Matthews dutifully fielded questions about it. "We didn't have a meeting or anything," he said. "Everything just stopped — and that's the way it should be. . . . It was evident what we should do. And that's to cancel. . . . We're a family. There's not even a consideration of anything else . . . Stefan has had a tragedy. We've had tragedies before in the band and it's been the same

SYDNEY BURTNER/THE OBSERVER

thing." Matthews went on to stress the importance of life, love, family, and "our brotherhood" (Morse, "Tragedy").

The band was back on the road in October, with Soul Coughing as their opening act. The *Boston Herald* reviewed their show on October 2, saying, "That they played so well and jubilantly — in light of the recent and unspeakably tragic death of bassist Stefan Lessard's infant daughter — perhaps truly does point to the healing power of music" (Rodman, "Dave Matthews"). The band's performance also demonstrated the level of consummate professionalism and spiritual strength that Lessard and the rest of DMB had achieved.

Back in Charlottesville, tragedy struck yet again; this time, it involved a musician who had once been close to DMB. On September 20, Haines Fullerton, 37 years old, was found dead in a pool house adjacent to an apartment building. He had died of a gunshot wound to the head. The police ruled it a suicide. According to several sources, Fullerton had quit bartending and had been living off the royalties he received as cowriter of "#34." Charlottesville was shocked. C-VILLE *Weekly* quoted a spokesman as saying that Matthews was experiencing his grief privately, and would not be making a statement about the death (Fox, "Arts Watch").

Many months later, Matthews spoke about music and healing in general: "Music will always be a source of healing. It is really like therapy for me. Death is dark and leaves great big holes, but it's also a wonderful way to remind us just how abbreviated life can be and how we should count our blessings. Sometimes you have to consciously remind yourself how important friends and family are" (Roos, " 'Crash' Course").

The DMB fall tour hit major East Coast cities. The band played the Letterman show again in October, performing "So Much to Say," even though Dave was clearly sick and could barely sing. He was bundled up in a coat because the famed Ed Sullivan Theater, where Letterman is taped, is notoriously cold inside. The tour extended through the Midwest, then concluded with a run on the West Coast. G Love and the Special Sauce opened for DMB at some of the later gigs. On the last dates of the tour, the band played Seattle, San Francisco, and other big centers along the West Coast. They sold out the Universal Amphitheater in Los Angeles on November 15 and 16.

The first of these two LA gigs was Carla Cain's first DMB show, and she returned to the amphitheater for the second one. She was 30 at the time. Cain was in the outer backstage area before the show began on both nights. She described the scene: several open courtyards dotted with tables bearing chips and salsa; the band's logo projected onto the side of the building backstage; a bar; walls adorned with *Crash* posters. There were few people on hand before the show. "The general atmosphere was festive," says Cain, "full of anticipation. Everyone was speaking in hushed tones, anxiously hoping for a glimpse of one of the band members. The crowd was all ages, although I expected a really young crowd. Carter came out and sat with a table of girls. I remember a couple of false alarms, of people saying, 'Oh, wait. There's Dave.' And then it wasn't. When Dave did walk nonchalantly through the crowd to introduce the warm-up band, everyone missed him. Then they started saying, 'Was that Dave? Was it him?' It was kind of funny." Cain found the two shows to be incredible. "I didn't know they did all that improvising. It was a cross between a rock

Silver Bowl, May 1995

J. TAYLOE EMERY

show and a jazz show — a pop/rock band with a jazz sensibility. It was really refreshing."

Ryan Senter was also at that show. Later, he hung out with Dave and other band members in a hotel lobby. He remembers being in the lobby at 3 A.M. and seeing almost all of DMB ranged in front of him: "There was Leroi, Carter, Boyd, Dave, and Henry [Luniewski, the drum tech]. Carter and Boyd left. I sat down and asked Dave some questions." The two proceeded to have a discussion about spiritual beliefs. Senter told Matthews he thought that a lot of his songs had very spiritual connotations, and when Senter asked him specifically about "Christmas Song," Dave replied that he thought Jesus was great because he stood up against the whole world.

On the second night of the LA gig, Cain as well as Senter again found themselves in the outer backstage area. During the encore, Matthews came out alone and played "What Will Become of Me" as a solo; then the rest of the band joined him. About 90 minutes after each of the two LA shows, Matthews came out to meet the fans. The second night, says Cain, he was immediately mobbed. "When he came out to greet people, Dave looked really good, with ivory skin and brown eyes, and wispy, curly black hair. Really good-looking close up. I hadn't anticipated how good-looking he'd be. He was a lot taller than I thought, tall and statuesque, wearing a stylish black leather jacket." Both nights, Bruce Flohr of RCA assisted Matthews in greeting enthusiasts. As throngs of people glommed onto Dave, begging him to kiss or hug them, or sign their tickets, or draw pictures on their shirts, Matthews sweetly and humorously obliged for at least an hour. Just being next to Matthews was enough to render fans of all ages speechless. Surprisingly, there were children present, despite the lateness of the hour. After a fan had the chance to speak to Matthews, Flohr would gently urge him or her aside, saying, "Spread the love, y'all, spread the love," thereby making room for the next person in line. The sight of Matthews tirelessly interacting with his fans after playing a three-hour show was an unforgettable one for many. He was unwaveringly kind, and always asked questions and made funny comments. Informal and conversational, Dave showed genuine interest in his supporters.

A big feature article on Dave and DMB was published in *Rolling Stone* on December 12, 1996. In it, Dave's mother noted that her son could have a career as a comic actor if his musical career ever faltered (Colapinto). On December 16, 1996, Matthews signed with a talent agency in Los Angeles that handles actors. He had selected the Ilene Feldman Agency as his theatrical representative ("Tenpercenteries").

Dave and Tim played an acoustic show in mid-December in New York, and DMB continued to do holiday tour dates. Their New Year's Eve show was again held at Hampton Coliseum, in Hampton, Virginia. Béla Fleck and the Flecktones opened for DMB and jammed on several tunes that night; some fans reported that together the two bands did the best version of "Lie in Our Graves" they'd ever heard.

And there was some good news about DMB on the touring circuit. Concert promoters, doing their year-end tallies, discovered that DMB had helped Hershey Stadium in Pennsylvania earn the title of "#1 stadium in America with a capacity of 40,000 or under." The Dave Matthews Band had drawn 18,926 people to Hershey Stadium at the end of September, and their show was proclaimed one of the highlights of the year (Tom Powell). But, more importantly, *Pollstar* magazine identified DMB's as one of the top-selling North American concert tours for 1996. The band ranked number 12 in 1996: playing 81 shows, they'd earned $20.6 million.

Perhaps the most telling sign that the band's meteoric rise to stardom was a reality came in the form of an invitation to play at the White House. The Dave Matthews Band was asked to perform at President Bill Clinton's second inauguration gala in January 1997.

10
KEEPS ON GROWING

As 1997 dawned, DMB had an even greater momentum going than they'd had the year before — and 1996 had been stellar. Accolades had continued to pour in during the last quarter of 1996: Matthews placed third in the Acoustic Pickstyle Guitarist category and second in the New Talent category in a poll conducted by *Acoustic Guitar* (Mettler). Carter was heralded by *Modern Drummer* as the #1 Up and Coming Rock Drummer of the year (William F. Miller, "Carter Beauford"). *Crash* went double platinum in November, and held its own in the mid-50 range on *Billboard*'s Top 200 Albums list.

One incident that occurred during the holiday tour summed up the band's unique demographic draw. In Omaha, Nebraska, a 39-year-old woman attending the general-admission Civic Auditorium Arena show with her 20-year-old son was trapped in pit gridlock near the front of the stage and had to be lifted over the barrier by a guard. She said: "I knew I was slightly claustrophobic, but I didn't know it could get that bad. People were pushing from the back on the people up front." Security had refused to help her until others in the crowd had intervened on her behalf. As it turned out, she didn't require medical attention, and ended up watching the show from the bleachers. Omaha's public-events manager released a statement saying that although DMB's had been "a mild mannered show," if you hadn't been to a concert in a while, it was a good idea to learn how a general-admission show operates before buying

LOU BARON/PORTICO PUBLICATIONS LTD.

193

a ticket ("Crowd"). So, people who hadn't been to a rock concert in years were coming to see DMB: plenty of 20-year-olds across the country (not just that one Omaha DMB fan) were bringing their parents to see the band.

On January 7, 1997, DMB was nominated for three more Grammys. "Too Much" was named in the Best Rock Song category. *Crash* got a nod as Best Rock Album. "So Much to Say" was nominated as Best Rock Performance by a Duo or Group. The awards were to be presented on February 26 at the 39th Annual Grammy Awards ceremony, held in New York. But, as dizzying as that news was, band members had other things on their minds: namely, the president.

The presidential gala was held on January 18 and 19. The inaugural festivities got under way in tents and buildings on the Mall behind the White House grounds; DMB played on that first night. The gala itself was held on the second night at the USAir Arena in Largo, Maryland; it was televised on ABC. Other performers on the inaugural roster included Stevie Wonder, Kenneth "Babyface" Edmonds, Trisha Yearwood, Aretha Franklin, James Taylor, Sandy Patty, Kenny G, Kenny Rogers, and Yo-Yo Ma (Holland, "D.C."). The Dave Matthews Band had several fans in the White House inner circle; the Gore daughters, Chelsea Clinton, and Roger Clinton had all professed their admiration for the band.

Actor/producer Michael Douglas introduced the quintet for the cameras, noting that DMB had achieved success by playing at colleges; they'd built a career the old-fashioned, grass-roots way. The television special filmed that night included DMB performing "Too Much."

Ticket prices for inaugural events averaged $100. However, one such event promoted by Voters for Choice (with Mary Chapin Carpenter, Joan Osborne, Ani DiFranco, and Keb' Mo') carried a best-seat price tag of $2,500 (Holland, "D.C."). Postgala parties followed the official gala, and these were sponsored by major corporations (like MCI) and the Record Industry Association of America. At some point in this seemingly endless stream of celebrations, DMB met the Clintons and the Gores.

In a year that a dance version of the "Macarena" was named top-selling single, DMB placed number 18 in the album category in *Billboard*'s Best-Selling Records of 1996. And although they did not win, DMB was nominated for an American Music Award in the Band (Duo or Group) category. They released the video for "Crash into Me" — a surreal romp in a meadow and a forest — to support the hit single.

After the inauguration, DMB took some time off. Dave and Tim Reynolds went on a national acoustic tour for part of January and all of February. Hitting smaller venues, mostly 1,000- to 2,000-seat houses, the dynamic duo played three hours per night with no backup. Tickets for their shows were hard to get in major cities. Their February 22 LA show, for example, sold out in four minutes.

The duo made some innovative choices in compiling their set lists. They even included a cover of "Cryptorchid," a Marilyn Manson song. Dave introduced another new tune that had a couple of morphing titles: "Captain of My Ship"/ "Crazy," depending on when you heard it. He and Tim bravely faced their audiences equipped only with two acoustic guitars and a few microphones. Dave sat on a stool. Tim stood. And that was about it for production values. Their performances on this tour were frequently interrupted by shouted professions of love for Dave and/or song requests; sometimes this happened at inopportune

Marquee, February 22, 1997

JAMES A. STEINFELDT

Dave and Tim

JAMES A. STEINFELDT

moments — in the middle of a quiet, acoustic ballad like "Christmas Song," for example. Yet Matthews and Reynolds were undaunted by periodic rudeness and fan zeal: they knew how to deliver a unique concert experience that would overcome all interruption. Their Zen-master concentration and devotion to the music prevailed. Also included in their shows was some revelatory Davespeak; tales of airborne bowel movements in Amsterdam were told on several occasions. The 1997 Dave and Tim Tour exceeded those of previous years in terms of attendance and number of performance dates.

The entire Dave Matthews Band got together again for the Grammy Awards. Presented by the National Academy of Recording Arts and Sciences, the ceremony was held at New York's Madison Square Garden on February 26. Nominated in three categories, DMB won for "So Much to Say," judged Best Rock Performance by a Duo or Group. The band's win was not televised; the awards in that category had been presented earlier in the day. But during the televised evening special, a picture was broadcast of them receiving the award — their moment of triumph. Nearly six years after DMB had been launched, they won their first Grammy — for a song, written in 1992, that had been part of their initial repertoire. Most DMB fans felt that such recognition was long overdue. (One of the song's co-writers, Peter Griesar, was away on vacation, and didn't learn of the award until sometime in March ["Grammy Thanks"]).

On the day the band won their Grammy, another DMB story was revealed to the public. It briefly confused DMB tapers, and it involved another lawsuit — this one worth more than $10 million in damages. The *Record* of Bergen, New Jersey, reported that in November of 1996 lawyer Jules Zalon of Essex County had been hired by DMB. Since that time, Zalon had investigated New Jersey record stores engaged in the illegal sale of DMB bootlegs for as much as $65 apiece. As a result of Zalon's efforts, Bama Rags had sued four record stores in November (DeMarco).

With further investigation, Zalon was also able to track the supply of bootleg tapes to a storage facility in Manhattan, near Madison Square Garden. More than 75,000 illegal

DMB tapes and CDs were found stashed in this makeshift warehouse under the name of distributor Gnarly Music. At the end of February, with Bama Rags' approval, Zalon filed a lawsuit in US District Court in Newark, New Jersey, charging Gnarly Music with copyright infringement. The claim for over $10 million in damages sought $100,000 for each song recorded without permission (DeMarco).

Industry insiders found the move to be unprecedented. They also acknowledged that piracy is a major problem: as much as $300 million in sales is lost per year due to bootlegging. In February 1996, Zalon stated that DMB had decided to stop entrepreneurs who were criminally making a profit; the band had made a commitment to do so. A spokesperson for the Recording Industry Association distinguished the difference between legal taping and bootlegging. Most musical acts, the association believed, recognize that "there's a big difference between fans taping for their own use and the illegal exploitation of artists" (DeMarco).

Supporters of DMB were initially puzzled, but then agreed that bootlegging was illegal and that the band had guts to go after this criminal element on the fringes of the music industry. Would tapers who were only trading their wares with other fans still be allowed to tape DMB shows? The answer came from Red Light Management: Yes. There was a collective sigh of relief. Fans were appeased. Tape trading continued.

Remember Two Things went gold on March 10, 1997, after having sold 500,000 units. Most independent records top out at 200,000, at best. This milestone was yet another indication of DMB's soaring popularity.

In March, the band hit the late-night television circuit to promote "Crash into Me." Playing both the *Tonight Show* and the *Late Show with David Letterman*, they charmed millions with their sultry interpretation of the ballad. Dave even managed to coax a wild animal while appearing on Jay Leno's show.

Dave's status as a popular-culture icon was solidified by his appearance on the April 16 edition of *Politically Incorrect with Bill Maher*. This TV show typically addresses timely topics and current events, eliciting candid opinions from a revolving series of guests. Matthews was joined by fellow pop-culture luminaries Judith Regan, Carl Reiner, and Clarence Page.

The broad topic of this installment of *Politically Incorrect* was: Why does puberty start earlier among American girls than among those in other countries? That question led Maher's guests to take a sweeping look at the aftermath of the sexual revolution of the 1960s. There was wild applause and screaming when Matthews came out; the show couldn't get under way until the audience had quieted down. Dave wore a blue button-down shirt with a white T-shirt underneath, and light brown pants. He was to sit next to Reiner, and as soon as he had settled in, he smiled and told Reiner that this was his first talk show and he was scared.

Maher got things going by telling the studio audience: "Folks, he's not going to sing." Dave interjected: "I wish I was, though. I'm more comfortable doing that." Dave's star power was so evident in the crowd's reaction to him throughout the show that after one commercial break, Maher quipped, "Welcome back to *American Bandstand*." At several points in the discussion about sexual activity and youth, Dave's innate humor shone through. During the freewheeling conversation, he was asked by Regan if he respected women who threw themselves at him. He answered that he spent half the time telling young female fans that he was old enough to be their uncle, and the other half kicking himself for saying that. *Politically Incorrect* is filmed in Los Angeles; Bruce Flohr was on hand to walk Dave through the taping procedures.

A week later, a major article appeared in the *New York Times* about DMB's bootlegging lawsuit. It revealed that a minor DMB boycott had developed as a result of the suit. Attorney Zalon had expanded his investigation to include more of New England; he had entered 40 stores in Connecticut, Massachusetts, and Rhode Island accompanied by a federal marshall. They had grabbed any DMB bootlegs they found, and threatened to sue to the tune of $100,000 for every illegal album. Zalon then offered each store a chance to settle out of court and requested up to $15,000 from each establishment to handle the costs of the civil complaints and the investigation.

The store owners were livid. Some boxed up DMB CDS and sent them back to RCA, vowing never to carry the band's products again. A Darien, Connecticut, record store named Johnny's put up a sign in its window that read "Boycott Dave Matthews — Fight Corporate Greed." There were testimonials from other independent record stores that had been served notice; the retailers were greatly distressed and felt this action would ruin their businesses. A spokesman for a store in Massachusetts declared, "What we're upset about is that he went right for the jugular, saying we're all a bunch of crooks. If not for small, independent stores, Dave Matthews wouldn't be where he is today" (Strauss). *Live! Music Review*, a bootleg journal out of Arizona, joined the boycott.

Coran Capshaw released a statement about the affair in which he allowed that Zalon had perhaps been overzealous: "We had never seen the demand letter that was given to stores. It stepped beyond where we were intending to go. We're going to move away from this whole money thing and just concentrate on stopping the bootlegs." Capshaw also pledged to settle the outstanding lawsuits without any monetary damages to the store owners — just an injunction prohibiting future bootleg sales. In addition, Capshaw revealed that DMB was likely to release some official live albums of its own (Strauss). The story was covered by MTV news, as well. Some reporters pointed out the irony of the situation: DMB had built its reputation as a taper band, and had, seemingly, invited the problem by allowing taping in the first place.

Lessard had this to say of the bootlegging brouhaha: "The problem is when these tapes are sent out of the country to some place where there's no copyright law, and they're produced in mass quantities, and sold for like $30 a CD, which is a ripoff for fans. It rips us off. It rips fans off, and in reality, it rips the stores off." He also remarked on the poor sound quality of most of them, and the deceiving color graphics on the covers, which often made the CDS appear as if they were official DMB releases (Catlin, "Dave

Matthews"). Releasing a live DMB CD, Lessard agreed, would help solve the problem. "If we let people tape, and if we can get a couple of albums out on our own label, then there should be such a supply that we can say 'Let them sell their bootlegs' and hopefully no one will buy them and people will realize 'Oh, my God, I have the same tape'" (Rodman, "Tangled").

Perhaps this entire affair spurred the Recording Industry Association of America to further action. This organization is the body primarily responsible for CD-piracy prosecution in America. In July, they busted a warehouse in Long Island City, New York, scooping up 425,000 illegal recordings, including some DMB, Phish, and Bob Dylan. It was the largest bust in RIAA history (Holland, "Long Island").

Happily, new DMB music was on the way to market. The single of "Tripping Billies" premiered on *Billboard*'s Modern Rock Tracks list the week of May 31 at number 31. The video debuted on MTV, and included live footage of a December holiday-tour concert in Philadelphia; fans were glad to see the live-concert experience evoked in a video.

Yet another press piece stirred things up again for DMB in the summer of 1997. It involved a follow-up feature that ran in *Westword*, a Denver alternative paper, and was picked up by a few other newspapers nationwide. In this feature, scribe Joshua Green profiled former *Rolling Stone* writer Jim DeRogatis and tried to get to the root of his animosity towards DMB. Green interviewed Matthews, as well. The article was called "Love That Dave: Critics Hate Dave Matthews, But That Doesn't Mean You Should" — a curious title, since so many critics seem to love DMB. The cover of the *Westword* issue in which the article appeared featured the headline "Dave Matthews Trades Blows with *Rolling Stone*." This was a hyperbolic description of the article's content. DeRogatis did go into detail about his disdain for DMB's music, and Matthews was quoted, but the two hardly "traded blows." By this point, DeRogatis, who had been fired from *Rolling Stone*, had not been with the publication for a year. Matthews generously allowed that writing music criticism is a tough task: "It's a difficult thing — to be a critic and to have your own voice. Who's to say what makes a good critic? It's a job I'm happy to leave up to you all" (Green). In the end, both DeRogatis and Matthews expressed the view that *Rolling Stone* does not belong in any pantheon of music journals. DeRogatis concluded: "*Rolling Stone* sucks royally." Matthews quipped: "*Rolling Stone* always has both thumbs packed firmly in their asses" (Green).

This was hardly a new topic, even though it was billed as one. Dave had spoken about the *Rolling Stone*/DeRogatis situation before. In 1996, he remarked: "You know, *Rolling Stone* likes to think it's on the cutting edge of journalism. But how on-the-edge can you be when you've been an overfed pig for 20 years? Anyone who thinks *Rolling Stone* or *Spin* exist for any other reason except to make money is fooling themselves. That's why they have more pictures than words" (Ransom).

Matthews had already weighed in on the topic of reviews, as well. Speaking of *Rolling Stone*'s DMB coverage, he declared: "What can one say? 'Nice of you to mention us.' When people say 'It's a bad review,' I ask, 'How bad a review?' And if they say 'scathing,' then I'll read it. If it's mediocre, I don't spend much time thinking about it. It's a very strange thing to me whenever critics come out and say anything. Certainly the process of making music and playing it for people is a very innocent thing" (Mervis, "HORDE").

The band spent the rest of the summer doing just that — making music. Their six-week summer tour began on June 3, 1997, in Richmond. In this short stretch of time, DMB would cover 19 states and play to stadium crowds. Most dates were sold out. They stayed focused on their audience's response. "We just want our music to make people happy," insisted Dave. "I don't care if people love us because they think I'm speaking directly to them, or if they like the way it sounds, or if it just makes them want to dance. We send it from our hearts, so however it lands in someone else's heart is fine" ("Dave Matthews Band Is Thriving").

Matthews explained the reason for the abbreviated tour schedule: "We certainly could go on a longer tour. But we're going to work on another album instead. We're going to take some time and reflect and go into it prepared" (MacDonald). "Crash" rose to number 44 on the *Billboard* CD charts again, due to the excitement generated by DMB's summer sojourn.

The rain poured down during the first show of the tour, but they still delivered a great performance, as promised: the tickets guaranteed purchasers a good show — rain or shine. After completing a few dates in New York, New Jersey, and Connecticut, DMB did the Letterman show again, on June 10. They surprised everyone by playing the emotional "#41," and not "Tripping Billies," their current single.

The band played two nights at Jones Beach — June 10 and 11 — and on the first night, John Popper guested on a long version of "Seek Up." Béla Fleck and the Flecktones opened for them for the first three weeks, and DMB played a steady, triumphant set of shows that extended through the middle of June and generated critical accolades nearly everywhere. Some of the highlights of their June reviews: The *Patriot Ledger* of Quincy, Massachusetts, called DMB "the most successful jazz-rock fusion outfit ever" (Jay Miller). The *Providence Journal-Bulletin* stated that "mostly the band scored, thanks to the powerful dynamic between its members, and they managed to keep the right balance between lengthy jams and the shorter, punchier tunes" (Smith, "Dave Matthews Showcases"). The *Washington Times* effused, "In an age of body-pierced wailers and 40-foot lemons, Dave Matthews is a beacon. Catch the band next time around" (Susie Powell). The *Washington Post* reported that "Jimi Thing," "Ants Marching," and "Crash into Me" were "among several tunes that benefited from the spirited and sometimes spontaneous interaction among the musicians, including guest banjoist Béla Fleck" (Joyce, "Dave Matthews: A World"). The *Asbury Park Press* maintained: "Despite not releasing an album for over a year and presenting little new material, the Dave Matthews Band's technical skill and improvisational edge kept things fresh, vibrant and exciting for a sold-out audience" (Jordan).

For a long time, DMB has supported Greenpeace, the

international environmental activism group. In 1996 and 1997, during DMB stadium shows, Matthews made a plea on behalf of the organization that usually went something like this: "From what I understand, if you give a dollar to Greenpeace, even if you sin, you'll get into heaven. If there is one." Matthews asked for donations to the cause at every show.

Describing the summer-tour production values, Matthews said, "We still have the same sound and light guys that we have always had and they know how we play. The band has grown, but the focus has stayed the same, and it's fun to rock a really big house. People wonder if we miss bars and clubs, and we do miss them, but I think maybe the fans who have been with us for a long time miss them more than we do" (Niesel). The band played a couple of new songs over the summer: a Daniel Lanois cover called "For the Beauty of Wynona," and a Dave song called "The Weight of the World."

Los Lobos joined the tour as opening act on June 20, and stayed on until the tour ended in July. Afterward, a member of Los Lobos commented that the band had enjoyed the stint with DMB, and felt that "the Dave Matthews Band . . . were all great people" ("Los Lobos"). At Denver's Red Rocks amphitheater over the Fourth of July holiday, DMB was again joined by John Popper. The *Rocky Mountain News* reported: "the evening added to Dave Matthews Band's reputation as a dynamic live act. The group's fierce jamming skills were blended to catchy standards . . ." (G. Brown, "Matthews").

The band also won a rave from the *Salt Lake Tribune*. In spite of a gnarly traffic jam caused by fans pouring into the concert site, the paper's reviewer concluded that "the time spent with Mr. Matthews and company was well spent"; he also thought "Tinsley and Beauford were especially enjoyable to watch. Tinsley's enthusiasm while playing his Cajun-spry violin brought the crowd to a boil. And Moore's tenor saxophone added just the right amount of texture" (Brophy).

The Orange County edition of the *Los Angeles Times* favored the performance of Los Lobos but concluded, "The

Dave Matthews Band . . . has a number of things going for it. Matthews has a quirky and engaging voice as well as the ability to write a ballad as memorable as 'Crash into Me.' Plus, bassist Stefan Lessard, and particularly, jazz-based drummer Carter Beauford are masterful support musicians" (Matsumoto). The show got a mixed review from the *Sacramento Bee*: toiling in 100-degree heat, DMB had achieved "an artistic triumph but an entertainment disappointment." The *Bee* reviewer described the band's set list as consisting of "free-flowing, improvisational tunes that was remarkable in its musical complexity"; however, he continued, DMB needed to bump up its production values (Carnes). But Matthews did do his bit to entertain that night, despite the heat. He read a sign out loud declaring one audience member's marriage proposal to another. He also had to chide a guy for shoving people ahead of him towards the front.

A *Seattle Times* review read: "When a band reaches the last performance of a long tour, the final show usually goes one of two ways: either the band is totally burned out, completely hates one another and can't wait to go home, or — in the case of Dave Matthews and his team at the Gorge last Friday night — they just couldn't play enough." The extended jams with Los Lobos members David Hidalgo, Cesar Rosas, and Steve Berlin were "possibly the best moments of the show" (Phalen). All in all, the response to DMB's summer run was extremely favorable. *Pollstar* magazine rated the tour as one of the top 25 best-selling tours of the first half of 1997.

Just one glance at the DMB 1997 Summer Tour binder — and its comprehensive listings of five-star hotels and precise catering calls at each venue on the road — brings to mind the 1993 touring conditions described by Jim Bailey. With overnight stays at hotel chains such as Four Seasons, Marriott, Hilton, Ritz Carlton, Westin, and Intercontinental, the band and crew got to relax in style when not traveling or on stage. Sound checks usually occurred between 3:00 and 4:30 in the afternoon. (As on past tours, Ultra Sound handled the audio, and the lighting was designed by TMS.) The nightly catering call varied between

7:00 and 8:00 P.M. Although DMB still had to endure a lot of driving, their general comfort level had certainly improved.

Legions of DMB fans tell stories of the band's kindness towards its faithful supporters. There are stories about Leroi arranging seats for fans in San Diego — people who'd traveled a long way to get to the venue, only to discover they'd lost their tickets. Boyd has signed autographs for hours at a time, even stopping in the middle of a long jog to scrawl his name for an admirer. Steven Walkuski, a 16-year-old Connecticut drummer, has a recent Carter story. Walkuski had made a large banner that said "Carter Is God" and displayed it at the June 8, 1997, Hartford Meadows show from his seat in seventh row center. He held his sign up before the performance began; Carter glimpsed it, and smiled. A DMB employee sought out Walkuski and asked for the banner — they wanted to give it to Carter after the show. Walkuski obliged, and, when the show was over, he was contacted by yet another DMB employee who presented him with a gift from Carter: the three drumsticks he'd used that night. Carter also autographed four paper plates, adding the words "thank you," for Walkuski and his friends.

Christa Zofcin was invited to hang out backstage at the July Sacramento show, and she came away impressed by every member of the band. She recalls how sweet and full of life Stefan was, and how eager he was to play his music. Zofcin also notes the true friendships that existed between the techs and band members: for example, Stefan and tech Henry Luniewski are close friends. Dave, Zofcin reports, was "incredibly sweet, hilarious, genuine, and a generous host." During a backstage meal, he urged her, "Have all the sushi you want." When a crew member offered her a drink, Dave jokingly intervened: "What are you doing giving her a warm beer?" Matthews kept the crew roaring with laughter, and seemed to enjoy hanging out with them. He asked Zofcin for her input on the set list — which he completed right before the show — and even incorporated one of her suggestions. Later, he asked, "Got any more song requests?" She was struck by his open, friendly nature and his intelligence: "Dave is really perceptive — he notices everything." Dave's drawing skills also attracted her notice: "He took time drawing pictures for fans, trying to give everyone a masterpiece." She could tell that he truly liked talking to fans, and he treated everyone with respect — the crew, the fans, his fellow band members.

In the summer of 1997, *Remember Two Things* and *Recently*, the band's five-song EP, were issued by RCA nationwide; the release date was timed to coincide with the band's summer tour. Evidently, a new deal had been arranged with Bama Rags; RCA had bought the albums from Bama Rags and released them under its own label. "Crash into Me" became part of a movie soundtrack — it was featured in the Alicia Silverstone vehicle *Excess Baggage*. And the video for "Crash into Me" was nominated for a 1997 MTV Music Video Award.

Culturally, DMB has made its imprint. The band is a major Internet presence, but DMB also pops up in other places. The band was mentioned in a *Newsweek* article about Brad Pitt (he's a fan). Their songs are played as bumper music on talk-radio shows (even by conservative Rush Limbaugh) and at sporting events nationwide. The line "Crash into Me" now appears in personal ads across America — a sort of siren call to a potential lover.

Boyd became an advertising icon in the late summer of 1997. He participated in a nationwide ad campaign for Jansport backpacks. The photo used was of his bare muscular back and the back of his head, but everyone knew who it was; the words "boyd tinsley" and "violinist/dave matthews band" also appeared in the ad, along with "Back" and "Pack." The campaign targeted "high school and college students and even younger kids," according to *Adweek* (Ebenkamp), and the ad ran in 31 magazines.

The band has also made a mark in the world of higher education. Cory Olson of Rush City, Minnesota, is just one of many young musicians who have studied DMB in the context of a college-level music-theory course. In Olson's class, the band's music was used as a springboard for a discussion of classical-music elements in rock. The entire class came to the conclusion that DMB was probably the most musically rich rock group working today.

John Athayde is now in a band called Tilae Linden. His love for DMB, and for performing, led him to pursue a career as a professional musician. He now plays guitar, mandolin, piano, and numerous other instruments; he sings, as well. There's a violinist in Tilae Linden, an uncommon feature for a rock group. The DMB connection is obvious. Tilae Linden has even done a few DMB covers in homage. They are also influenced by Celtic folk music and the British band James.

Early DMB supporter Joshua Nicholas Tolson now runs a web site dedicated to the band. His passion for professional photography is also linked to the group; his shots of DMB appear throughout this book. Tolson has combined two consuming interests, the Internet and photography, and used them to explore and promote a third: DMB.

By 1997, the band had made a resounding impact on popular culture, not just the music industry. As we've witnessed, their influences can be seen in the Internet, education, and advertising. Phrases from their songs are now part of the common vernacular. Younger musicians are modeling their instrumentation on DMB's. The band's importance reaches beyond the brilliance of their music: they have become a fixture of popular culture.

11
'TIL WE DANCE AWAY

And the band plays on. Upholding a tradition, DMB played the Farm Aid Benefit on October 4 at Tinley Park, outside of Chicago. Matthew Winer, a 27-year-old Chicago native, attended the nine-hour event, which featured twelve bands. It was his first DMB concert. Winer reports: "When we first pulled into the parking lot, there were lots of high-school-age fans there. You could tell lots of people made the trip just to see the Dave Matthews Band." The band's performance, Winer maintains, was "a definite highlight of Farm Aid. People went nuts when they came out. It was an intense performance. They really gelled the crowd. Boyd, the violin player, was amazing. DMB put on a great show." The 1997 Farm Aid Benefit raised over $1 million in relief funds. Fall 1997 tour highlights included opening for the Rolling Stones in November and December.

The band also released their first live double CD on October 28, 1997. Titled *Live at Red Rocks, 8/15/95*, the release succeeded in fulfilling the ardent hopes of many longtime DMB fans. After being weaned on live tapes, the desire to hear a high-quality CD recording of the live DMB experience is shared by legions of the band's enthusiasts — another positive effect of the taper culture.

The seventeen-track CD demonstrates DMB's masterful jam and improv technique in live performance, circa 1995. Tim Reynolds makes a guest appearance at the show, playing electric guitar. Euphonious surprises include a brief rendition of John Denver's "Sunshine on My Shoulder" sung by Dave in the intro to "Recently," as well as Leroi's playful "Somewhere over the Rainbow" extended sax solo in "Lie in Our Graves." Carter's drumming solo at the beginning of "#36" is also a standout. Leroi's solo on "#36" includes a brief nod to Vince Guaraldi, with a few notes from "Linus & Lucy." The Red Rocks show was a solid and exciting one from start to finish. Tech credits are noteworthy: Dan Healy was in charge of the live recording; and the CD was mixed by John Alagia, Doug Derryberry, and Jeff "Bagby" Thomas at Alpha Beat Studios in Washington, DC. Several more live releases are forthcoming in this new series of live DMB performance CDs.

Two other releases involving DMB debuted in the fall of 1997. A CD called *Live on Letterman: Music from the Late Show* — billed as featuring "one-of-a-kind performances" by 14 artists or bands who'd appeared on the CBS show over the years — premiered. DMB's cut was a rendition of "Too Much." The other release, a soundtrack for the film *Scream 2*, included a studio version of "Help Myself," a major event, which many fans had been awaiting. Tim Reynolds performs with the band on the tune, continuing the DMB tradition of incorporating Reynolds into recorded releases.

DMB's third RCA studio CD was recorded in the San Francisco area during the fall of 1997. That CD (and the big tour to support it) became the focus for 1998. Steve Lillywhite again served as producer, performing his unique technical magic on the new material the CD contains.

Matthews explains his philosophy on the progression of the band's studio recordings: "If you sit down and say that you have to go in a new direction, that's like shooting yourself in the foot. I think we just try to make a good album, and we are only trying to please ourselves. I don't know what anyone else wants. I only know what I want. If we sell 100 records, that's fine. I don't make any rules because once you do that, you cut out all the possibilities" (Niesel). In keeping with DMB's live improvisational approach, Matthews embraced the idea of in-studio innovation: "I think the next album we can experiment a lot. . . . I certainly feel the next album we can pull things out of it that we haven't seen before, see how far we can stretch the fact that people will buy our albums again. Or maybe we can take it to a place where people will say [the heck with] this" (Trott).

The individual members of DMB, of course, also have personal priorities to focus on.

Lessard — accompanied by his wife, Josie — became the only member of DMB to move away from Virginia. While the band was recording *Under the Table and Dreaming* and *Crash* in Woodstock, New York, Stefan grew fond of the place. "I always wanted to go to college, so since I didn't do that, I had a chance to make a move and went there," to Woodstock (Catlin, "From Frat Houses"). Lessard still visits Charlottesville often. In 1997, DMB's traditional holiday-tour plans were altered due to the happy circumstance of Josie's pregnancy.

Beauford put the finishing touches on a solo project in the summer of 1997 up at Bearsville. It was something he'd been working on for a long time. He commented in 1996: "I finally got some equipment that will help me put it together. I bought a computer and some software so I can write music. . . . I've been writing melodies and bass lines and putting songs together." The project is "fusion-oriented." When asked if any of this would change his DMB drumming style, Carter laughed and replied, "Hell no! Don't worry, the playing will be there. That's who I am" (William F. Miller, "Carter Beauford"). Carter Beauford's instructional video about drumming made waves when it was issued in the late fall of 1997. Entitled *Under the Table and Drumming*, it was released on DCI Music Video. Extensive discussion of drumming techniques and insider info about song development is included in the two-volume video set, which is priced at $60.

Tinsley, after having those stunning shots of his back plastered on billboards, LA lifeguard stands, and the sides of New York City buildings throughout the late summer of 1997, presented an award at the MTV Music Video Awards ceremony with Matthews. Boyd's charismatic appearance was a highlight of the event (held on September 4, 1997) for many DMB supporters.

Matthews has told the *Richmond Times Dispatch* that

his future plans involve Charlottesville: "I figure that I will have down-time later in my life, when I'll be still . . . I do think that when I'm maybe making music and not touring so much — down the line — that I'll probably do most of my down-time in Charlottesville and Central Virginia, because I definitely see that as home" (Gatewood). Dave once — in 1995 — modestly assessed his future for a Norfolk newspaper, mentioning the possibility of resuming his working life behind a counter: "Speaking for myself, I try to keep my perspective a realistic one: that things pass. Any illusions of grandeur will eventually slam into our faces, whether it's 10 years from now, four years from now, or next month. It's self-preservation, so that when I'm back to bartending, I won't be smashing my head against the wall, going 'I've been mistreated'" (Wright). Matthews ended 1997 with a televised duet with Mick Jagger and the Rolling Stones on December 12, which was shown around the world as part of the "Bridges to Babylon" broadcast. The tune? "Wild Horses." And 1998 began with the good news that Dave had been nominated for a Grammy for songwriting on "Crash Into Me," while the band as a whole received a nomination in the performance category.

Moore has started taking saxophone lessons again, practicing with master teacher John Purcell of the World Saxophone Quartet. Although Moore has known Purcell for years, the two lived in different places and rarely saw one another. They hooked up again, however, backstage at the Dave Letterman show, and Purcell now helps Moore stay in shape, to maintain muscularity, especially while touring. Purcell also hopes to assist Moore — to balance his many instruments and to find additional Selmer saxophones. About Moore, Purcell opines: "He's an integral part of the Dave Matthews Band, yet he's also known as Leroi Moore, the saxophone player. He likes to be colorful on all his instruments" (Granados).

Code Magenta has a new CD in the works; the trio is excited about the release of their second recording. Dawn Thompson and Greg Howard continue their longstanding musical collaboration with Moore. Thompson underscores, "I've always loved playing with Leroi." Howard concurs:

"Leroi has always impressed me as someone with a unique voice on the tenor saxophone. There were a lot of horn players around but no one could have complemented the sounds Dawn and I were making better than him."

Dave assures fans who may worry that all these independent endeavors could lead to the dissolution of DMB: "The thing is, we love playing together so much. That's sort of the core of everything. We all may work on other projects but we will always get back together. To kill this horse to get on another one is a dumb idea" (MacDonald).

And what's become of all those people who witnessed the genesis of DMB? John D'earth, Dawn Thompson, and Robert Jospe still play at Miller's and D'earth tours with Bruce Hornsby as the "Big Dog" or "Trumpet Slacks."

Tim Reynolds moved from C'ville to Santa Fe, disbanding TR3 in September of 1997.

Greg Howard performs at Miller's on Monday nights now, filling Tim Reynolds' old weekly spot.

Ron Lessard now works for the Leonard Peltier Freedom Campaign and is a lobbyist for American Indian rights. The campaign was supported by Mother Theresa and the Dalai Lama, among millions of others. He performs frequently with jazz pianist Bob Bennetta.

Ross Hoffman is a partner in the company that manages the pop-rock group Hanson.

Lydia Conder still runs Gallery Neo in Charlottesville.

David Wellbeloved, Jamie Dyer, and Dan Sebring are working together again as the Hogwaller Ramblers. They've been playing Sunday nights at Eastern Standard. "It's almost like Fellini's," Wellbeloved says. Other former Hogwaller Ramblers have given the group's revival their blessing. Wellbeloved also hosts a news-talk radio show on C'ville's WINA; his newest CD, *Elvis Watching*, has a 1998 release date. The new Ramblers have played gigs at Miller's.

Peter Griesar is now in a band called the Ninth, which is based in Charlottesville and includes former members of Pie Boy and Hedonistic Cravings. They've been doing some recording and have played in New York. Stefan Lessard sat in with them pretty regularly in the first part of 1997.

Coran Capshaw and Red Light Management are now

successfully handling many other groups — like Agents of Good Roots, who are also on the RCA label — in addition to DMB. Their current roster also includes Gibb Droll.

Cristan Keighley hopes to start a C'ville record label; its first releases would be *The Afrikan Drum Festival* and a Charlottesville compilation featuring artists such as Corey Harris, Tim Reynolds, Shannon Worrell, Jamie Dyer, and Nickeltown (formerly the Treefrogs). "I've compiled a lot of wonderful recordings over the years," Keighley remarks, "and it's past time to share them."

After graduating from UVA, Roy Thigpen went to work as a communications analyst. Because DMB's initial fan base was drawn from the college crowd, many of their early fans are either still in college or attending grad school; others are recent graduates.

Victor Cabas still teaches and plays the blues. He hasn't acted in a while. Richard Hardy moved west.

Miller's, the venue where it all began, remains a vibrant part of the C'ville music scene. Dawn Thompson commends the club's owners, Steve and Dave Tharp, for "being so supportive and encouraging of music. If Steve knows the musicians are good, he says, 'Go for it.' It's an open atmosphere where you can try things and not worry."

As far as the general ambience of the bar is concerned, Tina Panella, a Miller's waitress, reports that "Miller's is still known for its relaxed atmosphere and the regulars. People can come in and say, 'I'll have what I usually have,' and we'll know what they mean. We've always got good beer on tap and the service is kind of casual. I think people are proud to be from Charlottesville — proud that the Dave Matthews Band is another great thing from a place full of talented people." Panella has a master's degree and wants to teach elementary school. She relates a story about a 14-year-old girl who sent a fan letter to Dave in care of Miller's. "We have it posted in the back, in case he comes in." However, Panella does not recommend sending DMB mail to Miller's. That letter has gone unread by the person it's addressed to for months.

C-VILLE *Weekly* (whose offices are currently in the pink warehouse) still publishes stories on the Dave Matthews

Band. The paper is sometimes accused of being anti-DMB. Of c-VILLE *Weekly*'s DMB coverage, which began in February of 1992 and continues today, editor/publisher Hawes Spencer comments: "Every time we mention DMB, big factions either think we love them or hate them. We have no long-standing opinion. People are interested in their stories and that's why we profile them." Spencer's staff has yet to land a direct interview with Matthews. "Every six months, we ask to interview Dave. I'm usually told, 'They're busy in the studio.' I can understand it. They don't have much to gain from talking to us."

In June of 1997, c-VILLE *Weekly* published a humorous article that referred to Dave Matthews as "one of the biggest luminaries to emerge from Charlottesville since the revered Jefferson" (Mahoney).

As he approached death in 1826, when he no longer had the energy to leave Monticello, Thomas Jefferson declared, "All is circumstance. All is circumstance."

Perhaps that's true for everyone. But it's also what you do with what you've got, how you cope and grapple with what life throws at you; it's what you make of the circumstances that come your way.

As one of the most talented and innovative bands working today, the Dave Matthews Band has done pretty well. They make the best of what's around.

THE RAGING OPTIMISM AND MULTIPLE PERSONALITIES OF DAVE MATTHEWS

By John Colapinto*

1. MR. A PSYCHS UP

In a dusty parking lot 100 yards behind the stage of DeVore Stadium, where 10,000 fans await his appearance, Dave Matthews begins his preperformance ritual. The location is Southwestern College in Chula Vista, California, another stop of the 1996 H.O.R.D.E. Festival, and the leader of the Dave Matthews Band is cranked. Beloved by fans for his achingly lyrical songs (and dismissed by some critics as a bland, Hootie Nation jammer), Matthews offstage is a guy neither his defenders, nor his detractors, would recognize. "I feel *good*!" Matthews yelps in a full-throated James Brown. He leaps and shimmies, tossing his gangly, goofy, loose-jointed frame down the narrow aisle of his tour bus. From here, Matthews glides into an imitation of fellow H.O.R.D.E. act Lenny Kravitz, thrashing at a low-slung air guitar and tossing imaginary dreadlocks. For a moment,

---

* From *Rolling Stone*, December 12, 1996. By Straight Arrow Publishers Company, L.P. 1996.

he's a gyrating stripper, then he's the ninja master from his favorite martial-arts movie, chopping the air, bellowing: "You have hurt my students. I will kick you hard in the intestines!"

Alex Stultz, the twenty-three-year-old merchandising manager, barely glances up from his magazine. After nearly four years with the Dave Matthews Band, he's seen this more times than he can count. He's heard Matthews' rapid-fire repertoire of voices, impersonations, accents; he's seen Matthews' dead-on imitations of Germans, crazy professors, Brazilian exiles, stuffy Brits; and he's heard Matthews' endless stream of toilet jokes — a raft of anal-fixated japes that from a less boyishly enthusiastic twenty-nine-year-old might be offensive and weird. But coming from Matthews (whose younger sister, Jane, affectionately calls him Mr. Anus), the unceasing allusions to his bowels — and the manic, high-speed, free-associative monologues — all come off as more funny than weird. So much so that it's not hard to imagine Matthews, in another life, succeeding as a Jim Carrey-like comic. Indeed, six years after Matthews began to supplement his full-time bartender job with musical gigs, his mother is still making backup plans for him. "If this rock & roll thing doesn't work out for David," she says, "he could become a comedic actor."

That won't be necessary. With sales around five million (and counting) for his three records, *Remember Two Things, Under the Table and Dreaming*, and the recently released *Crash*, Dave Matthews' musical career is working out just fine — far better, in fact, than anyone had reason to expect, given the improbabilities of just about everything touching Dave Matthews and his band.

Five years ago, when the rest of the music world moshed to shredding grunge bands, Matthews was leading a virtually acoustic outfit: Carter Beauford on drums, Leroi Moore on sax, Stefan Lessard on bass and Boyd Tinsley on violin. Accomplished players all, they blended their disparate influences — jazz, fusion, funk, and rock — with the rhythmic, lilting folk music that reflected Matthews' formative years in South Africa. The band's sound bore greater affinities to sixties hippie bands like Fairport Convention than such grunge role models as the Stooges, Black Sabbath, and the Sex Pistols. The spirit of Matthews' songs, too, could not have been further from that of his rage-ridden grunge confreres. Good vibes radiate from the titles: "The Best of What's Around," "One Sweet World," "Lover Lay Down," "I'll Back You Up." But Matthews' lyrics, sung in his wafting, Sting-like croon, are more likely to limn bittersweet emotions. In the song "Tripping Billies," which has become a virtual anthem for his fans, the singer entreats: "Eat, drink, and be merry / For tomorrow we die."

Music critics, for the most part, hate it. But audiences have embraced the band with a fervor that the group's multiplatinum sales only hint at. Following the group from venue to venue, compiling notes on the ever-changing set lists, making band-sanctioned bootlegs that are traded with fellow Daveheads via the Internet, the group's fan base — mostly well-scrubbed college kids and tie-dyed latter-day hippies — have appointed DMB (along with Phish and Blues Traveler) as torchbearers for the Grateful Dead. It's a legacy the Dave Matthews Band is living up to, thanks to the strength of its live show, which it has honed during five years of relentless touring.

Back on the bus, Matthews dispatches the last of his phantom ninja attackers. Minutes later, he is facing the DeVore Stadium crowd with his band mates. Their entrance is met with a cheer that hits the stage like a gale-force wind. "Hey, how y'all doin'?" Matthews asks, as if he's just happened upon a few friends. "We're the Dave Matthews Band, and we're from somewhere in Virginia."

With that, Matthews begins the staccato guitar figure that opens the song "Drive In Drive Out." For the next ninety minutes, the band unreels an unbroken skein of entwined sax and fiddle lines anchored by Lessard's bass, Beauford's rock-steady drumming, and Matthews' agile riffing. It's a tight but improvisational sound that seems to draw this crowd of ten thousand into an intimate circle, in which Matthews is the center, the "party guy," as he puts it later, the entertainer. Only by listening to the words of "Drive In Drive Out" would you guess at the singer's ambivalence. "I hear more than I like to," he says with a growl, "so I boil my head in a sense of humor / I laugh at what I cannot change. . . . When all that I want is so badly to be / By myself again."

2. THE RACIAL BONUS

Dave Matthews' speaking voice is, like his music, a weave of accents and influences, a laconic Southern drawl one moment, a precise British inflection the next. Matthews' image is equally tough to pigeonhole. His oversize T-shirts and baggy shorts say hip-hop; the necklaces (beads, shells, fossils) shout hippie; his close-cropped dark hair is too short to justify the description "brush cut," too long for a skinhead 'do.

Matthews' protean image, it turns out, fits him well. He was born January 9, 1967, in a suburb north of Johannesburg, South Africa, where both sides of the Matthews family have deep roots. When David was two years old, his family moved to the New York suburb of Yorktown Heights, where Matthews' father, a physicist, worked for IBM. For one year in 1974, the family lived in Cambridge, England, before returning to Yorktown Heights.

Matthews, who much of the time brims with the potential for a joke or a laugh, grows quieter when he speaks about his father. Matthews calls him, with obvious pride, "one of the granddaddies of the superconductor," and describes a loving and close-knit family that included, besides Jane, an older sister, Anne, and a brother, Peter. But the family peace was disrupted early in Matthews' life when his father, John, developed lung cancer. "We figure he might have got the disease from the radioactive material he handled," Matthews speculates. His father died when Matthews was ten.

This was not the only tragedy to visit the Matthews family. Shortly before the release of Dave's 1994 breakthrough album, *Under the Table and Dreaming*, Anne died, the victim of a tragic incident that also claimed her husband. Matthews asks that the details of their deaths not be published for the sake of her two children, ages six and nine, whom he and Jane are raising. Although Matthews has never spoken publicly about the tragedy, he dedicated

Under the Table to Anne and included in the CD's jewel box a photograph of himself and his nephew.

Matthews says that these experiences have inevitably colored his songs. "I think a lot of the reason my choruses conclude, 'Make the best of it' — or maybe, 'Be grateful, anyway' — is because the different tragedies that hit our family were also an *inspiration* for me," he says. "They make me want to live now, *desperately* — and to try to affect things positively."

Having returned to Johannesburg with his mother and siblings after his father's death ("For family connections and support," he says), Matthews was an indifferent high-school student whose antics earned him the lash at his British-modeled private school. His time was devoted not to schoolwork but to noodling on the guitar, drawing, and listening to music.

"It wasn't like the rest of us, however," says Jane about her brother's passion for music. "He listened very purpose-fully. He knew every word to every single Beatles album." He also fell in love with the indigenous African pop music and was especially drawn to the emphasis on drums. "I'm very into percussion," he says. "That's the way songwriting started for me: imitating different folk music that I found, drumming in African — or even Irish — music, and trying to move with the guitar rather than just strumming and singing a vocal line over it." Matthews prefers to play unplugged: "Electric guitar is not as much a percussive instrument as an acoustic is. I feel at home with an acoustic because it's hollow; it's got a drum quality."

To avoid South Africa's compulsory military service, Matthews returned alone to the United States, in January 1986. Although he had become a U.S. citizen at thirteen, he still considers South Africa his spiritual home. He says that his mother, a painter and a former architect, helped to shape his views on South Africa's segregationist apartheid regime. "She was involved in the Quaker church," Mat-thews says, "and was extremely aware of the political scene and very involved. It was an integrated church and often a place for a political voice . . . to protest the govern-ment. We were brought up, very aggressively, that bigotry and racism are *evil* things, and they stem from fear." During his later trips to the country, Matthews himself became active in protesting the crumbling apartheid regime: "I would go back and stay with friends, and political conversations were going on because they were all in college now. My friends would go to marches, and I would join them. It was a really interesting, vibrant time. The theater and music we'd go to see was always a voice of opposition. Going back there now and seeing the striving for freedom is such an amazing thing."

Matthews says that his later decision to enlist three black men for his band reflects, at least obliquely, his experience as a white person growing up in segregated South Africa. "I approached Carter, Leroi, and Boyd because they were the most fantastic musicians I'd ever seen," Matthews says. "But if the way our band looks onstage — two white guys and three black guys all playing together — sends out some kind of positive racial message, that's a bonus."

Upon his return to the United States at nineteen, Matthews lived in New York. He took a job as a temporary clerk at the IBM research center where his late father had worked. Matthews did not attend college and says that his mother and sisters were not pressuring him to firm up a plan in life. "We didn't really know what he was going to do," says Jane with a chuckle, "but I always assumed it would be something fabulous."

His extended family was not so understanding. He recalls how his South African uncles used to hassle him. Matthews slips into an Afrikanee accent: " 'David, you've got to have a *foundation*,' " Matthews laughs. "It got to the point where they'd ask me what I was going to do with my life," he says, "and I'd just say, '*Nothing*.' That'd really piss 'em off."

3. HOMEGROWN

Like such musical breeding grounds as Athens, Georgia, and Seattle, the compact city of Charlottesville, Virginia, is a congenial place for the nurturing of bands. A college town of some fifty thousand, it's a laid-back city of green lawns and tree-lined avenues — a place well stocked with music-hungry students and complete with hole-in-the-wall bars and restaurants where pickup bands spring up with all the fecundity of the local kudzu.

It was to this town that Matthews migrated, in 1986, along with his family. "Before I was born, my dad taught in Charlottesville," Matthews says, "which comes around to why we ended up there."

Though he bridles a little at the description, Matthews, who then sported a long ponytail, doesn't deny that he was something of a hippie. "I'd draw and wander, draw and wander," he says. "That's kinda all I wanted to do, was walk around. For me that was my college, just making enough money to get from one place to the next place, going back to South Africa, working temporary jobs." A brief stint at community college (where he excelled at philosophy but little else) didn't take. Vague plans to attend art school also evaporated. Meanwhile, he indulged his hearty appetite for transcendental and consciousness-raising substances. "A little dabbling in everything," he says with a grin. "Smoke a little something with somebody; drink a little something with someone else; whatever's going around. Whoever's there."

In 1987, he took a job as a bartender at a local Charlottesville bar called Miller's. The step hardly seemed one that would put him on the path to multiplatinum pop stardom. But Miller's was a hangout for local musicians who played gigs on the small stage at the front of the room. Among them were local music teacher and hornman John D'earth, who later put out a solo record and now plays in Bruce Hornsby's band; guitar virtuoso Tim Reynolds, whom Matthews later recruited to play second guitar on his band's albums; and a fine saxophone player named Leroi Moore — a saturnine, Buddha-shaped presence who sat across the bar from Matthews on many nights. "We used to get into these weird conversations about South Africa," says Moore. "We'd mostly get drunk and talk about how evil apartheid was. I had no idea that Dave was a musician. Not the slightest idea. He was just the bartender."

"My friends in South Africa knew I played guitar because I played all the time; that's all I did," Matthews says. "But no one in Charlottesville really knew." Gradually, he let his secret be known among his new friends at Miller's: "I sat in with Tim Reynolds a few times, and I played with John D'earth. I started to open up." One day, Matthews let everyone know that he'd also been writing songs. "It's weird," he says. "After a trip to South Africa, I cut off all my hair. Somehow that gave me the confidence to show people my stuff."

Miller's regular Ross Hoffman was among the first to spot Matthews's songwriting talents. "He was the guy who pushed me," Matthews says. "He was the one who'd say: 'No, don't smoke that pot. Finish that verse. Finish that song.' He was my musical mentor, the guy who said, 'You should do this.' "

When Matthews decided in late 1990 to put together a band, he approached his old customer Moore. Having joined the school band as a sax player in the seventh grade, Moore was by now one of the most respected and sought-after saxmen in Charlottesville. "He said he wanted to do this project," Moore recalls. "He wanted to make this demo. I said, 'Sure, I'm down with that.' "

At the same time, Matthews enlisted drummer Carter Beauford. Moore and Beauford had grown up as good friends on the same street in a middle-class black neighborhood in Charlottesville. In their postcollege years, they played together in bands. "We sort of grew up musically," says Beauford, a cheerful man of thirty-nine whose barrel chest and meaty arms suggest the athleticism and power of his drumming. By 1990, Beauford was playing in several bands — fusion, jazz, a swing orchestra — as well as appearing on Black Entertainment Television's BET on Jazz channel.

For a bass player, Matthews turned to D'earth, who recommended one of his music students, Stefan Lessard, a sixteen-year-old prodigy and the only other white musician in the band besides Matthews. Raised in a cash-strapped hippie family that spent its early years migrating between California and Rhode Island, Lessard settled near Charlottesville when his parents became followers of Swami Satchidananda, who established an ashram nearby. Lessard lived out of a trailer from the age of five until he was ten.

"A bunch of hippie potheads," Lessard says with genuine affection. "These are my childhood memories."

Violinist Boyd Tinsley, recruited just weeks after the band formed, grew up right around the corner from Moore and Beauford, and had studied history at the University of Virginia, where he jammed at the locally famous "hippie frat house" Sigma Nu. "Lot of brothers were doing Bob Dylan covers," says Tinsley. "Neil Young covers, Grateful Dead."

The Dave Matthews Band's first gigs were at a miniscule restaurant, Eastern Standard, down the street from Miller's. Within weeks, crowds were lined up outside the door, listening. The band then landed two weekly slots at Trax, a local nightclub, and Flood Zone, a club in nearby Richmond, Virginia. Now the audiences were more than nine hundred people a night — every night. The clubs' owner, Coran Capshaw, took immediate notice. He signed on as the band's manager and told it he wanted it to take a "different route" to success. A bearish man with a wiry head of graying hair, Capshaw is the veteran of some four hundred Dead shows. He detected in DMB something of the Dead's free spirit, but, more important, he saw an outpouring of passionate devotion from fans. Capshaw set out to grow the band on similar principles to the Dead's: through a grass-roots following built on the strength of Dave Matthews Band's live show. Record labels came sniffing, but Capshaw turned them down. Instead, he booked the band at every paying gig in the Southeast. "I doubt ICM, William Morris, or CAA would put them in a frat house," Capshaw says. "I did, and I put them in resorts and at beach clubs. . . . Lots of people have an ego problem with that."

Not Matthews and the boys. He calls the band's frat days "good work." But it was also an education for Matthews in American college life. "Boy, was *that* the educated class!" he laughs, then imitates the sound of someone vomiting. "The hurling, puking, tertiary education that every good American should have."

Soon, the band was playing two hundred nights a year, "three or four hours a night," Matthews says, "five or six nights a week." It often crossed paths with a band on a similar mission, Hootie and the Blowfish. "We have real respect for each other," Matthews says, "because we played on the same circuit. Our music is clearly different from theirs. But they are such nice guys, and they know the score. These are not guys who say to you, 'We are badass players.'"

The Dave Matthews Band *are* badass players, and word spread fast. "People were bootlegging our shows and sending tapes to their friends," Tinsley says. "People in Colorado knew about us [before DMB toured there]. We'd never been to Alabama before. We'd go to this place, and cars would be lined up down the road, and there'd be all these people going to this big club. We'd be sitting in our red van saying, 'Oh, my God!'"

By late 1993, Capshaw thought the band had built a big enough fan base to warrant signing a major-label deal. (The 1993 independent CD *Remember Two Things* had just been released and would go on to sell 366,000 copies.) The band's major-label debut, *Under the Table*, was released in 1994 and went to number 11 in the *Billboard* two hundred, driven by the hit "What Would You Say." The band deliberately didn't release a video of the song to MTV until more than two months after the record's release. "I wanted people to be a fan of the *band*," Capshaw says, "not the single." The band's label, RCA, went along with the unorthodox strategy. "We could have sold hundreds of thousands more copies of *Under the Table* if we'd wanted to go for the fast buck," says Bruce Flohr, the label's West Coast A&R man. "But the idea was to bring along the core base of fans, then add new ones."

The strategy seems to have worked. The band's sophomore RCA disc, *Crash*, released last April, debuted at number 2 in *Billboard* — robbed of number 1 by fewer than five thousand units by their old buddies Hootie and the Blowfish. But *Crash* ran afoul of some critics, who dissed the album as boomer-friendly rock. Matthews laughs off the critical backlash. "I don't really read reviews that much," he claims. "Really, really, really crappy ones — I like to read those. A guy from New York *Newsday* gave us the best insult. He said our success was somewhere between America's tolerance for Barney and France's love for Jerry Lewis.

I was like, 'At least we're up there.' I mean, that was right when Barney was *burnin'*, just tearing it up; and Jerry was still as big as he always will be in France." Meanwhile, the Dave Matthews Band sold out all thirty-five thousand tickets for its two-night stand in October at New York's Madison Square Garden; the first show sold out in three hours.

4. THE WILD DOGS

Late in the summer, Dave Matthews has returned home to Charlottesville to begin a rare three-week vacation. He will be flying off to St. Maarten in three days with his girlfriend of four years, Ashley.

He gets off the plane at 10:30 P.M. and an hour later is at his old stomping grounds, Miller's, where he joins his sister Jane and a few friends to watch Tim Reynolds play his regular Monday solo gig. Back in the room where Matthews tended bar for years, it seems, for a short while, as if he never left; then strangers begin to recognize him. He is approached by a string of well-wishers — including a dark-haired, black-clad girl who has been sitting along the wall, scribbling in a notebook. She slips him a piece of paper that includes a quote from Kierkegaard, her phone number, and the P.S.: "You *need* to see *Trainspotting*. . . . P.P.S.: With me." Later, out on the sidewalk, where he's weaving a bit from a string of tequila shots and some herbal stimulation shared with a friend, Matthews looks at the note, then says to Jane: "She definitely seems like an intense person with a strong mind." Then he adds with a laugh: "And a giant, illuminated sign over her head saying: DON'T COME ANY-WHERE NEAR THIS GIRL. DANGER!" With that, he wobbles off into the night to Jane's house, which is nearby; his final destination: her guest bed.

Last year, in an effort to stake out his own retreat, Matthews moved into a house in the secluded foothills of the Blue Ridge Mountains. The day after he arrives home, Matthews drives out there to check on the place. The house, a hermit's retreat, is at the end of a winding, narrow, dirt road and perched on the side of a waterfall. A converted flour mill built in 1750, it comes with sixty-five acres and a price tag of $500,000. He strolls around, inspecting the grounds and making plans. "I've got the design in my mind," he says, "for simple three-room cottages with lots of light, high ceilings, so that friends of mine, people who need a place, and artists, can come and live and just have a place that they can do their art and don't have to worry about money."

But Matthews is a long way from starting his artists' colony. During the past six months, he's spent perhaps two nights here. Packing boxes sit, still full, in the mill's vast, loftlike interior, and the place has a lonely aura. The few personal touches are a set of dusty museum display boxes containing the African cicadas that Matthews collects as a reminder of his homeland. The singer's CD collection, which has not yet been removed from its packing box, offers a catalog of Matthews' influences: Pink Floyd, Peter Gabriel, the Beatles, U2, INXS, Traffic — as well as a cache of South African and other international musicians: Vusi Mahlasela, Ali Farka Toure, Baaba Maal, Abdullah Ibrahim, Juluka.

Matthews walks over to a brocaded antique sofa that Jane recently bought for the place. He picks up a guitar that leans against the wall. Alone, far from the stage and the cheers of his fans, Matthews coaxes from his melodies a melancholy that he says was often the impulse behind the songs. Between playing soulful, slowed-down versions of his hits, he talks about the price he has paid for musical success. "Sometimes I get a little afraid that being on the road — and in this separated position — that I will lose sight of some of the things that were inspirational to me when I was bartending and meeting people," he says. Matthews also says he's beginning to feel the pressure to keep coming up with hits. He plays the riff to "What Would You Say" and looks up. "See, I look at that and think, 'Where did I come up with that lick?' I've also been plagued by the song 'Recently.' I want to write another lick like that. I don't know what I was thinking. I wish I could figure it out. When I get one, I think, '*Phew*, I got another one I like.'"

Matthews then plays the chords to "#41," a song from *Crash* that reflects the new album's darker mood. "Remember," he sings in a voice abraded by too many cigarettes, too many days on the road, "when I used to play for all the loneliness that nobody notices now."

Still fingering the guitar, Matthews reveals that this song was written around the time that he was undergoing a messy split over money with his mentor, Ross Hoffman. "I was thinking about where I come from, and why I wrote songs and what was my inspiration," Matthews says. "And how I was now in this situation where those things that I'd done, I so loved, had now suddenly become a source of incredible pain for me. Suddenly there's all this money and people pulling, asking, 'Where's *mine*?' The wild dogs come out. The innocence of just wanting to make music was kinda overshadowed by the dark things that come along with money and success." Then Matthews, catching himself, smiles — and like one of his songs, he turns the melancholic moment, searching for the upside. "So it's a song about looking back," he says, "but at the same time, a song that's still adamantly looking forward and going, 'But I'm still going to carry on, regardless.'"

ON THE ROAD ... 'W/ THE DMB, PART 1

BY JACK BAILEY*

C-VILLE *Weekly*, June 30–July 13, 1993

"Not everybody gets this band when they first hear it. I always thought it was good, and then at one show I was suddenly like, 'Hold on a second. This is important,'" says Mr. Coran Capshaw, manager and booking agent for Charlottesville's own Dave Matthews Band.

Of course, if you are already a part of the jumping, gyrating crowd that has been packing Trax nightclub each Tuesday night for the past two years, then you understand what Mr. Capshaw is getting at. They come at you from almost every conceivable direction — jazz, funk, country, blues, and straight-ahead rock and roll. You agree that the music of the Dave Matthews Band is important — at least on Tuesday night.

But what of these guys during the other six days of the week? Where do they go? What of their daily existence away from home? What's it like to be in a band on the cusp of the big time? Thanks to the kindness of Mr. Capshaw and the openness of the musicians and crew, you now get a behind-the-scenes look at the whirlwind life on the road of Charlottesville's dominant musical force.

* * *

The first lesson you learn is that the schedule is in a constant state of flux. You arrive at Trax on Wednesday at

---

* Reprinted by permission of C-VILLE/Portico Publications Ltd.

4 P.M. as per your instructions from road manager Fenton Williams only to find yourself waiting and waiting as loose ends are tied up and more loose ends are revealed. Instructions are yelled from office to office inside Mr. Capshaw's headquarters. "Did anybody get the oil changed in the van? No? Why not? It'll have to wait until tomorrow in Richmond. Did you call AAA for the trip ticket?" "It's being taken care of. Settle down." "Let's get this load-out started. Where's Bagby? Where's Boyd?" "Have you seen the notebook with the mailing list?" "I think it was in the box with the T-shirts. Can I borrow your lighter?"

The fifteen-passenger Ford Clubwagon and accompanying trailer are finally loaded and ready to roll just after 5 P.M., but the first ride is a short one to the home of bassist Stefan Lessard, where the heavy funk of Miles Davis's *Doo Bop* is spilling out of the windows and Stefan is dozing next to a book about the Oglala Sioux. After a brief tour of his backyard garden, during which he feeds you bits of different plants, it's back to the van for Richmond. Or so you think. First there is the requisite stop for gas, sodas, snacks ranging from chips and dip to Kraft macaroni and cheese, and the one constant throughout the journey — plenty of cigarettes. At last the tour is under way.

But wait a minute. The van seems conspicuously empty. In fact, the only band members present are Stefan and drummer Carter Beauford. The other passengers are the aforementioned road manager Fenton Williams, soundman Jeff Bagby, and merchandising coordinator Alex Stultz. The other band members — saxophonist Leroi Moore, fiddle player Boyd Tinsley, and guitarist/vocalist Dave Matthews — have been left to their own devices on this first leg of the journey.

The trip to Richmond's Flood Zone is uneventful. The tape deck is still working at this point, and the conversation revolves around the esoteric jazz which Stefan has brought along from home. Carter's wealth of knowledge about all things musical begins to reveal itself as he recognizes and names the various sidemen on the tape according to their different styles of play. "Hey Fonzy (Stefan's nickname), that sounds like Scofield. And that sounds like Bill

Frisell." "Yeah, it is. Turn this up. Carter, listen to this change right here. I think that's a really cool change." You start to realize that these guys hear a lot more in music than you do. They're really listening.

Arriving at the Flood Zone is much like arriving at home for these guys. Since it is also under the aegis of Mr. Capshaw's entertainment conglomerate and since the band plays here weekly to crowds numbering seven hundred or better, the Flood Zone is a sort of home on the road for them.

But there's no time to waste. The load-in begins almost as soon as the van stops. Everybody works. Everybody. As the equipment is wheeled and carried into the club, the genuinely friendly Carter strikes up conversations with two natural gas workers who are parked nearby. These men in their mid-forties politely decline his invitation to the show but are charmed by his easy-going nature and are soon laughing along with him like they are old friends.

Boyd arrives a few moments later in the company of Mr. Capshaw and a young lady named Lisa. He gets involved immediately setting up his equipment and preparing for soundcheck. Dave arrives riding a wave of manic high energy, encouraging everyone in sight to enjoy some candies from his tin of Altoids. He does this with a high-voltage flair of ceremonial grace that includes a sweeping bow at the waist and elicits laughter from everyone present.

"HEY HEY, HO HO, CHECK ONE TWO, CHECK TWO TWO TWO, HEEEYYY, HO, CH CH, CLUCK, AAHHYUH!" Bagby is checking the mikes and his voice echoes through the cavernous interior of the Flood Zone. You will realize as this journey continues that the twenty-year-old Bagby is an integral part of this band and is easily as important as anyone onstage. His conversation is peppered with sound-manspeak like "dB," "4K," and "constructive phasing" which belies the empirical intelligence hidden behind his profanely wry attitude.

You go around the corner to Bottoms Up Pizza for dinner with Fenton and Mr. Capshaw to try to get a handle on what the movers and shakers behind this band are all about. Mr. Capshaw, who looks a helluva lot like Bob Dylan doing an ad for L.L. Bean, regards Fenton as "like my little brother," and their casual, sarcasting baiting of one another underscores the closeness of their relationship. When a reference to Kenneth Brannagh's film adaptation of Shakespeare's *Much Ado About Nothing* flies past Fenton without his understanding, Mr. Capshaw intercedes in his defense saying, "He's making history, not reading it." Behind his jovial tone, you get a sense of how seriously these men believe in the future of the Dave Matthews Band phenomenon.

Back to the offices of the Flood Zone and you meet the band's lawyer, Christopher Sabbec. A University of Georgia law graduate employed in the Richmond area by McGuire, Woods, Battle, and Boothe, Chris is the first lawyer at this firm to be involved in entertainment law. He admits that having the Dave Matthews Band as a client is quite a coup for him. He speaks fondly of his mentor Bertis Downs — a Georgia law professor and also attorney for R.E.M. — who helped him realize that he could, in fact, combine his love of music with his career as a lawyer, and he relates the chance encounter at the Van Riper's Music Festival where he was asked to record the band's performance on the D.A.T. equipment he had set up to record the now defunct Charlottesville-based band Indecision. He agreed, and thus the genesis of a partnership came to life. His enthusiasm for the music is contagious as he projects the brightest possible future for the band.

Dave wanders in and flops into a chair to work out the songs for tonight's first set. "I usually do the set list, but mostly that's because no one else does. It's not a question of creative control," he responds to your queries on the subject. He mumbles, "I'm obsessed, he's obsessed" (pointing at everyone in general and no one in particular), "and you're obsessed, we're all obsessed, we can't help it." And those maniac eyes burn, and that devilish smile flashes out of nowhere, and you have to laugh with him because you get the feeling he's right.

At 11:10 P.M., after deciding it's absurd to wait any longer, the band takes the stage without Boyd because he has not returned from a last-minute trip to People's drugstore. They rip into their first tune amidst wailings of "Booyyd! Where's Boooyyyydd?" from the Richmond faithful.

Boyd wanders casually onto the stage around 11:20, fiddle in hand, and joins the chorus of the second tune, "Granny," as the crowd erupts with applause and cheers. He responds with a wave and a huge, toothy smile and makes up for his tardiness by bringing out the good stuff, including a serious, foot-stomping, hoe-down romp through his solo on "Recently."

The break between sets involves much wandering through the labyrinthine backstage area with its myriad of confusingly interconnected halls and stairways until you find yourself back in the dressing room, from which David has just emerged and is headed back downstairs, singsonging over his shoulder, "Carter, I'm onstage, baby!" Carter sings right back to him, "Yeah, I'm with you, brother!"

The second set goes off without a hitch: Dave singing as the dense swarm of females directly in front of the stage swoons and sways with him; Boyd bowing his fiddle for all he's worth; Leroi standing motionless back in the shadows behind dark glasses, only stepping into the light to take a solo or add his vocal; Carter pumping rhythm out of his drums with both arms and legs; and through it all Stefan providing the funkiest of underpinnings over which all of their improvisations can take place.

Most of the load-out in Richmond is accomplished by Bagby and Alex, and this provdes to be true throughout most of the week. Because they do it most often, they know the pack best. So at the different venues along the way, while the entire band is generally helpful and involved in carrying the different cases and racks to the trailer, it is undeniably Bagby who orchestrates this cumbersome nightly event.

After the 11 A.M. wake-up call from the front desk and further wake-up calls provided by Fenton and much milling around in the lobby and many aimlessly smoked, pre-breakfast cigarettes, the van finally takes to the highway a little after 2 P.M., headed for a club called Ziggy's in Winston-Salem, North Carolina.

Life in the van can get more than a little tiresome. According to Bagby, "There's nothing to do on the van except eat, sleep, and smoke." Coupling this apothegm of truth with the fact that seven of nine passengers are smokers, it's not too surprising that the atmosphere in this vehicle, enhanced by a Mystic juice bottle strapped to the shoulder harness with duct tape as a MacGyveresque ashtray, gets more and more stale as the days drag on.

On this first major day of travel, replete with hangovers from the long night before, the road-hardiness of these men comes through as the conversation pinballs from one topic to the next with nary a segue in between. The only sustained subject for discussion is the previous night's performance which is playing on the tape deck. (Bagby tapes most of the shows through the soundboard.)

As the show plays through, they complement each other on licks they particularly enjoyed or on particularly innovative changes. Dave tells Stefan, "You should play on this Intro." "I always lose you guys on that. I never know how many times you're going through it." "Yeah, Fonzy, you should play on that. It's just four times through." They iron this out, and the conversation spins off in another direction as Bagby begins a sardonic soliloquy plotting the slow torture of an incompetent monitor assistant from a club on last week's tour schedule. His tale is winding, technical, and tangential but soon has everyone laughing — more at his cocksure attitude than from a spirit of complicity. Between blasts of his high-pitched machine-gun cackle, Dave manages to ask, "Why is this funny? I don't even know what you're talking about. What the hell does 'thermal lock' mean?"

* * *

"Carter, do you have any Alka-Seltzer?" whines Dave from the backseat.

"I've just got the regular kind. I don't have what you need."

"The regular kind is what I want. Can I have some? I think I'm dying back here."

As the Alka-Seltzer is passed through the van, Dave begins singing joyfully from the backseat, "I love Carter! I love Carter! Carter is my Jesus!"

You're thinking, "This guy Dave is completely crackers! Carter is my *Jesus*? Get a grip on yourself, man." But suddenly this outburst reveals that one truth you've been trying to put your finger on since yesterday. These guys really do love each other, that's how they do it. That's how they sleep three to a seat in the van with arms and legs splayed in every direction — something your family could never accomplish on its vacations because your sister was such a brat. That's how they survive the goading sarcasm directed at each other throughout the long days and nights on the road. That's how they can laugh at their own persistently puerile jokes about women who are either "ugly, gorilla-faced mopotamusses" or "phat." (You have learned at this point that despite the phonetic similarity, "phat" does not mean "fat.") It is instead the opposite of "ugly, gorilla-faced mopotamus." The meaning of which is obvious to all but the thickest of readers. But, you are digressing. Back to the love thing.) They love each other and they love the music.

"The music is why I do this," says Carter over double bourbons after one show. "I love the music and everything about being in the music business. I've been playing since I was three years old, and I can't imagine doing anything else." In fact, Carter has done something else. He was an elementary and high school history teacher for twelve years in school districts in Albemarle County, Winchester, and Winston-Salem, North Carolina. He says he sometimes misses teaching because so much of what he does now involves nonverbal expression and silly banter with fans, and he occasionally yearns for a plain, old, intelligent conversation. There is no way of knowing what sort of scholars came and went through the doors of Carter Beauford's classroom, but only a few moments with him is enough to safely assume that they went away a lot hipper than they came in.

When Carter talks about the things he loves, he practically glows. Mention his daughter, and the trademark smile grows wider than you've ever seen it, and he gushes about her and their upcoming trip to the beach. "She is my everything!" he says and pronounces her name slowly, "Breanna . . . Simone . . . Beauford," savoring each word as if he could somehow conjure her out of thin air.

When he talks about music (and he can do so forever), the words seem to come from a mystical place inside himself. He talks about not counting time but "feeling the one" and improvising over and around it while always "holding onto the one." "It's a hard thing to learn or explain. You have to be able to feel it inside. It's like having an internal metronome," he says. He laughingly recalls the band's early days and how much tighter they have become as a unit. "Dave used to be into this thing of dropping beats because he wasn't used to playing with a group. Sometimes he'd even drop whole measures, and we'd have to try to get back to the one. Then he'd realize what had happened and try to adjust, and we'd be all over the place."

While he stresses that they are constantly trying to play better, Carter has nothing but praise for his fellow bandmates. He is emphatic about including Bagby as a band member, saying how much they have learned from him about sound. "His board is like an instrument that he plays. We wouldn't sound half as good without Bagby."

* * *

The van pulls into Winston-Salem, North Carolina, in the late afternoon, backs up to the door of Ziggy's, a nightclub near the campus of Wake Forest University, and it's time for another load-in. After spending the day in the van, everybody gets right to work hauling cases and lifting amps. Bagby begins another cryptic conversation about EQ bypasses and such with the house soundman and soon this open-air pavilion is filled with his bellowing cadence, "CHECK ONE TWO, HEY HEY HO HO, CHECK TWO TWO TWO."

Bagby tells you that he got this job by being in the right place at the right time. When the band's former soundman took a month off to get married, Bagby, who had been working monitors, was asked to fill in for a while. A while turned out to be a permanent arrangement as he and the band members got along well, and they liked the sound he mixed. He tells you that he learned what to do behind all those knobs "mostly by paying attention." This self-effacing commentary strikes you as a little odd coming from someone who admits to sleeping and playing hackysack throughout most of his formal schooling. "No, school just wasn't too happening for me," he laughs.

Everyone is out of cigarettes. Everyone except Alex that is. This twenty-year-old University of Richmond student is like some kind of repository of cigarettes. He doesn't smoke any more or any less than anyone else on the road, but he always seems to have plenty to share. Alex, whose speech pattern incorporates the word "yo" the way other people pause for a breath between phrases, says that traveling with this band is like a dream job for him. "My parents think this is the most ridiculous job ever, yo, but I've always been into music, and I've always wanted to do something like this. I don't want to be onstage or anything, but I really like the whole behind-the-scenes aspect of it, yo," he says. Watching him dance and sell shirts night after night proves him truthful.

Some Kentucky Fried Chicken is consumed just before soundcheck by everyone except Boyd who seems to be silently rethinking his decision to become a vegetarian. He sticks to his guns, however, and after a successful run-through of *One Sweet World*, you all head for the Comfort Inn.

During the hour or so while people are showering and changing clothes, you find Boyd sprawled in front of the television watching the news. As the trip continues you notice that Boyd, with a degree in history from UVA, is something of a political buff and buys and reads newspapers at every stop along the way.

He talks about his life as a musician, on the road all the time, and says he misses his wife a great deal, but he says, "This is what I do. I'm a musician, you know. Touring is part of it. Sure it can be a grind at times, but ideally that grind disappears when we hit the stage, because the music is what it's all about."

Boyd says that he hopes to contribute more to the band in the future in terms of songwriting. *True Reflection*, a composition of Boyd's which is performed regularly by the band, is, he says, "a very personal song that kind of just came out of me, you know." Its straightforward message is a "nice counterpoint to Dave's songs which are sometimes a little more difficult to figure out," he says.

Soon it's time to pile back into the van for the short ride to Ziggy's. You all roll in and go to the somewhat cramped dressing room where the required cooler of icy Budweiser is waiting along with several bottles of Evian Spring Water, virtually all of which is consumed during the course of the show. There is not much intake of alcohol before and during the show — maybe a few beers here and there, but they are no more likely to be rip-snorting drunk onstage than you are to be staggering around the office in the middle of the day.

No set list has been put together tonight, so they simply decide as a group which two songs to play first and take the stage, leaving the remaining songs to be determined through the course of the show.

The band has played here before and has something of a following in this Carolina town. The crowd of 503 knows the music well and swings and sings as much as any crowd at Trax or the Flood Zone. Ziggy's is basically the only game in town for live music around here since Baity's Backstreet — the hair-and-leather club up the street — burned under auspicious circumstances. (Rumor has it that by a freak coincidence the big-screen TV was removed the same night the club went up in smoke. Lucky.) But Ziggy's patrons don't seem to miss it and are having a ball in the cool night air.

During the break you return to the dressing room where the band members are relaxing and kicking around ideas for tunes to open the second set. Apparently the need for a set list is not critical tonight as they prepare to go on a second time without one. A couple of friends drop in backstage to say hello to Dave and the boys. One of these guys fires up a joint and offers it around, but his offering is not met with any great enthusiasm from the band.

Wait just a doggone second! This is rock-and-roll. Everybody's supposed to be whacked out of his skull the whole time, right?!? What's going on here?

"This is not a very drug-oriented band," says Fenton. "Until we get paid and loaded-out, I've got work to do. I usually don't even drink until the end of the night."

Carter's response is similar to Fenton's. "Some people will tell you they play better when they're high," he says, "but I'm telling you, nobody plays better high. I'm not knocking it or anything; people can do what they want, but you've gotta have it together onstage. You shouldn't do it on the job."

Boyd echoes Carter's sentiments on drug use, saying, "I can't imagine trying to play stoned. I've got to be in control of the little bit of mental capacity I've got. Without that, I'd be lost up there."

After the show, while the band is packing up, Fenton takes care of the financial dealings wiith the Ziggy's management who are enthusiastic about tonight's crowd and want to know when they can book the next gig. They are instructed by Fenton to Call Mr. Capshaw in Charlottesville. Certainly something can be arranged.

The band members safely back at the hotel, a trek across the highway to the International House of Pancakes is suggested and undertaken. So begins the parade of breakfast food across your palate which will continue for the remainder of the trip. It seems like breakfast is the only meal these guys take seriously, and when they are not eating microwaveable delights from the Circle K, they can be found at the nearest I.H.O.P. or Waffle House. The latter is the preferred venue for breakfast fare.

Friday, after brunch at you-know-where and the oil-change that was put off until Richmond and a stop at a music store (where Bagby is lauded by the owners for a superior job with the PA at Ziggy's), the van rolls onward to Mug-Shots, a college bar in Greenville, North Carolina. The tiny room is awkwardly arranged, and the stage backs up to a plate glass storefront. The difficulties this space provides lead to a late soundcheck, which allows very little time for a shower and a change at the hotel.

David has been getting more excited as each passing day brings him closer to a rendezvous with his girlfriend, Ashley Harper, in Athens, Georgia. He foregoes his opportunity for a shower, preferring instead to call every possible number where Ashley might be and leave very polite messages on several different answering machines announcing his arrival in Athens and dictating instructions on where she can reach him.

"I'm insane for this woman!" he tells you while stabbing at the buttons on the bedside telephone.

Back at Mug-Shots, they launch into the set list Dave has prepared on the drive over. The crowd is small but enthusiastic and has grown to the room's capacity before the end of the first set. During the break, a quick survey of some listeners reveals how this music is affecting people up and down the East Coast. Lauren Wooten remembers hearing them first while working at the Atlantis in Nags Head. "We were all like, 'Yeah, yeah, Dave Matthews, big whoop' and then we just got slammed. It was one of the busiest nights I can remember in that place."

Laurie Oliphant, an East Carolina University student, said she had heard they were good and decided to see for herself. Although she described herself as "not fanatical about music," she said she really likes the band. "That saxophone has such a romantic sound. Romance and lust are the same thing, right? I really like the violin, too," she added. You wonder if Laurie would like to come back to the hotel to see your etchings.

JACK BAILEY/PORTICO PUBLICATIONS LTD.

PART 2

Saturday is a travel day with a long trip to Athens, Georgia, ahead. You're lurching along I-85 with Leroi at the wheel. The tape deck has eaten one tape, and no one dares feed it another. Easy listening and oldies fill your ears along with the measured tones of Linda Wertheimer and the breathy phrasings of Garrison Keillor at the low end of the dial. Moods pick up considerably as you near Athens, and Carter finds a station playing the likes of Aretha Franklin, Clarence Carter, the Reverend Al Green, and Stevie Wonder. Everybody is really grooving on this stuff, and Bagby bemoans the dearth of good radio stations in Charlottesville.

The prospect of a night off in Athens pleases everyone, and almost immediately upon arrival at the hotel, plans are made for a night out. Ashley and some friends from Atlanta have arrived, and while her friends join you and the rest of the band for drinks, Dave and Ashley stay behind because according to Dave, "We have an important matter to discuss."

It turns out to be a quiet evening in Athens because UGA summer school does not start until Monday, but the drinks are tall and strong, and the chance to relax in the elegant, high-ceilinged salon of City Bar is relished.

Back at the hotel after last call, the mood is lighthearted and a joint is passed around among the Atlanta contingent. Once again, drugs don't seem to be a dominant theme on the road for the band members, coming primarily from friends and fans along the way. This ain't no traveling medicine show.

Sunday's gig is an afternoon debutante party in Lawrenceville, Georgia, for UVA student Laurin Morgan. Her parents have pulled out all the stops for their adored deb, and under the huge yellow-and-white tent you find gaming tables for craps, blackjack, and roulette as well as a plexiglass cash-grab booth with a couple of hundred bucks in U.S. greenbacks flying around inside. Behind the tennis courts is a tethered hot-air balloon giving rides to the revelers. Up the hill under yet another party tent, a barbecue and corn-on-the-cob feast has been prepared for your dining pleasure. No alcohol is being served by the hosts; however, allowing for the resourcefulness of college students, the aroma of cheap bourbon floats on the air around some people the way Charlie Brown's buddy Pigpen trails dirt and grime.

Seriously Sound, the contracted production company, has subcontracted this assignment to a lesser organization, and Bagby is fuming with frustration as the mikes feed back, and he is called on to solve problems which he feels should not even be happening. True to form, though, he works it all out in the end, and the show isn't delayed more than a few minutes.

The crowd is initially more interested in the opportunity to gamble than they are in dancing. Dave asks if anyone "would like to use this area in front of the stage for anything other than dancing, please feel free to do so since no one is using it for dancing." He rambles on, "Bring your milling and mingling up a little closer to the stage because

Dave plays roadie

JACK BAILEY/PORTICO PUBLICATIONS LTD.

when you're all back there we get paranoid that we smell bad, which we probably do, but come down here anyway and use this area for whatever you like as long as it's not dancing." He raises one arm, sniffs his armpit and says, "It's not that bad. Really." The crowd responds to his gentle jesting, and soon the floor is filled with people singing and dancing.

During the break between sets, you ask some of the non-UVA students what they think about this band. Smith Watkins, a UGA coed studying international business who likes to doodle in her spare time, said she is drawn by "the unique sound of Dave's voice and the violin." She went on to say that Dave Matthews Band is something special in Athens. "The bands around here all sort of blend together after a while," she said. "But Dave is really popular here — at least among my friends."

Smith's boyfriend, Chris Lanter, a good-natured behemoth from Atlanta, said Dave and the rest are popular because "they're all such great musicians and it shows in their style of play. The combination of different instruments — like the sax and the violin — really sets them apart too."

Perhaps the most intelligent commentary on the band's ever-burgeoning popularity came from Chris's sister Catherine, who agreed with her brother about their talent as musicians but focused on their improvisational skill as the key to their success. "They play around with the music so that the songs are varied and fresh each time you hear them."

The show is over by 8:30 P.M., and you sprawl on the grass next to the van to catch the end of game 6 between the Bulls and the Suns. David leaves for Atlanta with Ashley and some friends, promising to return to Athens tomorrow in time for the load-in at the Georgia Theater. Mr. and Mrs. Morgan thank everyone profusely for a job well done and attribute the strong turnout in spite of the absence of alcohol to the presence of the Dave Matthews Band. "Usually if you don't serve alcohol at these parties a lot of people just won't show up, but thanks to y'all everybody came and had a great time. Thank y'all so much for playing," she said.

The van motors back to Athens with much excitement over Paxson's three-pointer to win it all for the Bulls and the prospect of what is effectively another night off in Athens. The excitement is somewhat short-lived as you learn that the bars stop serving at midnight on Sundays in this Georgia town, but you go out anyway and make the best of it, knocking back a couple of adult beverages with Carter, Leroi, and Fenton.

Returning to the hotel, you find Stefan playing guitar in his room. Carter joins him with another guitar, and they jam through some Latin music which Stefan has been fooling around with at home in his free time.

Carter is enthused by what he hears and encourages him to add this to the band's repertoire. "Fonz, you've got the kickin' Latin chords, man. You've got to bring your stuff out." Stefan says he is going to keep this stuff to himself for a while.

Stefan is something of an enigma, and with his penchant for horticulture and his obviously monogamous devotion to his girlfriend Josie, with whom he has lived for about a year, you think that this earthy youth might be better suited to a more domestic existence rather than the nomadic musician's life which he leads. He attended the Tandem School in Charlottesville, but did not finish because, he says, "I have a really tough time turning down gigs, and it got to a point where we were playing so much that I couldn't go to class."

He was accepted into the music program at VCU for jazz performance after getting his G.E.D., but he only attended for about ten days because he wanted to keep playing with the Dave Matthews Band. Carter insists that since Stefan's emphasis at VCU was to be on performance, he is getting a better education by going on the road with the band. "When I first met Fonz," recalls Carter, "he was like fifteen or sixteen and playing upright bass better than a lot of older cats I know who'd been playing longer than he's been alive."

Strong praise coming from a man who is the house drummer on Black Entertainment Television's jazz programming and has sat in with musicians too numerous to mention here.

Does Stefan agree with Carter about his education on the road? "Sometimes . . . sometimes," he says thoughtfully. "I like taking classes and learning new things, and if we get to a point where we're not touring all the time I'm sure I'll go back to school. But I do get a lot out of working with the guys in this band."

Monday night's show is at the Georgia Theater in Athens so without the need for travel you have the opportunity for some wandering through the town. After lunch at the Grill, a twenty-four-hour diner that for some inexcusable reason doesn't serve breakfast after 11:00 A.M. (Go figure!), you stroll with Carter, Bagby, and Alex over to a hip little clothing and jewelry store called Spiral, where Fonz has already purchased gifts for Josie. Alex and Bagby purchase a few items and depart to feed the parking meter and to visit the record store a few doors down. Later you will find them on the sidewalk in front of Spiral hacking the sack.

In the meantime Carter is charming both clerk and customers alike and scribbling down names for inclusion on the guest list, while also buying enough incense to last a lifetime and choosing gifts for a friend back home.

It's getting late and it's time to go hitch up the trailer for yet another load-in. The set-up and a souncheck are underway inside the huge, old theater space minus its first twenty rows of seats which have been removed to create a dance floor of sorts in front of the stage. Two mammoth pillars of speakers abutt the stage on either side, and you can't wait to hear Bagby crank those babies up.

The house soundman recalls hearing the band play once before and is not sure, but "Didn't you guys used to have a piano player? What happened to that guy?"

He's right. Peter Griesar did play piano in this band. Good question soundman! What happened to Peter?

According to Carter (and his statements are confirmed by the others as you ask them separately during the remainder of the journey), "Peter is a much more domestic person and didn't enjoy traveling so much. So he left the band."

You think back to the Flood Zone and remember that Dave drove himself to Richmond in Peter's car, so you figure there's no more to it than that. But you make a mental note to stop by Miller's, where Peter works, when you return to Charlottesville just to see if he has anything to add. Peter is taken aback by your question, coming as it does out of nowhere. His somewhat cryptic response is, "Rather than withhold information from you, I'd rather not answer the question. It would take too long to explain." When you tell him what the band's consensus is — that he preferred not to travel so much — he says, "Yeah, that's pretty much it. That just wasn't what I felt like I should be doing at that time." (Hmm . . . curious.)

There is time before the show for a real dinner — the only sit-down-and-be-served-in-a-restaurant meal that is not breakfast. The cuisine is Italian and everybody carbo-loads on salads and pasta. Everyone is present except Boyd, who ate earlier and walked back to the hotel, and Leroi, who went to find a liquor store and will be waiting at the hotel when the rest of you return from dinner.

Backstage at Georgia Theatre the band is working out a set list as people begin filling in. A club employee urges the band to take the stage and get started so folks will hear the music outside and come in. His friendly manner fails to mask his doubts about their ability to draw a crowd. This same gentleman will be more than a little embarassed and surprised when he has to open the balcony to accomodate the 694 payers who come to hear the show. He should have listened to Smith. She said they were popular among her friends, but she never said she had so many. Who knew?

This music-town crowd loves what they hear. Roberta Henderson, UGA Tri-Delt sorority girl says that, even in a town that boasts roughly three hundred bands, "This band is my favorite. I saw them when they played at Chi Phi, and I danced 'til five in the morning. Are you really gonna print that?" Don't worry, Roberta, your mama won't read this. "The music is so easy to move to," she continues, "it's almost like *it* moves *me*. And it's really easy to relate to the songs. Like *Seek Up On Emotion* — love that one especially."

You expect tonight to be pretty low key after the show, considering the return trip to Charlottesville slated for tomorrow, but you're wrong. You're all up until close to dawn drinking and talking about musicianship.

Leroi, who has until now been reluctant to talk to you, feels comfortable enough with your presence at this point to share some of what he feels as a musician. He says he wants to be both "an artist and a craftsman" with his horn. "I want to be like a carpenter who can build the Taj Mahal or an outhouse, and if they're both sound and solid then one is as good as the other," he says. He tells you of the frustration he feels when he thinks people aren't listening and don't fully appreciate the music, and he tells you how there are always those who surprise him when they compliment specific changes within a performance and seem to really get it.

9:00 A.M. comes pretty quickly and there's no time for that extra few minutes of sleep. Leroi quite literally bounces Carter out of bed when he rushes into the room and takes flight like some kind of kamikaze wake-up call. You grab your bag in a daze and sleepwalk to the van, cursing whoever replaced your tongue with the floor from a Mexican prison during the night. You say a quick prayer that Fenton is awake enough to drive and follow it with a prayer of thanks that Leroi is not behind the wheel. And you go right back to sleep.

You wake up enough to inhale a burger and some fries, and then you sleep again until crossing the Virginia-Carolina state line. Not far from home.

So what did you learn about David? What makes this guy tick? You think back over the week and realize that with Dave what you see is what you get. He doesn't act like a guy whose name is attached to a band that could cross the threshold of stardom any day now. He acts like a person and responds best to people who treat him like one. He likes the lithe and willowy Ashley because "she has no agenda" and says he gets sick of the "psycho-betties who want to know what I think about while I'm peeing." You ask him why he does what he does and he responds in his characteristic offhand manner, "Because it's better than bartending."

Home again at Trax, Fenton heads for Mr. Capshaw's office with briefcase in hand for the weekly debriefing. They have been in touch by telephone a few times during the week, but they sort through the details face to face anyway. The band is watching *Beavis and Butthead* while Bagby readies for soundcheck and Alex assembles his mobile T-shirt shop.

You say goodbye to everyone individually while waiting for your ride home even though you will be in attendance for tonight's performance.

Tuesday's turnout is a solid six hundred plus crowd of hometown devotees who seem oblivious to the fact that this thing is catching on out on the road.

Before falling asleep for the night, you think about what lies ahead for the Dave Matthews Band. Richmond again tomorrow, New York after that, our nation's capitol for the weekend, studio work for the CD, and the H.O.R.D.E. shows in August. You sort of want to keep going with them. You remember all the timekilling antics in the van: Bagby's pneumatic launching of a key ring from his navel, seeing who can get their teeth around a roll of duct tape, and the impromptu wrestling matches of which Fenton always seem to be the target.

As you fade from consciousness, one thought muscles its way to the foreground of your mind — Steve Perry was right! The road really *ain't* no place to raise a family!

WORKS CONSULTED

Abraham, Andrew. "Picks and Pans: *Crash* — Dave Matthews Band." *People* 6 May 1996: 25.

"Albermarle Says Man Found Dead at Pool Took Own Life." *Daily Progress* [Charlottesville, VA] 24 Sept. 1996.

Ali, Lorraine. "Sound and Vision Pop Music: Grunge-Free Work from the Tongue-in-Cheek Pilots; Dave Matthews Band Also Has Its Cheeks Stuffed in a Cheesy Video with a Theme Heavy on Gluttony." *Los Angeles Times* 5 May 1996, home ed.: 61.

Allan, Marc. "Herky-Jerky Quippy Quirky: Having His Own Way with Life's Rhythms and Sounds Animates Dave Matthews' Hot Selling Songs and Performing Style." *Indianapolis Star* 18 June 1996, city final ed.: D1.

____ . "The Dave Matthews Band Has Music World's Attention." *Montgomery Advisor* 5 Sept. 1996: 5C.

"American Music Awards." *Washington Post* 26 Jan. 1997, final ed.: Y4.

Appleford, Steve. "H.O.R.D.E. Cuts a Wider Groove; Pop Music: Dynamic Sets in by Lenny Kravitz, the Dave Matthews Band, and, Especially, Rickie Lee Jones, Give the Alterna-Festival a Rush of New Energy." *Los Angeles Times* 29 July 1996, home ed.: 1.

"Arts Watch." *C-VILLE Weekly* [Charlottesville, VA] 10–24 Aug. 1994: 6.

"Arts Watch: Grammy Thanks in Part to D.M.B.'s 'Sixth' Member." *C-VILLE Weekly* [Charlottesville, VA] 25–31 Mar. 1997.

Athayde, John M.P. E-mail to the author. 30 July 1997.

____ . Telephone interview. 5 Aug. 1997.

Atkins, Ace. "The Bottom Line." *C-VILLE Weekly* [Charlottesville, VA] 23 Oct. 1993: 5.

____ . "Dear Dear Charlottesville: Niggling Questions Answered about the New Local Music CD." *C-VILLE Weekly* [Charlottesville, VA] 18–24 July 1995: 34.

Atwood, Brett. "Video Nets, Ticketmaster Fight Aids: Lifebeat Show Raises $500,000 for Cause." *Billboard* 7 Oct. 1995.

Augusto, Troy. "Dave Matthews Band." *Daily Variety* [Hollywood] 15 Dec. 1994.

Bailey, Jack. "On the Road . . . 'w/the DMB, part 1." C-VILLE *Weekly* [Charlottesville, VA] 30 June–13 July 1993: 7–9.

____ . "On the Road . . . 'w/the DMB, part 2." C-VILLE *Weekly* [Charlottesville, VA] 14–27 July 1993: 7–8.

"Beatles Rank Number One on the Infoseek Internet Band Chart: Infoseek Announces Today's Hottest Musical Bands." *Business Wire* 26 Feb. 1996.

Becker, Lawrence D. "Local Band Begins Rock'n'Roll Ascent." *Observer* [Charlottesville, VA] Summer 1992, Our Town sec.: 88+.

____ . "Reynolds Plays with Rare Mix of 'Chops and Heart.'" *Observer* [Charlottesville, VA] 11 Nov. 1993, Charlottesville This Week sec.: 10.

Beckerman, Jim. "Wish We Were Dead." *Record* [Bergen, NJ] 21 Oct. 1996: Y1.

Beeler, Tony. "Dave Matthews Prank Fools Hopeful Students." *Cavalier Daily* [Charlottesville, VA] 2 Apr. 1996: 1.

Bellafante, Ginia. "Fame, We Wholeheartedly Embrace You." *Time* 30 Jan. 1995: 91.

Benedetti, Winda. "Band on a Run; Dave Matthews Band Brings Phenomenal Sound to the Gorge Friday." *Spokesman-Review* [Spokane] 10 July 1997, Spokane ed.: D1.

Bessman, Jim. "Dave Matthews Back with a Bang: RCA's 'Crash' Follows Still-Strong Label Bow." *Billboard* 23 Mar. 1996.

"Best of '96: Lyle Lovett, Dave Matthews Band." *Wisconsin State Journal* 2 Jan. 1997: 14.

"Best-Selling Records of 1996." *Billboard* 18 Jan. 1997.

Blackwell, Mary Alice. "Backstage: Boyd Tinsley Tries Fiddling to Fame." *Daily Progress* [Charlottesville, VA] 3 Jan. 1992.

____ . "Dave Matthews Band Is No Longer 'Dreaming.'" *Daily Progress* [Charlottesville, VA] 23 Sept. 1994: 3+.

____ . "DMB's Affection for Fans No Joke." *Daily Progress* [Charlottesville, VA] 5 Apr. 1996.

____ . "DMB Tunes Used for Crowd Control." *Daily Progress* [Charlottesville, VA] 23 Dec. 1994.

____ . "New Release by the Dave Matthews Band Hits the Charts in a Big Way." *Daily Progress* [Charlottesville, VA] 7 Oct. 1994: 3, 19.

____ . "'Two Things' to Put Smile on DMB Fans." *Daily Progress* [Charlottesville, VA] 5 Nov. 1993.

Bledsoe, Wayne. "Rockin' on Violin; Tinsley Learned to Merge the Music with the Instrument." *Knoxville News-Sentinel* 8 Sept. 1996: T4.

Booth, Philip. "Band Thrives on Improvisation: Musicians from Jazz and Classical Backgrounds Merge Influences with Rock for Chart-Topping Success." *Tampa Tribune* 30 Aug. 1996, final ed.: 20.

Borzillo, Carrie. "Lonestar Enjoying Shining Success: Grass-Roots Marketing Benefitting BNA Act." *Billboard* 27 Apr. 1997.

____ . "MTV, Radio Wake to Rusted Root: Mercury Act Rewarded for Nonstop Touring." *Billboard* 29 July 1995.

Bothner, David W. "Fans or Felons? The Tape-Wielding Groupies Trade Tunes for Love, Not Money." *Buffalo News* 8 Dec. 1996: 1F.

Brace, Eric. "Eddie from Ohio: Habit-Forming." *Washington Post* 8 Aug. 1997: N10.

Brophy, Steven M. "Matthews Concert: Getting There Isn't Half the Fun." *Salt Lake Tribune* 5 July 1997: B5.

Brown, G. "Chance Encounter in Club Was Start of Acoustic Combo." *Denver Post* 17 Feb. 1997, 2nd ed.: E8.

____ . "The Happy Hippie Matthews Tries a Different Sound." *Denver Post* 30 Oct. 1996, 2nd ed.: G8.

____ . "Matthews Band Jams with Guest on Rocks." *Denver Post* 4 July 1997, 2nd ed.: B3.

____ . "2 CD Hits Putting 'Why Store' in National Spotlight." *Denver Post* 22 Nov. 1996, 2nd ed.: F15.

Brown, Mark. "Coming in from the Cold Road; Rock: By Way of South Africa and Virginia, the Dave Matthews Band Finally Brings Its Music out West." *Orange County Register* 8 Dec. 1994: F3.

____ . "Matthews Suite." *Orange County Register* 4 Aug. 1995: 8.

Buk, Askold. "Drummer Boy." *Guitar World Acoustic* 19 (1996): 41.

Burtner, Sydney. "Lawsuit, like Stardom, Hits Dave Matthews and Coran Capshaw: $3.1 Million Requested." *Observer* [Charlottesville, VA] 19–25 Oct. 1995: 1+.

____ . "The Money Side of Music: Local Talent Sells the Dave Matthews Band." *Observer* [Charlottesville, VA] 11–17 Aug. 1994: 6+.

Cabas, Victor. Telephone interview. 14 Aug. 1997.

Cadigan, Mark J. "The (Dave Matthews) Band; Lead Singer Downplays His Role in Rock's Boundary-Crashing Quintet." *Boston Herald* 27 Sept. 1996: S15.

Caputo, Salvatore. "Road Tested Dave Matthews Band Hasn't Had

Time to Savor 'Overnight Success.' " *Arizona Republic* [Tucson, AZ] 14 May 1995: F4.

Carnes, Jim. "Matthews Lost in Jam, Forgets Its Expo Fans." *Sacramento Bee* 10 July 1997, final ed.: F1.

"Carpal Tunnel Syndrome." *Compton's Living Encyclopedia.* 1996 ed.

Catlin, Roger. "Campuses Welcome Dave Matthews Band." *Daily Progress* [Charlottesville, VA] 8 Feb. 1995.

____ . "Dave Matthews Band Cracks Down on Stores That Sell Bootleg Tapes." *Hartford Courant* 5 June 1997: 37.

____ . "From Frat Houses to Amphitheaters; Dave Matthews Band Brings Summer Tour to the Meadows Sunday." *Hartford Courant* 5 June 1997: 21.

Chenoweth, Avery. "Hey! Dave Matthews!" C-VILLE *Weekly* [Charlottesville, VA] 4–10 Oct. 1994: 7–8.

Colapinto, John. "The Raging Optimism and Multiple Personalities of Dave Matthews." *Rolling Stone* 12 Dec. 1996: 52+.

Conder, Lydia. Telephone Interview. 25 July 1997.

____ . Letter to the author. 28 July 1997.

Considine, J.D. "Eclectic Guitar." *Guitar World Acoustic* 19 (1996): 39+.

"Cool. Excellent. Thanks." *Newsweek* 3 Feb. 1997: 50.

Cornish, Chris. "Artist Interviews: Carter Beauford." *Cyber-Drum* Online. 12 Aug. 1996.

Crashing the Quarter. MTV. 18 May 1996.

"Crowd Crush Alarms Fan." *Omaha World Herald* 5 Dec. 1996, sunrise ed.: SF39.

Daly, Sean. "Dave Matthews Band, Live: Performance Review." *Rolling Stone.* Online. 30 Dec. 1996.

"The Dave Matthews Band." America Online Interviews. 11 May 1996.

"Dave Matthews Band Begins '96 on a High Note." *Business Wire* 5 Jan. 1996.

"The Dave Matthews Band." MTV Online Interviews. 22 Feb. 1995.

"The Dave Matthews Band Biography." RCA/BMG, 1995.

"Dave Matthews Band Eases Bootleg Policy." MTV *News.* MTV Online. 25 Apr. 1997.

"Dave Matthews Band Is Thriving: The Group Has a New Hit Album, *Crash,* That Follows up on the Band's 4-Million-Selling Debut." *Orlando Sentinel* 14 July 1996: F2.

Dave Matthews Band Newsletter. Sept.–Nov. 1994; Apr.–May 1995.

Dave Matthews Band: Under the Table and Dreaming: Guitar, Vocal with Tablature. Port Chester, NY: Cherry Lane Music, 1995.

D'earth, John. Telephone interview. 7 Aug. 1997.

Deck, Stewart. "Dave Matthews Band: The Next Stars?" *C-VILLE Weekly* [Charlottesville, VA] 5–18 Feb. 1992: 25.

Deeds, Michael. "Dave Matthews Fans Have Something to Cheer About." *Idaho Statesman* 4 Oct. 1996: S4.

DeMarco, Jerry. "Band Lawsuit Steps Up Attack on Bootleg CDs." *Record* [Bergen, NJ] 26 Feb. 1997: A1.

"DMB CD Release Party at Plan 9." *Daily Progress* [Charlottesville, VA] 11 Nov. 1993.

"Dummies Video Hits a Nerve." *Gazette* [Montreal] 13 Oct. 1996, final ed.: D10.

Ebencamp, Becky. "JanSport to Ride Bare Backs: Elgin DDB Repositions Backpacks on a Cast of Celebrity Skin." *Adweek* 16 June 1997.

Emery, J. Tayloe. "Here and Loafing in Las Vegas: The Search for the American Dream." *C-VILLE Weekly* [Charlottesville, VA] 20–26 June 1995: 12–13.

Farber, Jim. "Matthews' 'Crash': It Isn't Pretty; Oddball Group's New Album Is the Scene of Mass Musical Destruction." *Daily News* [New York] 30 Apr. 1996: 37.

Farrell, Matthew S. Telephone interview. 18 July 1997.

Fields, David. "Tinsley Takes His Violin through Full Musical Range." *Observer* [Charlottesville, VA] 22–28 Aug. 1991, Our Town sec.: 5+.

Findlay, Prentiss. "The Dave Matthews Band Comes 'Crash'ing into Town." *Post and Courier* [Charleston, SC] 25 Dec. 1996, preview ed.: 16.

Flaherty, Mike. "H.O.R.D.E. Is Their Shepherd: Blues Traveler Keeps the Dead Flag Flying (Whether They Like It or Not)." *Entertainment Weekly* 25 Aug. 1995–1 Sept. 1995: 20.

Fox, Jonathan. "Arts Watch: Well Known Musician Found Dead; Police Rule It a Suicide." *C-VILLE Weekly* 1–7 Oct. 1996.

____ . "Dave on the Stand? Legal Maelstrom Swirls around Charlottesville's Hottest Singer." *C-VILLE Weekly* [Charlottesville, VA] 24–30 Oct. 1995: 8+.

____ . "Dave Matthews Now a Player in Lawsuit." *State* [Richmond, VA] 16 Nov. 1995. Rpt. in *C-VILLE Weekly* [Charlottesville, VA] 21–27 Nov. 1995: 13.

____ . "Legal Thang: A Timeline of the Dave Matthews Lawsuit." *C-VILLE Weekly* [Charlottesville, VA] 16–22 Jan. 1996: 30.

____ . "Matthews in the Middle . . . No More." *C-VILLE Weekly* [Charlottesville, VA] 16–22 Jan. 1996: 30.

Fusco, Kevin. E-mail to the author. 25 June 1997.

Gallo, Phil. "Dave Matthews Band." *Daily Variety* [Hollywood] 7 August 1995.

Gatewood, Chris. "Way More Matthews These Days: Band Comes Home to Begin World Tour." *Richmond Times-Dispatch* 25 Apr. 1996, city ed.: D4.

Gillen, Marilyn. "Lillywhite Moves beyond the 'Drum Thing': Producer Brings Vocals-First Approach to Morrisey Set." *Billboard* 26 March 1994: 113.

"Grammy Thanks in Part to D.M.B.'s 'Sixth' Member." C-VILLE *Weekly* [Charlottesville, VA] 25–31 Mar. 1997.

"Grammys List." *BPI Entertainment News Wire* [New York] 26 Feb. 1997.

Granados, Christine. "Leroi Moore." *Windplayer* 56 (1997): 15–23.

Grant, Kieran. "Matthews Back with a Crash!" *Toronto Sun* 11 May 1996, final ed.: 45.

Green, Joshua. "Love That Dave: Critics Hate Dave Matthews But That Doesn't Mean You Should." *Westword* 10–16 July 1997: 77+.

Griesar, Peter. Telephone interview. 25 July 1997.

____ . Telephone interview. 31 July 1997.

Gulla, Bob. "Dave Matthews." *Discovery Guide to the BMG Music Service* Feb. 1997: 7.

Hardy, Richard. Telephone interview. 31 July 1997.

Herbert, James. "Crash Landing Tailgate Party May Leave Listeners Reeling from Too Much Fun." *San Diego Union-Tribune* 2 May 1996.

Holland, Bill. "D.C. Is Booked Solid with Inaugural Events on Tap." *Billboard* 25 Jan. 1997.

____ . "Long Island Bootleg Seizure Is Largest in RIAA History." *Billboard* 6 July 1996.

Howard, Greg. E-mail to the author. 26 July 1997.

____ . E-mail to the author. 12 Aug. 1997.

"Hot 100 Recurrent Airplay, Weekly." *Billboard* 13 Jan. 1996.

Huntley, Johnathan. "Road Warriors: Travel Is a Way of Life for the Agents of Good Roots." *Roanoke Times and World News* 14 June 1996, metro ed.: 1.

"Influences from a Life on the Move: This Band Refines Simplicity." *Record* [Bergen, NJ] 6 July 1996.

"Joel Jones Presents 'Site Specific' One-Acts." *Observer* [Charlottesville, VA] 18–24 July 1991: 7.

Johnson, Steven C. "Influences from a Life on the Move; This Band Refines Simplicity." *Record* [Bergen, NJ] 7 June 1996: 3.

Jolson-Colburn, Jeffrey. "Arista Top Label of the Year: 'Exhale' Heavy Breather." *Hollywood Reporter* 19 Dec. 1996.

Jones, Wendy Price. "Matthews to Headline Benefit." *Daily Progress* [Charlottesville, VA] 4 Sept. 1992: 3.

Jordan, Chris. "Tweaking the Old Favorites." *Asbury Park Press* 18 June 1997: 5.

Joyce, Mike. "Dave Matthews: A World of Rhythm." *Washington Post* 17 June 1997, final ed.: E2.

____ . "Dave Matthews Finds Success." *Washington Post* 4 Nov. 1994: N15.

Keighley, Cristan. Telephone interview. 28 July 1997.

Kelley, Michael. "Matthews Band Builds on Individuality." *Commercial Appeal* [Memphis] 3 May 1996, final ed.: E14.

"Killer Breaks Silence on Hani Assassination: South Africa Amnesty Panel Hears of '93 Plot to Spur Anarchy." *Chicago Tribune* 13 Aug. 1997: 6.

Lessard, Ron. Telephone interview. 10 Sept. 1997.

Lichtman, Irv, ed. "The Billboard Bulletin." *Billboard* 15 Oct. 1994: 110.

____ . "Nice Man Exits Music, Makes Deal with Giant." *Billboard* 10 May 1997.

"Los Lobos Enjoy 'Nice Guy' Aspect of Tour." *Ottawa Citizen* 26 July 1997: H2.

MacDonald, Patrick. "Last Stop: The Gorge; Dave Matthews Ready to Work on Next Album." *Seattle Times* 10 July 1997, final ed.: D7.

Mackie, John. "Disc Man: How to Make a Record, with Super-Producer Steve Lillywhite." *Vancouver Sun* 29 Apr. 1993: D3.

Mahoney, Jeff. "Dave and Me." c-ville *Weekly* 24–30 June 1997: 12+.

Marzullo, Katy, and Mark Leta. "Dave Matthews Band." CREX, *Creative Existence* Jan.–Feb. 1995: 8+.

Matera, Mariane. "Interview with Dave Matthews." *Richmond Music Journal* Feb. 1994.

Matsumoto, Jon. "Dave Matthews Band Outshined by a Band with Teeth: Los Lobos." *Los Angeles Times* 7 July 1997, Orange County ed.: 2.

Matthews, Dave. "Building an Audience from the Grassroots." *Musician* June 1995: 14, 18.

____ . "Raves." *Rolling Stone* 24 Aug. 1995: 32.

McLennan, Scott. "Smash or 'Crash'? Dave Matthews Band Trying to Avoid Sophomore Slump." *Telegram and Gazette* [Worcester, MA] 6 June 1996: C1.

Mcleod, Harriet. "State of the Union: Virginia Is Second Home for Band with Blend of Rural Soul." *Richmond Times-Dispatch* 18 Feb. 1996, city ed.: J1.

Mehle, Michael. " 'Crash' Test Dave Matthews Band Goes from Grassroots to Greatness with Another Promising Album." *Rocky Mountain News* [Denver] 28 Oct. 1996: 6D.

_____ . "Dave Matthews Raises Pulses at Red Rocks." *Rocky Mountain News* [Denver] 16 Aug. 1995: 58A.

_____ . "'Opening Band Blues' Warming Up a Crowd Can Be a Chilling Experience." *Rocky Mountain News* [Denver] 10 Jan. 1997: D20.

Mervis, Scott. "Crashing Through: Virginia's Dave Matthews Band Grew from Grassroots to Multi-Platinum." *Pittsburg Post-Gazette* 14 June 1996, sooner ed.: 2.

_____ . "HORDE Dave Matthews: The Boy Next Door." *San Diego Union-Tribune* 25 July 1996: 3.

Mettler, Mike. "Profile: Dave Matthews." *Guitar Player* 30.8 (1996): 29.

Miller, Jay N. "A Winning Fusion of Jazz and Rock." *Patriot Ledger* [Quincy, MA] 13 June 1997: 21.

Miller, William F. "Carter Beauford of the Dave Matthews Band: Next in Line." *Modern Drummer* Oct. 1996: 40+.

_____ . "Matthews on Beauford: So Much to Say." *Modern Drummer* Oct. 1996: 60.

Minge, Jim. "Dave Matthews Band Stretches out on New Disc." *Omaha World Herald* 12 May 1996, sunrise ed.: 3.

_____ . "1995 Leaves Rich Legacy of Choice Pop Sounds." *Omaha World Herald* 7 Jan. 1996, sunrise ed.: 3.

"Modern Rock Tracks, Weekly." *Billboard* 15 July 1995.

"Modern Rock Tracks, Weekly." *Billboard* 17 Feb. 1996.

"Modern Rock Tracks, Weekly." *Billboard* 20 Apr. 1996.

"Modern Rock Tracks, Weekly." *Billboard* 31 May 1997.

"Monticello Avenue." Charlottesville, VA, Online. 19 June 1997.

Morse, Steve. "Hootie Falls to Matthews Band Surge." *Boston Globe* 10 May 1996, city ed.: 66.

_____ . "How Dave Matthews Found His Groove." *Boston Globe* 26 Apr. 1996, city ed.: 63.

_____ . "Tragedy Interrupts Dave Matthews Band's Winning Summer." *Boston Globe* 27 Sept. 1996, city ed.: D14.

"MTV Premieres 'The Dave Matthews Band: Crashing the Quarter Special.'" *Business Wire* 15 May 1996.

Niesel, Jeff. "Hear! On Top of the Charts and Dreaming; Pop: Dave Matthews Forsakes Fashion and Makes His Kind of Rock-Jazz-Folk Hybrid." *Orange County Register* 4 July 1997: F45.

Niesslein, Jennifer. "Dave Matthews Band: They've Arrived." *C-VILLE Weekly* [Charlottesville, VA] 20–26 June 1995: 8–11.

_____ . "DMB: A Timeline." *C-VILLE Weekly* [Charlottesville, VA] 20–26 June 1995: 9.

_____ . "Dear Charlottesville Shindig." *C-VILLE Weekly* [Charlottesville, VA] 1–7 Aug. 1995: 34.

Norris, Jane Dunlap. "Band Has Three Nominations." *Daily Progress* [Charlottesville, VA] 8 Jan. 1997.

Nunes, Mark. "D'earth Enlivens Local Jazz Scene." *Observer Magazine* [Charlottesville, VA] 29 Aug. 1991: 2+.

"Offstage Theater Featured in Upcoming Skyline Illustrated." *Observer* [Charlottesville, VA] 18–24 Oct. 1990: 11.

Oland, Dana. "Samples Still Love Live Music." *Idaho Statesman* 31 Jan. 1997: S3.

Olson, Cory. E-mail to the author. 28 June 1997.

____ . E-mail to the author. 29 June 1997.

Panella, Tina. Personal interview. 14 July 1997.

Pareles, Jon. "Recordings View: Dance Vamps with a Light Touch." *New York Times* 26 May 1996, late ed., sec. 2: 27.

Passy, Charles. "Dave Matthews Band Finds Varied Musical Paths." *Palm Beach Post* 1 Sept. 1996, final ed.: J1.

"Paul Shaffer." America Online Interviews. 25 Nov. 1996.

Peskin, Mindy. E-mail to the author. 12 Aug. 1997.

____ . E-mail to the author. 7 Sept. 1997.

Petrozello, Donna. "Alternative Rock in Mainstream: Number of Radio Stations Carrying the Format Multiplies." *Broadcasting and Cable* 20 May 1996: 51.

Phalen, Tom. "Matthews' Tour Ends Upbeat." *Seattle Times* 14 July 1997, final ed.: F5.

"Pollstar Lists Top Concerts for 1996." *United Press International* [Fresno] 27 Dec. 1996.

"Pop Charts: Compiled from a Sample of Retail Sales Reports and Airplay in the Five Boroughs and Nassau and Suffolk Counties; Compiled from a National Sample of Sales Reports Collected and Provided by SoundScan." *Newsday* 30 June 1996: C22.

Powell, Susie. "Dave Matthews Band Fits into Its Special Groove." *Washington Times* 17 June 1997, final ed.: C13.

Powell, Tom. "Hershey Stadium Earns Another No. 1 Ranking: Hershey, PA's Hersheypark Stadium." *Amusement Business* 16 Dec. 1996: 45.

"Predictions of Stardom." C-VILLE *Weekly* [Charlottesville, VA] 20–26 June 1995: 11.

Provencher, Norman. "Matthews Band Stays Adventurous: Nothing Is Straightforward." *Gazette* [Montreal] 9 May 1996, final ed.: B5.

____ . "Telling Rock'n'Roll Stories with a Southern Gothic Twist." *Ottawa Citizen* 15 Feb. 1997: D1.

"Quakers." *Collier's Living Encyclopedia.* 1996 ed.

Randall, Mac. "Ping-Pong and Wood Blocks: The Making of Dave Matthews' 'Crash.'" *Musician* Sept. 1996: 88.

Randall, Willard Stern. *Thomas Jefferson: A Life*. New York: Holt, 1993.

Ransom, Kevin. "Neo-Hippie Sound Puts Eclectic Band on Top." *Detroit News* 20 June 1996.

_____ . "Remember 2 Things Release Party." *Daily Progress* [Charlottesville, VA] 11 Nov. 1993.

Riemenschneider, Chris. "Dave Matthews Band: One of H.O.R. D.E." *Austin American-Statesman* 18 July 1996: 14.

Robicheau, Paul. "Matthews Band Is Poised for Takeoff." *Boston Globe* 6 Feb. 1995.

Rodman, Sarah. "Dave Matthews Band Makes It Look Easy: The Dave Matthews Band with Soul Coughing at the Fleet Center, Boston, Last Night and Tonight." *Boston Herald* 2 Oct. 1996, 3rd ed.: 35.

_____ . "Tangled up in Tape: The Dave Matthews Band's Battle for Recording Quality Ends in a Nightmare Confrontation with Bootleggers." *Boston Herald* 10 June 1997, Arts and Life sec.: 37.

Roland, Tom. "So Much to Say: The Dave Matthews Band Continues to Invent New Sounds." *Tennessean* 10 Sept. 1996, city ed.: D3.

Roos, John. " 'Crash' Course: With So Much Being Said about Him, Dave Matthews Tries to Steer Clear of Complacency." *Los Angeles Times* 4 July 1997, Orange County ed.: 26.

_____ . "With This Band You Get Moe for Your Money; Pop Music: Quartet with 'No Boundaries' Prides Itself on Extended Jams with Several Styles Thrown into the Mix." *Los Angeles Times* 26 Feb. 1997, Orange County ed.: 2.

Rosenberg, Madelyn. "Old Friends in Concert: 'When We Start Playing, It's the Same, Like It's Always Been' — Tim Reynolds." *Roanoke Times and World News* 6 Feb. 1997: 1.

"R.S.I." *Concise Columbia Electronic Encyclopedia*. 1994 ed.

Ruggieri, Melissa. "Richmond Next Musical Mecca? Hometown Bands Are Making Good, or Trying Anyway." *Richmond Times-Dispatch* 27 Mar. 1997: D3.

Sanminiatelli, Maria. "Dave's Back — In School." *Daily Progress* [Charlottesville, VA] 30 Apr. 1996: 1.

Saxberg, Lynn. "Dead's Jam-Band Spirit Lives on in Moe." *Ottawa Citizen* 22 Apr. 1997, final ed.: B10.

Scharnhorst, A. "A Story of Success, Chapter 2: Dave Matthews Band Is Selling Again after an Early Peak." *Kansas City Star* 10 Mar. 1995, metro ed.: 10.

Scribner, Sara. "Record Rack." *Los Angeles Times* 28 Apr. 1996, home ed.: 62.

Scully, Sean. "Success No Longer a Dream for Dave's Band." *Daily*

Progress [Charlottesville, va] 27 Sept. 1994: B1–B2.

Senter, Ryan. Personal interview. 9 July 1997.

Shapiro, Craig. "At Home and Abroad: Charlottesville-Based Dave Matthews Band Riding High with New Album." *Virginian-Pilot* [Norfolk] 3 June 1996, final ed.: E1.

Silverman, Taije. "Making the Jump to Stardom: Catching Up with Dave Matthews." *Observer* [Charlottesville, va] 11–17 Aug. 1994: 18–19.

Sinclair, Tom. " 'Crash' Landing: Another Intricate, Intimate Disc from Dave Matthews." *Entertainment Weekly* 3 May 1996: 77.

____ . "Dave's World." *Entertainment Weekly* 7 Feb. 1997: 69.

Smith, Andy. "Dave Matthews Showcases Eclectic Mix." *Providence Journal-Bulletin* 13 June 1997: B4.

____ . "Dave Matthews, Tim Reynolds Pack in Crowds." *Daily Progress* [Charlottesville, va] 2 Feb. 1997.

Snider, Eric. "Don't Try to Peg the Dave Matthews Band." *Sarasota Herald-Tribune* 30 Aug. 1996: T9.

Spencer, Hawes C. Telephone interview. 4 Aug. 1997.

Stout, Gene. "Dave Matthews Band Humbled by Success." *Times Union* [Albany] 5 June 1997, three-star ed.: P3.

____ . "Family Tree of Hip Bands Has One Root." *Stuart News-Port St. Lucie News* 29 Nov. 1996: D12.

____ . "Group Aims for the Root of Music." *Times Union* [Albany] 23 Jan. 1997, three-star ed.: P8.

Strauss, Neil. "The Pop Life." *New York Times* 23 Apr. 1997, late ed., sec. C: 10.

Sudo, Philip Toshio. *Zen Guitar*. New York: Simon, 1997.

"Tenpercenteries." *Daily Variety* [New York and Hollywood] 16 Dec. 1996.

"Teri Hatcher to Host This Week's 'Saturday Night Live.' " *Austin American-Statesman* 18 Apr. 1996: E3.

Thigpen, Roy. E-mail to the author. 23 July 1997.

____ . E-mail to the author. 24 July 1997.

Thompson, Dawn. Telephone interview. 4 Aug. 1997.

Tolson, Joshua Nicholas. Telephone interview. 28 July 1997.

Triune Music Group and Ross E. Hoffman v. Robert Coran Capshaw. Circuit Court for the City of Richmond, va. 12 Sept. 1995.

Trott, Robert W. "Matthews Puts Aside Ambivalence to Enjoy Himself." *Chattanooga Free Press* 18 Aug. 1996.

"'20–20–20–20–20' Dave Matthews Band Is More than Solo Performance." *Charleston Gazette* 26 Aug. 1996: P3B.

VanHorn, Theresa. " 'Crash' Course on a Local Band: Dave Matthews Is Dreaming of Fame and Fortune Now." *Washington Times* 12 June 1997, final ed.: M2.

Vannoy, Emily. "Publicist Ambrosia Healy Puts Artists on Road to Success." *Cavalier Daily* [Charlottesville, VA] 17 Jan. 1997: 5.

"Video Monitor, Weekly." *Billboard* 4 Nov. 1995.

"Video Monitor, Weekly." *Billboard* 27 July 1996.

Violanti, Anthony. "No Glitz, Please, Just a Good Time with the Dave Matthews Band." *Buffalo News* 9 June 1996, final ed.: G1.

Waddell, Ray. "Dave Matthews Band Enjoying String of Sellouts on U.S. Tour." *Amusement Business* 7 Aug. 1995: 7.

____ . "Fifth h.o.r.d.e. Festival Stands to Gross $12 Mil: Horizons of Rock Developing Everywhere." *Amusement Business* 1 Apr. 1996: 1.

____ . "'95's Top 10 Promoters Take in $701,983,687." *Amusement Business* 18 Dec. 1995: 3.

Walkuski, Steven. E-mail to the author. 9 Sept. 1997.

Wellbeloved, David. Telephone interview. 24 July 1997.

Wertheimer, Linda. "A Profile of the Dave Matthews Band." *All Things Considered*. National Public Radio. 26 Jan. 1995.

Wester, Holly. "Good Idea Gone Bad." *Arkansas Democrat-Gazette* 6 Aug. 1996: 1E.

Winer, Matthew. Telephone interview. 2 Nov. 1997.

Wright, Rickey. "Living a Dream: The Band Knew They'd Make It, But Even the Leader Wouldn't Predict Just How Far They Eventually Would Go." *Virginian-Pilot* [Norfolk] 27 Dec. 1995: E1.

Zack, Ian. "Suit Filed against Dave Matthews' Manager." *Daily Progress* [Charlottesville, VA] 21 Oct. 1995: A1+.

Zofcin, Christa. Personal interview. 22 July 1997.

ACKNOWLEDGMENTS

First of all, I'd like to thank Robert Lecker of ECW Press for wanting to publish a book on the Dave Matthews Band. This book was his idea. Additionally, I must profusely thank all the people who agreed to let me interview them: Peter Griesar, Dawn Thompson, John D'earth, Richard Hardy, Matthew Farrell, Hawes Spencer, Cristan Keighley, Victor Cabas, Tina Panella, Mindy Peskin, John Athayde, Cory Olson, Kevin Fusco, Roy Thigpen, David Wellbeloved, Lydia Conder, Ryan Senter, Christa Zofcin, Matthew Winer, Steven Walkuski, Carla Cain, and Ron Lessard. Thanks to Greg Howard for corresponding with me. Thanks to all the people I spoke to who didn't want me to mention them. Special thanks to Ryan Senter for all the info and all the tapes; your input beginning in 1996 made it possible for me to write this book. Mindy Peskin, thanks for all your answers to my many questions. Christa Zofcin, thanks also for the tapes and for sharing your great backstage experiences. When I was in Charlottesville, I really appreciated the help of the Alderman Library staff at UVA, the staff of the *Observer*, the *Daily Progress*, and, especially, C-VILLE *Weekly*. The librarians at the LA Public Library also aided me. Thanks especially to reference librarian Rosita Kwan.

As I researched this book, Steven Walkuski came through with videos and lots of info when I needed it most. Thanks again, Steven. Thanks to Lindsay Heller, Brian Pace, and Steve Conover. Susan Goodell, you told me how to do this. Many thanks for all your encouragement in the summer of 1997. Danna Voth, thanks for all that BMG stuff and your continued moral support. Lori Goodman, thanks for talking to your brother and for all of your support. Also, to all the people in the DMB Usenet group (alt.music.dave-matthews), I'm very grateful to you. I also appreciate the Nancies for generously providing me with information back in the fall of 1996.

On a personal note: I must thank Beth Blickers, Jason Fogelson, Mike Lubin, William Clark, Andrew Miano (thanks for going to the Irvine show!), Robert Oppenheim, and — at ECW Press — publisher Robert Lecker, editor Mary Williams, Holly Potter, and Klara Banaszak. Tami Tirgrath and Tom Haun, merci! Indirectly related and yet so crucial (and you know how): thanks to my favorite band in Oregon, the Traceys. Leslie Ringold and Marty Porrecca, kudos. Marty, thanks for letting me carry your drums at the Whiskey and the Roxy last summer. Carla Cain, thanks! Elizabeth Wong, you're the best! Bill Adams, thanks for going with me to hear DMB/Béla Fleck and the Flecktones/John Popper at Jones Beach. Tony Lipin and Lauraleen Walker, thank you. To that amazing couple, supertalent Lily Mariye and supersaxophonist Boney James, thanks a million. Lily, you know, you *really* started all this by telling me to buy *Under the Table and Dreaming*.

More appreciation must go to: writer/producer Robert L. Freedman for the continuous friendship and encouragement he's given me for 20 years; the wonderful Julie Phelan, for friendship and support throughout this project, and always; J.J. Sanss-McSeuss, thanks for your support. To the rest of my friends who were so nice to me when I was "under the deadline and screaming," please know how much I appreciated your understanding throughout this project. To the entire Delancey family: love, kisses, and hugs. Thanks to the people at Red Light Management. Lastly, and most importantly, thanks to: Carter Beauford, Stefan Lessard, David Matthews, Leroi Moore, and Boyd Tinsley.

FYI: While I listened to more live DMB tapes than I can name here, for what it's worth, here is my top-16 list: Trax, 8/4/92; Flood Zone, 11/25/92; Wetlands (Dave and Tim), 1/29/94; Richmond Marriot, 12/31/94; Roseland Ballroom, 2/23/95; Roseland Ballroom, 2/24/95; Yoshi's radio show, 5/10/95; Hampton Coliseum, 12/31/95; University of New Hampshire (Dave and Tim), 2/19/96; Sony, Camden, NJ, 6/5/96; Madison Square Garden, 10/4/96; Seattle, 11/7/96; Universal Amphitheater, 11/15/96; Hartford Meadows, CT, 6/8/97. Thanks to all the tapers and traders who helped me acquire these great shows.

— Morgan Delancey